Marketing Navigation

How to keep your marketing plan on course

Edmund Bradford, Steve Erickson and Malcolm McDonald

 **(G)** Goodfellow Publishers Ltd

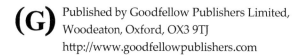

Published by Goodfellow Publishers Limited,
Woodeaton, Oxford, OX3 9TJ
http://www.goodfellowpublishers.com

British Library Cataloguing in Publication Data: a catalogue record for
this title is available from the British Library.

Library of Congress Catalog Card Number: on file.

ISBN: 978-1-908999-23-8

 Design and typesetting by P.K. McBride, www.macbride.org.uk

Cover design by Cylinder, www.cylindermedia.com

Printed by Baker & Taylor, www.baker-taylor.com

Contents

About the authors   vii

Acknowledgments   viii

Part 1: An Introduction to Marketing Navigation   1

1   A new way to steer your plan to success   2

A perilous voyage   2

Perilous marketing voyages   4

The causes of implementation failure   5

The end of dead reckoning in marketing   9

Implementation is a multi-billion dollar issue   10

Marketing Navigation: a new way to implement your marketing plan   13

The Marketing Navigation System   16

The Parker Case   17

The big threat and the big opportunity   18

The payoff from Marketing Navigation   19

Business strategy vs. market strategy   20

2   The Marketing Navigation System   22

The Marketing Navigation System   23

The Navigation Dashboard   24

The Risk–Commitment Matrix   28

The Risk–Commitment Diagnostic   30

The Marketing Helm   33

Using all the tools together   37

Working smarter with the Navigation System   38

3   The essential elements of an excellent marketing plan   43

Section 1 – What should appear in a strategic marketing plan?   45

Section 2 – The marketing planning process   53

Section 3 – Guidelines for effective marketing planning   70

Section 4 – Do marketing plans contribute to profitability?   79

Part 2: Using the Marketing Navigation System   89

4   How to plan your implementation journey   90

Step 1: Is your marketing plan ready for implementation?   93
Step 2: Do the implementation diagnostics   95
Step 3: Develop a change plan   109
Step 4: Use the plans to improve your position immediately   114
Step 5: Confirm your readiness for the next phase   117
Navigation Dashboard Example   122

5   Piloting your plan   129

What is a pilot?   132
How to pilot your plan   133
Navigation Dashboard example   138

6   Rolling out your plan   146

How to roll out your plan   149
The Winmap rollout   160
Navigation Dashboard example   165

7   Refining implementation   169

Why worry about refinement?   172
How to refine implementation   173
Confirming implementation is complete   183
Refining Winmap   183
Testing/evaluation   186
Navigation Dashboard example   187

8   The technology of testing   192

The importance of testing   193
The new technologies   195
Testing methods   195
Advanced testing with simulations   206
Using marketing simulations   210

Part 3: Summary and Implications 219

9 The new marketing leader 220

The real root cause of success and failure 221
What does good leadership look like? 229
Leadership's overlapping roles 232
The implications for leadership 232
Do we really care? 234
The competent CMO 235
The CMO of tomorrow 237

10 Conclusions 239

Implementation matters 240
Implementation is a process not a program 241
Planning is still vital 243
Strategy is implementation and implementation must include change 247
Leadership means being good at market strategy and change 248
The four key factors for implementation success 249
Seven steps to successful implementation 250
Finally...from Harrison to Hamilton and beyond 250

Appendix 10.1: An Implementation Plan Template 252

11 The seven steps to implementation success (fast track) 255

1 Learn to use the Marketing Navigation System (Chapter 2) 256
2 Plan your implementation carefully (Chapters 3 and 4) 256
3 Test your implementation plan with a pilot exercise (Chapter 5) 258
4 Rollout implementation (Chapter 6) 259
5 Refine the implementation (see Chapter 7) 261
6 Use technology to improve your implementation testing (Chapter 8) 263
7 Improve implementation leadership (Chapter 9) 265

The implications for leadership 267

Marketing Navigation: Quick Reference Guide 268

Part 4: Marketing Implementation Case Examples   269

Austro: Accelerated implementation   270

English Energy: Implementing a new market entry strategy   275

European eCards: Successful implementation of smart marketing   280

Global Language Partner Consulting: Charting an implementation
    course in China   284

Globalserve: Combining account management with change management 288

IEB: Implementing a new mindset   297

ITSalesco: The challenge of a complex sales-driven company   302

Kennametal: Keeping marketing plans on track   304

Lafarge Jordan: Re-cementing a leadership position   307

Medic: Implementation enlightenment in India   324

Oxford Learning Lab: Online implementation   329

Tuntex: A cautionary tale from the textiles industry   333

Index   **337**

About the authors

Edmund Bradford is a serial entrepreneur who has co-founded successful consultancies in strategic marketing and key account management. He is also a Director and co-founder of Market2win Ltd which produces simulation games to teach students and executives about strategy. Market2win was named as a finalist in the 2010 *Marketing Excellence Awards* by the UK's Chartered Institute of Marketing.

He has been involved with implementing strategic initiatives around the world for over 20 years, acting as both a consultant and senior executive.

In addition to his work with business schools, his company experience includes work with Brussels Airlines, Compass Group, GlaxoSmithKline, Jones Lang LaSalle, LloydsTSB, Parker Hannifin Corporation, United Utilities and a host of small enterprises.

He holds an MBA from Warwick University, England

Steve Erickson is Vice President Strategic Marketing for Parker Hannifin Corporation, a $13 billion global diversified manufacturer headquartered in Cleveland, Ohio. Parker's many motion and control technologies are used in thousands of applications for a wide variety of machines such as the F-22 Raptor, earthmoving equipment, ships, factory automation and air conditioning.

Steve has global responsibility for developing and supporting Parker's strategic marketing process in the areas of market intelligence, business intelligence and economic intelligence.

Before joining Parker in 1997, Steve held various positions in manufacturing and international business development in both the U.S. and Japan, including serving as Vice President of a Japanese automotive parts manufacturer.

Steve holds a BS in Mechanical Engineering (with highest honors) from the University of Nebraska and a masters degree (summa cum laude) from Trinity International University in Deerfield, Illinois. Steve lived in Japan for 10 years and is fluent in Japanese.

Malcolm McDonald MA (Oxon) MSc, PhD, D.Litt., FCIM, FRSA, until recently was Professor of Marketing and Deputy Director, Cranfield University School of Management in England with special responsibility for e-business, and is now an Emeritus Professor at the University as well as Honorary Professor at Warwick Business School.

Malcolm is a graduate in English Language and Literature from Oxford University, in Business Studies from Bradford University Management Centre, and has a PhD from Cranfield University. Malcolm has extensive industrial experience, including a number of years as Marketing Director of Canada Dry, and has written over forty books, including the best seller *Marketing Plans; how to prepare them; how to use them.*

Acknowledgments

This book is different because of the significant contributions of the following people:

Hussam Asmar, David Atkinson, Neil Bamford, Phil Borland, Kulwinder Bradford, Faas Broersma, Giorgio Burlini, Chris Cardell, Gary Cook, Ian Dunbar, Arif Fahim, Peter Fox, Francois Gau, Mostapha Hebbassi, Ian Helps, Peter Ivanoff, Charles Jacobs, Adrian Joseph, Andrew Kearns, Neil Kendrick, Kaouther Kooli, Jeroen Kurvers, Zhanhong Liang, Rich Nagel, Jodee Peevor, Marco Retel, Savannah Richards, Tomeka Robinson, Elena Roilou, Alistair Taylor, Ian White and Fred Wiersema.

We, the authors, thank you for helping us navigate through our journey.

Part 1

An Introduction to Marketing Navigation

1 A new way to steer your plan to success

■ A perilous voyage

On October 22, 1707 a fleet of 21 British warships commanded by Sir Cloudesley Shovell was sailing home towards Portsmouth, England. The ships were rounding the coast of Brittany in northwest France and heading into the English Channel. After three weeks at sea and battles with French and Spanish warships, the crews were looking forward to returning home.

However, the weather had been abysmal for days and had now turned into an Atlantic storm. As the rain lashed the decks, a dismal day turned to a dark night and the ships rolled in the heavy seas.

At 8pm, the 90-gun flagship, HMS Association, suddenly struck rocks. She went down in minutes losing all 800 men on board. Soon after, the 70-gun warship HMS Eagle and the 50-gun HMS Romney also hit rocks nearby and sunk, with just one survivor. Another ship, HMS Firebrand, also hit rocks but was lifted off by a wave. She struggled on but sank soon afterwards, losing more lives.

In all, 2000 men lost their lives that night. It was a titanic tragedy and one of the greatest disasters ever to befall the Royal Navy. News of the tragedy shocked the nation and an investigation was immediately commissioned to determine its cause.

So what went wrong?

The cause was a serious navigational error related to an age-old mariner's problem: measuring longitude. They simply did not know where they were!

The common method of navigation used at that time was called 'dead reckoning.' The navigator would estimate the ship's position based on an already determined previous position or 'fix.' The speed of the ship was estimated by dropping a wooden log into the sea that was tied to a rope with knots at regular intervals. The navigator calculated the speed by measuring the 'rate of knots' with a marine sandglass and used a compass to determine the direction of travel. When possible this was combined with astronomical observations and depth recordings to achieve greater accuracy. This was a very inexact science but there was simply no better method known to mankind.

The investigators discovered that as the fleet sailed toward the English Channel, Admiral Shovell had sought the advice of his navigation officers as to their position. He was told that the fleet was near Brittany. It was not. The fleet was, in fact, more than 90 miles off course and heading straight for the rocky shores of the Isles of Scilly, a small group of islands 28 miles southwest of Land's End, England. It was a tragic error that would have fatal consequences.

In 1714, alarmed at the continuing heavy losses to naval and merchant ships, the British Parliament sought to find a permanent solution to this intractable problem. It offered a substantial prize of £20,000 (over three million US dollars today) to anyone that could invent a way of measuring longitude to within half a degree. The race to win 'The Longitude Prize' was on!

There were two competing solutions. One was based on astronomy. It had been known for centuries that the moon, planets and stars travelled through the night sky on predictable courses, acting, it was said, as the Creator's clock. If the paths of the stars could be accurately measured and recorded, navigators would be able to determine their ships' positions. The Royal Observatory in Greenwich, England, was established for that very purpose. However, in addition to having an incomplete record of the paths of the heavenly bodies, astronomers also faced challenges with taking precise readings of their positions while on a rolling ship, with skies often overcast and the moon only being visible on 20 days out of each month. There was also the small matter of having enough skilled sailors who could reliably perform the complex mathematical calculations required!

The other solution was based on accurate timekeeping. Scientists had known for over 100 years that longitude could be determined based on the Earth's rotation. The Earth rotates 360 degrees (one revolution) in exactly 24 hours, which equates to 15 degrees per hour. Therefore, navigators knew that if the local time on the ship was, for example, one hour later than the local time at Greenwich, they were exactly 15 degrees west of there.

However, despite over 100 years of trying, no clockmaker had been able to manufacture a device that would perform reliably in the unsteady, extreme temperatures and varying humidity of a ship's environment.

This formidable engineering challenge was finally solved by John Harrison, a brilliant self-taught clockmaker who devoted most of his life to creating accurate marine clocks. After 40 years of development, he finally received his reward in 1772 when his fifth clock, the 'H5,' was trialled by no less a figure than King George III who pronounced it a triumph. As further confirmation, in 1775, the English adventurer Captain Cook returned from a three-year voyage of discovery praising its virtues.

Just one year later, on his 83rd birthday, Harrison died. He was one of the greatest inventors of his age. His maritime clocks not only saved thousands of lives and led to the birth of marine chronometers; they also laid a key technological foundation for the growth of global trade.[1]

■ Perilous marketing voyages

Fast forward 240 years to 2012. What does this have to do with modern marketing practice?

We spend a lot of time writing marketing plans specifying where we want to go. In the good plans (and some would argue the minority of plans) we also define a clear strategy for getting there. But how often do we implement those plans and get to our desired destination successfully?

To answer this question, in 2011 we conducted a survey of senior executives in 70 different organizations to find out their experiences with implementing marketing plans.[2] Our research revealed that very few plans were implemented fully and effectively. In fact, no one said they hit their targets all the time and only a minority (39%) of respondents said they hit their targets most of the time. Most respondents (61%) said they hit them just some of the time or rarely (see Figure 1.1).

Furthermore, implementation is not just about whether or not a plan hits its targets. A plan needs to hit its targets *on time* and here we uncovered another problem.

As Figure 1.2 shows, few respondents (39%) were able to implement their marketing plans on time (i.e. either 'most of the time' or 'all the time'). In other words, the majority (61%) of respondents said they do not typically implement their marketing plan on time. A sizeable minority (14%) said their marketing plan 'rarely' or 'never' gets implemented on time!

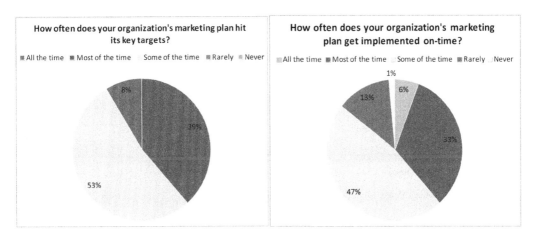

Figure 1.1: Hitting key targets   **Figure 1.2:** Staying on time

From analyzing the detailed responses, it is clear that the main problem area is sales goals. The majority (60%) of executives surveyed said they are typically behind schedule in this area. Next, hitting market share and profit targets on time is a problem for 50% of the respondents. For market share, this includes 21% who said they were typically 'significantly behind schedule' in implementation. So it appears that most marketing plans simply fail to deliver the promised benefits on time.

Taking a marketing plan through to implementation is one of the most perilous voyages that anyone can undertake. It cannot be good for your business or your career if your plan repeatedly hits the rocks!

■ The causes of implementation failure

Why is implementing a marketing plan such a perilous task? Where does it all go wrong? We believe that there are two major factors: commitment and risk.

The significance of commitment

In our survey we named five significant issues affecting implementation and asked how significantly each of these affected implementation. The results are shown in Figure 1.3.

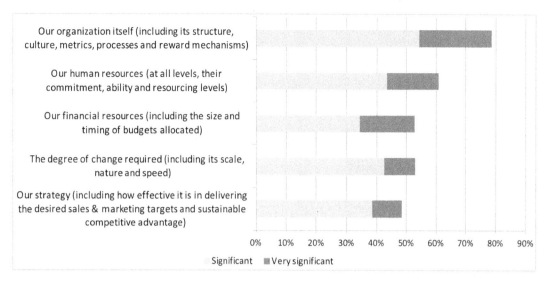

Figure 1.3: The key causes of implementation failure

The talent pool of 'human resources,' which includes people's commitment, ability and resourcing levels, was ranked second in importance with 61% of respondents saying it had either a significant or very significant effect on implementation.

Our experience also suggests that most practitioners involved in implementation programs readily report that commitment is key. But what is it?

What is commitment?

Commitment is an interesting concept, often thrown around at meetings and conferences.

Commitment is not something we either do or do not have. It is not a light switch that is either on or off. Marketers often assume they have it when they do not. And even if key stakeholders 'approve' a marketing plan for implementation, it does not necessarily mean that they are committed to it.

Commitment is a degree of buy-in, beyond approval, at the higher end of a continuum. In Part 2 we look at this in more detail.

How important is commitment for implementation success?

It is interesting to note that 'our organization,' which includes its structure, culture, metrics, processes and reward mechanisms, was overwhelmingly seen as the most important issue affecting implementation. Of the respondents, 78% saw this as either significant or very significant. Nearly a quarter of them said this was a 'very significant' issue.

Furthermore, the financial resources required to implement the plan, the degree of change required by the plan and the strategy within the plan were also significant issues for around half the respondents. Clearly, there is more to implementation success than 'commitment' alone.

Risks

In Part 2 we look at the most common causes of failure and use engineering principles to uncover the real root causes. We treat each of these potential failure points as risks that must be addressed. We can summarize these risks as follows:

The risks from an inadequate marketing plan: This is the most basic of risks, as important as having a well-built ship and a solid navigation plan before leaving port. Is the strategy solid? Is the market well understood? Are the value propositions compelling? Has the competitive response been correctly anticipated? Are the forecasts realistic? Is the timing correct? Have resource implications been thoroughly considered? With the Marketing Navigation approach, we address this risk prior to the implementation phase by providing a marketing plan diagnostic designed to determine whether your plan is ready to be implemented. If the marketing plan itself is not robust, it is certain to end up on the rocks!

The risks related to the *external* environment: Even a good strategy captured in a good plan can fail if the external environment changes dramatically (see Box 1.1). For example, the credit crunch storm of 2008–10 threw many implementation programs off course. Without realizing it, many plans were heading towards troubled waters.

The risks related to the *internal* environment: Even good plans will struggle in a difficult internal environment. This may be an organization that is resistant to change, that is split into many autonomous business units or that does not value marketing. Plans sailing in conditions like these will need a lot of hard work to stay on course.

The risks from inadequate leadership: Poor leadership is a sure way to stall a good plan. It may be a leadership team that does not understand marketing, that spends too much time analysing past financials and too little considering the future direction, or that is more interested in new ideas than implementing existing ones. This motley crew will ensure the plan never reaches its desired port. In Chapter 9 we look further at the important part that leadership has to play in overcoming these challenges.

To summarize, we have two major issues to think about:

- Commitment to implementing the plan.
- Risks to implementing the plan.

These are the two factors that will underlie much of our thinking.

Box 1.1: A £469m implementation failure

In 2004 the UK Government announced a plan to replace 46 local fire control centers with nine larger regional centers. The rationale behind this was to save costs, ensure more consistent service levels, increase response times – and ultimately save lives. They then spent the next six years implementing the plan using both internal civil servants and external contractors.

In 2007 a £200m contract to build the centers was won by EADS Defence & Security. In commenting on the deal, the company said, 'Our programme is focused on sensitive and effective change management, ensuring a seamless transition and that staff receive the best possible training to support efficient use of the new system.'

But in 2010 the scheme was abandoned.

Margaret Hodge, who chairs the MPs' Public Accounts Committee, said the project had been 'flawed from the outset' and one of the worst wastes of public money for many years.

'The taxpayer has lost nearly half a billion pounds and eight of the completed regional control centres remain as empty, costly white elephants.'

She said the project had been terminated 'with none of the original objectives achieved and a minimum of £469m being wasted'. Even now, the empty buildings cost the taxpayer £4m every month to maintain.

In a BBC interview, she said the problem came down to basic errors:

'They (the project team) never talked to the fire services properly. Lesson 1 is get buy-in from all the key people. Lesson 2 is the project management was just dire. A lot of money was spent on external project managers yet no one did proper project management. For example, a fire center was built before they had let the IT contract. The third thing that went wrong, which so often goes wrong in these sorts of projects was that it was a far more complex IT endeavour than they had thought. They were unable to get these 46 different systems to talk and work together.'

Source: BBC News, March 7 2007 and September 20 2011, British APCO Journal news, April 2007

■ The end of dead reckoning in marketing

How much consideration do you give to the issues of risk and commitment in your marketing plan? Perhaps you are better at some aspects than others. Maybe you know that these are important issues but are not sure how to deal with them. They are not fixed but change, like the weather, as the plan goes through its implementation journey. Risks can suddenly appear, rise in importance then fall away as the issue is addressed. Commitment can be gained and lost.

Most marketers are not trained in how to deal with these issues. We tend to rely on experience or 'gut' judgment in deciding what matters most and what actions to take. This is the marketing version of 'dead reckoning'. Our marketing plan tells us where we want to go and maybe how we are going to get there. But where are we on that journey? Are we on course to meet our objectives? Are we on time? What actions are necessary to keep us on course?

We propose that the underlying reasons why a plan is failing can be linked back to these risk and commitment factors. If these can be identified and managed dynamically, then the success of the plan can be more accurately predicted.

We marketers are like a captain of a ship expecting to see an island at a point in the journey but instead seeing it a day or two later than planned. We know we should have reached that target at that time and are not sure why we missed it.

In some cases, marketers are not concerned about implementation. If this is the case and the plan has been left entirely to another function or team to implement, the marketing department is reliant on the accuracy of the progress reported to them by others. Should we care? It depends on whether we are happy to risk our plan hitting the rocks or not. Without the right navigation aids to give us insight, we are just using the long outdated and ineffective method of dead reckoning.

So when, without good navigational aids, everyone around you reports that things are going fine and we will be reaching our target on-time, just think of Sir Cloudesley Shovell on HMS Association.

■ Implementation is a multi-billion dollar issue

Does all this matter? We wanted to know the impact of poor implementation so, in our survey, we asked what the costs of failure were to the various organizations that responded.

Figure 1.4 shows the estimated profit lost annually due to poor marketing plan implementation. Just over 40% of the responding organizations reported losing 10% or more of their profits, 25% were losing 15% or more of their profits and almost 20% saw an opportunity to increase profits by 20%. On average, nearly 13% of profits are being lost every year due to poor implementation.

This is a multi-billion dollar problem. If we apply this percentage across the Top 50 corporations of America, we estimate the total lost profits from poor implementation to be well over $50 billion. That is four times the annual profits of Apple!

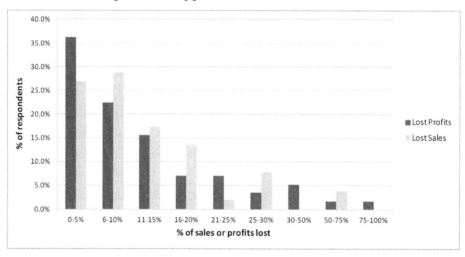

Figure 1.4: Lost profits due to failed implementation

Add to that the lost profits from the thousands of companies further down the American ranking and repeat it for the other global regions and you can see this is a considerable global goldmine.

Finally, this figure may be significantly below the true cost. There are significant invisible costs that we need to consider as well.

The invisible costs

When we think of the costs of failure we often think of just the hard monetary costs such as lower-than-planned sales and profits. However, these are just one part of the losses suffered by a business. There are other costs, both hard and soft, and both direct and indirect which may be difficult to quantify but which can also significantly impact the business.

We have laid out these cost areas in Figure 1.5.

1

Hard direct costs

Failure to implement a marketing plan results in many direct costs to the business. The most obvious of these are lower sales and profits than if the plan had been successfully implemented. Also, inventory may have been built up which cannot be sold and the fixed costs of the business (e.g., rent) will be spread over smaller product volumes sold. These will drive up the average cost per product. Cash flow may also be worse if, for example, the plan was to encourage early customer payment. Severe problems in delivering the marketing plan can hit the share price. These all have a monetary value and are the hard direct costs of failure to implement the plan successfully.

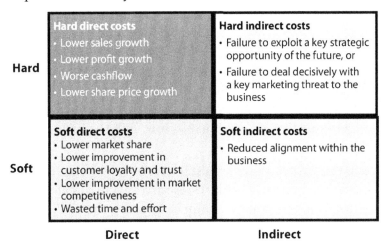

	Direct	**Indirect**
Hard	**Hard direct costs** • Lower sales growth • Lower profit growth • Worse cashflow • Lower share price growth	**Hard indirect costs** • Failure to exploit a key strategic opportunity of the future, or • Failure to deal decisively with a key marketing threat to the business
Soft	**Soft direct costs** • Lower market share • Lower improvement in customer loyalty and trust • Lower improvement in market competitiveness • Wasted time and effort	**Soft indirect costs** • Reduced alignment within the business

Figure 1.5: True costs of plan failure

Soft direct costs

There are also costs which occur as a direct result of unsuccessful implementation but which need to be translated into a monetary value. A plan may still be partially unsuccessful if it hits the sales targets but fails on the market share targets. This would be the case if the market itself is growing faster than the company's sales to that market. This drift down in market share will need to be translated into missed sales and profits. Also, delivery failures may hit the brand value, customer loyalty and competitiveness. Toyota's problems with both its braking systems and the Japanese earthquake resulted in it losing (at least temporarily) its #1 market share position. These are the soft direct costs of failure.

Hard indirect costs

By its very nature, the marketing plan looks both ahead and across into major strategic opportunities and threats that are facing the business. A primary purpose of the marketing plan is to point the business towards new opportunities and help defend it against external attacks. If the marketing plan is not correctly implemented, it is often these strategic areas that fail. This is because they often require the most coordinated and committed response from the executive yet have an uncertain future profit stream attached to them. We need only to look at the many failed corporate acquisitions to show how a strategy to buy market share can fail through poor implementation management after the acquisition has been made.

Soft indirect costs

These are perhaps the dark matter of implementation: hard to see and hard to quantify. One of these is reduced alignment in the business. The marketing plan acts as a rallying call to the business in establishing where the business is heading. No other document defines so clearly how the marketplace is evolving over the next few years and where the business needs to be positioned in the future. If the plan is not implemented well, business units will simply continue along their own paths. Alignment is such a serious issue that Kaplan and Norton (2006) have devoted a whole book to the subject.

In economics, the soft and indirect costs mentioned above can be called 'opportunity costs.' That is, if resources were directed more effectively, there would be an opportunity to improve the profitability of the business.

When we asked our respondents about the impact of poor implementation on their organization, it is interesting to note that two invisible issues scored higher than simple lost sales and profits (see Figure 1.6, *The greatest impacts of poor implementation*). The top five impact areas (with figures showing the percentage of respondents who said this had a significant or very significant impact) were:

1 Wasted time and effort (59%)
2 Failure to exploit a key strategic opportunity or block a key strategic threat (54%)
3 Lower sales growth (51%)
4 Lower profit growth (45%)
5 Worse cash flow (42%).

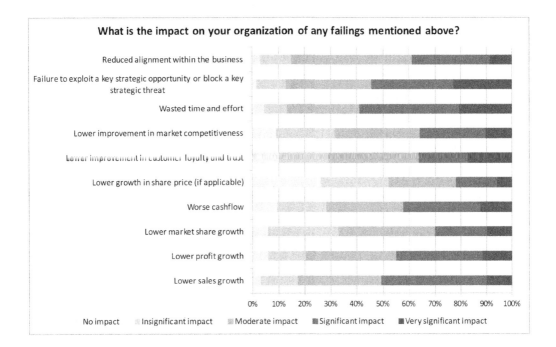

Figure 1.6: The greatest impacts of poor implementation

This shows the frustration felt by the marketing department when their marketing plans do not get implemented well, the missed strategic opportunity that this represents and its adverse effect on cash flow to the business.

We can conclude that although billions of dollars are lost from poor implementation, like the rocks of the Scilly Isles, the biggest impact areas are dangerously invisible.

■ Marketing Navigation: a new way to implement your marketing plan

Traditional marketing approaches follow a step-by-step approach to writing the marketing plan yet say very little about how to implement it. Typically they follow a 'Ready, Steady, Aim, Fire!' approach which roughly equates to gathering information (Ready), analysing the information (Steady), writing a plan (Aim) and then implementing it (Fire!). This would be fine if implementation were like a bullet: fast, unswerving and small. However, many strategic implementation programs are the opposite: slow, evolving and large.

Implementation is a complex and risky exercise more akin to a ship in heavy seas than a speeding bullet. The plan provides the course that the ship is supposed to take, but the world and weather changes as the plan goes into implementation. The plan must face the changing seas of customer needs, the shifting winds of political, economic, sociological, technological, legal and environmental change, the challenge of competitor ships and the hidden rocks of unexpected events. This means that plans are rarely able to sail on a simple straight course on their way to successful implementation.

This is before we consider possible problems with our own ship: the limited resources on board, the internal competition for the captain's favor, the motivation of the crew, the limitations of the engine and our slowness in changing course. In particular, implementation is very context-specific. The degree of risk rises with shorter timescales, fewer resources, larger change programs, less clarity, greater customer uncertainty and more competition, amongst other factors.

We have been involved in researching and implementing marketing plans for over 20 years in a variety of businesses, markets and geographies. Over that time, we have found that the solutions to implementation challenges often do not come from within the marketing profession at all. They come from other professions that have had to deal with resolving implementation issues of their own. In particular, we look to the engineering, change management and strategic account management professions for inspiration.

Wherever possible, we have adapted tried-and-tested ideas from outside to be deployed in marketing itself. As David Kord Murray (2010) would say, we are 'borrowing brilliance' from outside to find new ways of solving problems inside. We also believe this strengthens the marketing profession itself by filling important gaps in the planning process and raising the skills of marketing managers, enabling them to become successful implementation leaders.

We have also reflected on recent work we have done with large and small marketing programs. In particular, we have seen how the marketplaces of our clients have changed dramatically over recent years and are now far more unpredictable, complex and turbulent. If your marketing plans dealt inadequately with change in the past, they will surely be sunk by the turmoil of tomorrow.

To solve the problem of mediocre marketing implementation in an increasingly turbulent world, we believe that a new philosophy and a new approach is needed, one that gives fresh guidance to marketers on how to break down that big implementation step.

The universal principles of Marketing Navigation

We have based our thinking on four universal principles that we see not just in business but in everyday life. These are:

Marketers constantly need to know their current position in the implementation journey so they can determine if they are on course. Modern GPS devices make this simple whether you are steering a ship, driving a vehicle or taking a mountain hike. The better GPS systems also report new hazards that lie ahead, offer advice on better routes and indicate the estimated time of arrival. Marketers need their own version of implementation GPS.

Implementation is about risk management. Any aerospace manufacturer or construction company will tell you that implementation is all about predicting and managing the known risks. If you are developing a new aircraft or building a new tower, you think through the risks in advance, prioritize them, act on them and monitor them closely. If we can do the same with our marketing plans, our chances of success will be much improved.

We must be able to sense and respond to events. This means we must be able to sense unpredicted danger and act on it effectively. Sports coaches do this all the time. They start a game with a plan for defeating the opposition. But often that plan needs adjustment within the first few minutes on the field. As we know, the best coaches are brilliant at responding to unexpected turns of events. We need to be more like winning sports coaches in implementing our plans.

Fast and simple is superior to slow and complex. We need to deal with risk and commitment issues swiftly. This means our mechanism cannot be burdened with data overloads, should be easily understood by all and quick to respond. We need to be more like the crew of a racing yacht than the crew of the *Costa Concordia*.

Our approach is straightforward, flexible and powerful. We hope you will find it useful in navigating your marketing plans through competitive oceans.

■ The Marketing Navigation System

The Marketing Navigation System consists of four areas (see Figure 1.7).

Figure 1.7: The Marketing Navigation System

The Marketing Navigation Dashboard provides a single page summary of the main risks to implementation, the levels of commitment to implementation from key stakeholders, the implementation phase the plan is currently in, and whether the plan is on course, on time and on budget. It also lists the key actions necessary at any given time.

The Marketing Helm is a phased approach to implementation. Plans will move through the four phases over time, but they can move quickly between phases as well. It is more of a circular process than a linear one with testing at its heart. It is like the helm (i.e. steering wheel) of a boat that can be turned one way or the other to keep the implementation progress on course as it faces continually changing conditions.

The Risk–Commitment Diagnostic is a simple but powerful tool that identifies (a) the level of commitment to implementation from the key stakeholders and (b) the other risks that threaten implementation success. It then uses a testing approach to help decide the key actions required.

The Risk–Commitment Matrix uses the scores in the diagnostic to show if the plan is on or off course and, if necessary, the corrections required to get back on course.

The Marketing Navigation System has the following features:

■ It is **scalable** to all levels of implementation complexity. We have used the system in organizations ranging from a single person micro-business all the way up to multi-billion dollar global organizations.

1

- It provides **instant feedback** on how your plan is progressing. The System can be easily updated at any time, giving you immediate updates on implementation progress. Think of it as your personal implementation GPS device.

- It provides **useful advice** throughout the implementation journey. Based on your current position and the course you have set, it provides advice on the best route to your desired destination. It is like your personal radar helping you navigate around the worst hazards ahead.

- It is **simple** to install and operate. The system can be run manually or with standard spreadsheet software so you can start using it immediately.

In Part 2 of this book we will take you through the Marketing Navigation System in detail. We will show you how each part of the system works and how we apply the principles above to make the system work well.

In Part 3, we explain the implications of Marketing Navigation for anyone that aspires to be a successful strategic leader. The implications are enormous. We also provide a fast track chapter so you can get going with marketing navigation quickly.

In Part 4, we provide some real implementation stories from around the world. These are based on interviews with the actual people who have been at the heart of implementation. They show the enormous variety of challenges that have been faced and how those challenges have been overcome – or have sunk the plan! In each case, we asked the interviewee what advice they would give the readers of this book. Their stories and advice are fascinating. The lessons learned from their journeys are useful for all students and practitioners of marketing.

The Parker Case

One of the main cases we will feature in this book is that of Parker Hannifin Corporation.

In 2005 Parker, was already a successful $9 billion global corporation making industrial products for other global companies. It was well known for being one of the few US corporations that had consistently increased its dividends over the past 30 years. However, it was still early in its marketing journey. Marketing was done independently across more than 100 worldwide business units operating in markets as diverse as aerospace, industrial, energy, transportation and mobile equipment, to name just a few. A consistent marketing approach was not in place and there was limited pooling of knowledge and effort. This meant there was a lack of strategic focus on the best opportunities amongst its thousands of customers spread around the world.

Today, Parker is a $13 billion corporation and as we write this, has just reported all-time record net income and earnings per share.

How have they achieved this? A key focus throughout this period has been their relentless drive to implement the company's 'Win Strategy' which was introduced by their CEO, Donald E. Washkewicz, in 2001. In support of this, within the marketing area, they have implemented an internally developed strategic marketing approach which is now seen to be amongst the best in the USA. According to Ralph Oliva, Executive Director of the Institute for the Study of Business Markets, Parker is a 'powerhouse firm that has led the way...with innovations in value pricing, marketing process, and tools and techniques for improving marketing' (Oliva, 2012).

This has been an immense global implementation journey involving well over 100 separate divisions and thousands of employees. The principles built into the Marketing Navigation System have been vital to steering this initiative through to success and we will provide you with many examples from their journey.

■ The big threat and the big opportunity

There is an urgency to all this. Many commentators have said that the world has changed forever since the Lehman Brothers collapse of 2008. The financial storm of 2008–09 may have abated, but there are still unsustainable government and personal debt levels in many Western economies. The USA has the highest levels of debt of any economy. In Europe, the rejection of austerity governments in both French and Greek elections has further weakened the euro. The UK has huge trade and personal debts. There is political upheaval in the Middle East and the threat of civil unrest in China. Then, within our own industry, change continues to accelerate around us. Dealing with these rapidly unfolding events in a connected world will challenge all of us marketers in the future. Greater change will be a big threat that we all face with our marketing plans.

However, there is a big opportunity that we can leverage: technology. For the first time ever, marketers in companies both large and small can easily access smart tools that help implementation. We can war-game the strategy to make sure it withstands competitor reactions, run split tests of the strategy to see how to improve it as we implement it, remotely survey stakeholders to get real-time insights about implementation, use spreadsheets to manage risks, use portals, dashboards and databases to monitor progress ... and more. Without seizing on what technology can offer, our implementation programs will be overtaken by the future tsunamis. In Chapter 8 we will discuss further how such techniques can be integrated into the Marketing Navigation System.

■ The payoff from Marketing Navigation

The rewards from navigating your plan to success are huge. Not only are you more likely to hit your targets on time, you are also more likely to better exploit new strategic opportunities and ward off key threats to your business.

In just one example, Parker used this approach to develop and implement a plan to exploit a new opportunity with a capital equipment manufacturer. The plan involved developing, selling and implementing an integrated systems solution that would be delivered on-time, perform better and have superior support compared to the competitors' solutions. This was a high stakes opportunity involving the management of a complex network of stakeholders across multiple companies on two continents and the application of advanced technical skills.

But the results were dramatic. Before implementation, Parker was an 'also ran' supplier, constantly competing with two other vendors for pieces of the account's business. As a result of good marketing navigation it was able to win the lion's share of their business and developed a strong partnership relationship. It became a multi-million dollar sales success story for Parker, enabling it to become a major player in a target industry.

■ Business strategy vs. market strategy

Before we conclude, we should clarify something straight away. People often talk about 'strategy implementation' as if it only means one thing. However, strategy comes in many shapes and sizes – and is often misrepresented altogether! The key distinction we need to draw here is between two legitimate strategy exercises. One is the implementation of a business strategy and the other is the implementation of a market strategy. This book is about implementing the latter: a market strategy. The market strategy is one of the key strategies in the overall business strategy. Other strategies include the financial strategy, the HR strategy, the IT strategy, the operations strategy and the procurement strategy.

However, it is important to note that:

1 The market strategy should lead the business strategy (i.e. the business strategy itself should be 'market-led') and

2 The Marketing Navigation System explained here can be easily applied to any business strategy challenge.

Therefore, whether you are in marketing or not, this framework will help you become a better business leader.

Conclusions

Implementing a market strategy is one of the most challenging tasks marketers face and few plans successfully reach their goals on time. Billions of dollars are lost annually from poor implementation programs with further invisible costs on top.

Although there is much help available for marketers in writing a marketing plan, very little support exists for getting it implemented. We have used fresh research, new technology, our own work and the implementation experiences of senior executives from around the world to help fill this gap.

Setting forth to implement a marketing plan without some useful tools and models is like setting sail without navigation aids, radar and an up-to-date weather forecast. The Marketing Navigation System provides all these and will help you through the hazards that lie ahead. It will replace the dead reckoning methods that most marketers employ today.

Once you have mastered it, you will be able to reach your desired goals safely, leaving the competition to flounder behind you.

Notes

1 This true story is based on historical documents held at the Royal Observatory, Greenwich, London with additional information from *Compass: A Story of Exploration and Innovation* by Alan Gurney.

2 Survey undertaken by the authors on 84 senior executives in 70 different organizations across 17 countries, 2011.

References

Kaplan, R.S. and Norton, D.P. (2006) *Alignment Using the Balanced Scorecard to Create Corporate Synergies*, Havard Business School Press

Kord Murray, D. (2010) *Borrowing Brilliance : The Six Steps to Business Innovation by Building on the Ideas of Others*, Random House

Oliva, R. (2012) Members Meeting Insights from Parker Hannifin, Kennametal and Arizona Chemical, March 20, 2012, Ralph Oliva, Executive Director of the Institute for the Study of Business Markets.

2 The Marketing Navigation System

There is nothing more difficult to take in hand, more perilous to conduct or more uncertain in success than to take the lead in the introduction of a new order of things, because the innovator has for enemies all those who have done well under the old conditions and lukewarm defenders, those who may do well under the new.

Machiavelli, *The Prince*, 1446–1507

Summary

In this chapter, we:

- Provide an overview of the Marketing Navigation System and its key components namely:
  - ☐ The Dashboard
  - ☐ The Risk–Commitment Matrix
  - ☐ The Risk–Commitment Diagnostic
  - ☐ The Marketing Helm
- Explain why it works
- Define what we mean by being 'on course'
- Explain the principles for diagnosing your current position correctly
- Present a four-stage implementation model
- Explain how to get the most out of the Marketing Navigation System

■ Introduction

To help you maintain control of implementation, we recommend you use the Marketing Navigation System. This chapter provides a summary of the system, the key tools that it uses and the principles it is built upon. In Part 2, we will go into the system in more detail and show you how to apply it to your own marketing plan.

2

Key principles

The key principles that we will use in the chapter are to:

- ■ Borrow brilliance from elsewhere
- ■ Keep things simple with a one-page summary
- ■ Use risk and project management to *anticipate* problems
- ■ Use sense and respond to manage *unanticipated* problems
- ■ Use change management to keep everyone on board
- ■ Use traditional marketing tools in new ways.

■ The Marketing Navigation System

The Marketing Navigation System is a suite of tools to help you implement your marketing plan more successfully (shown in the center of the circle in Figure 2.1). It has four core tools:

- ■ The Marketing Helm
- ■ The Marketing Navigation Dashboard
- ■ The Risk–Commitment Diagnostic
- ■ The Risk–Commitment Matrix

The core tools are based on good demonstrated practice in a range of professions. We have identified the best practices, imported their essential ingredients into our system and adapted them for our use. These are shown in boxes on the outside of the circle.

The end result is a powerful system with solid foundations.

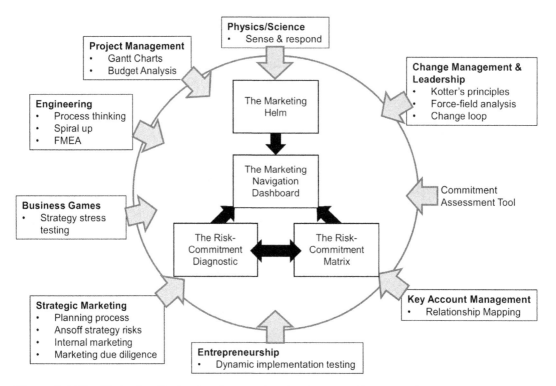

Figure 2.1: The Marketing Navigation System showing imported best practices

■ The Navigation Dashboard

At the heart of the system is a one-page Navigation Dashboard (see Figure 2.2). The Dashboard is an executive summary of the key issues and indicators that you need to watch. These issues and indicators are themselves gathered by other tools in the system. It is just like your car or boat, with a central dashboard in front of you which is itself connected to other on-board devices, systems and diagnostics.

The Dashboard is designed to be simple but powerful. It takes only a few minutes to update but can also support full-blown review meetings when necessary. It can therefore be used by marketers in small enterprises all the way up to large global organizations.

There are three key indicators on the upper left-hand side. These ask the three most important questions about implementation:

- Is our marketing plan **on course**?
- Is it **on time**?
- Is it **on budget**?

Marketing Navigation System

Navigation Dashboard

Plan/Project:
Owner:

Date:
Revision:

2

On Course?   Yes/No

The Risk-Commitment Matrix: Current Position

High

Risk

Low

Low   Commitment   High

Key Actions

Action	Who	By When	Done?

On Time?   Yes/No

Comments here

On Budget?   Yes/No

Comments here

The Helm

Implementation Phase: Pilot

Refine   Plan

Test

Roll-out   Pilot

Risk - Commitment Diagnostic

Top Risk Issues

Conclusion | GO/ NO GO

Ref	Desired State	Risk Area	Failure Threat	Test	Current Status	GO, NO GO

Top Commitment Issues

Conclusion | GO/ NO GO

Ref	Desired State	Stakeholder	Failure Threat	Test	Current Status	GO, NO GO

Figure 2.2: The Navigation Dashboard

If the answer to these three questions is 'yes' then the plan is being implemented well and you can afford to be more confident about its chances of success. If, however, any of these answers are 'no' then you need to take action.

On course?

What we mean by this question is, 'Are we confident the implementation of our plan will be seen as a success by the key stakeholders?'

This in turn means:

1 We know who the key stakeholders are

2 We know what success looks like for them

3 We know the risks involved in achieving that success

4 We know if each key stakeholder is committed to the plan.

For the moment, let us assume that we know 1 and 2 (we will come back to these later in this chapter). We can then go straight to summarizing our implementation risks and commitment to implementation.

This is done in the Risk–Commitment Matrix (see Figure 2.4).

On time?

What we mean by this question is: 'Will the plan be implemented on time?' A supporting question is, 'Are we where we are supposed to be now?' However, the first question is the key one as time may be made up or lost between now and the final delivery date. It is the same as any GPS system, where the estimated arrival time is a more important data item than the current position as it will tell us if we are likely to be on-time or not. This is a simple case of choosing 'Yes' or 'No' to the question.

In order to do this, basic project management needs to be done. This will typically involve some form of project plan showing key steps and tasks, timescales, milestones, current date and how complete is each task. From this rudimentary plan, a rough estimate of the delivery date can be gauged. More sophisticated plans (like Gantt charts) will also show resources, task connections and critical paths. You should also consider both the Risk–Commitment Diagnostic and the Marketing Helm before reaching your answer.

It is not the purpose of this book to reproduce these rudimentary project management tools. However, we do urge you to ensure you have at least a basic project plan established which you can update simply and frequently.

On budget?

The final key question asks, 'Will the plan be implemented within its budget limit?' The plan may be over budget now, but that is of less importance than knowing if the plan will be on budget when it is implemented. Again, this is a simple 'Yes' or 'No' question.

To get the right answer, you should be using a suitable budget tracking tool. These are often part of normal financial systems or project management software. Sophisticated tools will be good at apportioning costs (e.g., for part-time resources), forecasting costs (which may change every month as the project goes through implementation) and apportioning costs to key tasks/milestones in the project. Again, the reader needs to research such tools if required.

Alternatively, you can create your own basic version in a spreadsheet. The key thing is to ensure that you have a good way of comparing the actual cost with the budgeted cost for that period or task.

The other areas on the Dashboard should also be consulted before reaching your Yes/No answer.

'On course' vs. 'On time' vs. 'On budget'

Being 'on course' is the most important question of all since any risks to the delivery time or the budget will still be included as a risk item in this question. Normally, if there is a high risk of the plan being delivered significantly late or significantly over budget, it cannot be on course. However, there are two special cases when a plan can be late or over budget and still be on course:

1 When delays do not matter as much as the quality of implementation. For example, Steve Jobs delayed the launch of the iPad because the design 'didn't seem casual and friendly enough to scoop up and whisk away'(Isaacson, 2012). For Jobs, perfection in design was everything and implementation timescales can suffer if necessary.

2 When the budget limit is less important than ROI. Some experts emphasize the importance of *buying customers* rather than adhering rigidly to a fixed marketing budget. The thinking goes like this: If it costs you, say, $1000 in marketing activities to buy a customer but that customer then delivers, say, $10,000 in sales over their lifetime, why would you want to be limited by the budget? Surely, it makes more sense to divert more resources to marketing so we can buy more customers! This means raising the marketing budget. Fixed annual budgets are for those who do not know how effective their marketing

department actually is! For smart marketers, exploiting these opportunities quickly and delivering quality experiences to them is more important than sticking to predefined budgets.

The key here is to be a good marketer and really understand the needs of the key stakeholders. In project management, they use the cost, quality, time triangle (see Figure 2.3) with a movable ball to show where the needs lie for any particular project. For Steve Jobs the ball would be right on the base of the triangle, firmly in the quality camp. For smart marketers with good ROI systems, it would be in the bottom right corner, furthest away from cost. Where is it for your plan?

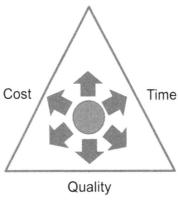

Figure 2.3: The cost, quality, time triangle

■ The Risk–Commitment Matrix

The Risk-Commitment Matrix (RC Matrix) separates the implementation risks into commitment and other risks.

Let us look at the commitment axis first. Rather than talk about commitment risk, in practice we have found it easier to simply talk about the level of commitment itself. The commitment axis therefore shows the degree of stakeholder buy-in to the implementation of the plan. High commitment, on the right-hand side, is good. Low commitment, on the left-hand side is bad.

The Risk axis considers all the other risks to implementation. High risk, at the top, is bad. Low risk, at the bottom, is good. As we saw in Chapter 1, these risks are numerous but generally fall under the headings of environment risks, funding risks and strategy risks. We will group these risks together and refer to them collectively as the Commercial Risks of the plan.

So, at any time, your implementation program can be in any of four positions (see Figure 2.4).

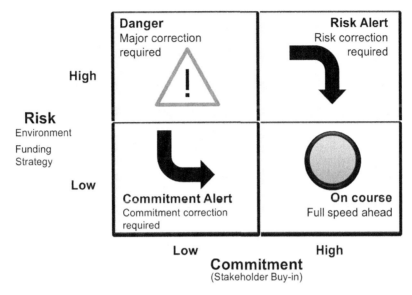

Figure 2.4: Four different positions on the Risk–Commitment Matrix

- **Low commitment + high risk = danger**. You have a dangerous combination of low stakeholder commitment and significant commercial risks. This is often the case when you assess your position at the start of an implementation program and have not had the chance to conduct your GO/NO GO tests. Nevertheless, this is the worst position to be in, and way off course. You will need to go back and rethink your marketing plan and its associated implementation plan so that you can plot a good route to getting back on course.

- **Low commitment + low risk = commitment alert**. You are low on commitment. Use the Marketing Navigation System to decide what actions you need to take to steer the plan back on course.

- **High commitment + high risk = risk alert**. Your plan has a high degree of commercial risk. Use the Marketing Navigation System to reduce the risks and get the plan back on course.

- **High commitment + low risk = on course**. You have the best combination of commitment and low risks. Get on with implementation but use sense-and-respond thinking to react quickly to unanticipated threats.

How do you know your position on the matrix? You need to do a Risk–Commitment Diagnostic.

■ The Risk–Commitment Diagnostic

Where do we sit on the Risk–Commitment Matrix shown in Figure 2.2? The answer comes from the Risk–Commitment Diagnostic (RC Diagnostic).

A summary of the items in the Diagnostic is provided in Table 2.1.

Table 2.1: A summary of the items in the Risk–Commitment Diagnostic

Item	Explanation	Inputs
Ref	A unique reference number for this issue	A detailed FMEA exercise*
Desired state	What successful implementation looks like for the key stakeholders	Change loop A relationship map to identify the key stakeholders Deep discovery interviews to understand their unmet needs
Risk area/ stakeholder	In the Risk Diagnostic, these are the areas of risk In the Commitment Diagnostic, these are the names of the key stakeholders involved in implementation	Risk assessment tool Commitment assessment tool
Failure threat	These are the specific threats to achieving the desired state (within the risk area or from the stakeholder). They are recorded as failure outcomes.	FMEA*
Test	A specific test that can be performed to evaluate whether the failure threat is real or false	Sense and respond Dynamic implementation testing Simulations
Current status	A brief description of current progress with the test	
GO, NO GO	The conclusion from performing the test. If the test proves the threat to be false, then the outcome is GO. Otherwise, the outcome is NO GO. The overall 'Conclusion' to the diagnostic can only be GO if all the outcomes are GO.	NASA launch control
* see Diagnostic principle #2: Identify the killer threats later in this chapter		

Although the Diagnostic can be operated as a stand-alone tool, for the best results it should be fed with the results from other tools, exercises and ideas. These are shown as 'Inputs' in Table 2.1. and will be explained further in Part 2.

The Diagnostic adopts three important principles:

Diagnostic principle #1: Start at the end

To do the Diagnostic well, you should use 'Change Loop' thinking. Roughly speaking, this says, 'Begin with the end in mind (Covey, 2004. Think about the desired state and then work back to decide what actions need to be taken to get there from the current state'. Here, the desired state is perceived successful implementation and we need to define what this looks like (question 2 in our 'On course?' questions above).

The 'desired state' can be a mix of implementation objectives and targets. Objectives are broad descriptive goals like developing a new website, improving the skills of the sales force, developing a new product or entering a new market. Targets are specific numerical goals like achieving a 10% improvement in sales, market share, profitability or customer satisfaction.

For Lafarge Jordan (see Part 4 of this book), the objective of their marketing plan was to develop 'a new brand proposition...with different cement products designed and targeted at specific customer segments.' This desired state was then broken down further into eight specific changes to the current state. These changes included: 'Link the product strategy to the application of the product...; Ensure good use of the Lafarge umbrella brand...; Gain a deep understanding of end-user applications...; Labeling in Arabic...' etc.

Getting the desired state right: a summary

- The desired state can be an objective or a target.
- Broad objectives and targets will need to be broken down into specifics.
- The desired state should be defined in a way that leads to dramatic success. Change loop thinking recognizes that if you start by analyzing the current state, then the vision often becomes just a modified version of it. It is more powerful and motivational to work back from the future, than to push the current state into the future.
- The desired states need to be clear and testable.
- The desired states may be different for different key stakeholders.
- The desired states will be different for different phases of implementation

We will discuss the last three points further in Part 2 of this book.

Diagnostic principle #2: Identify the killer threats

Marketers are familiar with identifying threats. We do it all the time when we do a SWOT (strengths, weaknesses, opportunities and threats) analysis. If you are unsure how to do a SWOT, segment by segment, we have included a form at the end of this chapter. However, we are often guilty of not doing enough to counter the threats. Often, a threat is listed during a brainstorming exercise, and once it is in the marketing plan it too often gets forgotten about.

Here we need to be more scientific. We need to recognize that implementation is a perilous voyage and the key threats need to be clearly identified and acted upon. How do we identify the most important threats? Let us look at how they deal with this issue in engineering.

A failure of any part of any aircraft can be dangerous. A failure of any part of any space craft can be catastrophic. By the time of the Apollo space program in the 1960s, NASA and its suppliers were perfecting a technique to identify and iron out all major failure risks. This technique was called failure mode and effects analysis (FMEA).

The idea behind the FMEA was to identify all the possible failure modes (threat possibilities) and score them according to their probability of occurring, their impact on the mission and their chances of avoiding detection. The engineers would then systematically take action on each failure mode to reduce its probability, impact and invisibility.

The Risk–Commitment Diagnostic uses FMEA thinking to identify the risks and commitment concerns that are most likely to lead to implementation failure. It is a short list of the pivotal issues that will either make or break implementation. Chapter 4 explains how to do an FMEA.

Diagnostic principle #3: Test the threats

How do we know if the threats are real or not? How do we know if a key stakeholder is committed to implementation or not? How do we know if a key competitor will kill our new product by cutting the price of their product?

We need to devise tests to sense the reality of the threat. Until the test is performed, we do not know if the threat is a potential issue or a real issue.

In engineering, tests are performed on a product or system to make sure it will perform when needed. In science, tests are performed to prove or disprove a hypothesis.

We need to do the same. We have a hypothetical threat that needs testing.

Our tests could be simple, like checking whether the stakeholder is willing to attend a key implementation meeting. Or they could be more complicated, like gathering intelligence on past competitor price moves. Whatever the actual test, the key idea here is that you devise a test that proves whether you are safe to proceed or not.

Diagnostic principle #4: Kill the threat, not the implementation

If any of your tests support the idea that the threat is real, then you will need to hold implementation and consider your next steps. Think of it like NASA's Mission Control Center during the Apollo program. You are asking for a 'GO' on all the key areas. If any of them report 'NO GO' then the conclusion is NO GO and you should stop the countdown immediately.

That is not to say you should kill the implementation altogether. Instead, you need to think how you are going to deal with this key threat. Once your solution has been decided, you can then undertake new tests to make sure it will indeed work. For example, for Oxford Learning Labs (see Part 4 of this book), the marketing strategy was to sell direct to paying customers via Google Adwords. However, as the strategy was implemented Giorgio Burlini realized the threat to its success was not insufficient traffic being driven to the Oxlearn website, but insufficient conversion of that traffic into enquiries. How did Giorgio work around that? He developed a new sales path and a new route to market. 'I started experimenting by putting links and video samples on YouTube. The most important thing I discovered from these tests was that if people found free samples, they would then buy my products.'

So, Oxlearn killed the threat to implementation, not by stopping implementation altogether but by finding new ways to convert online visitors to paying customers. Once this had GO written all over it, he accelerated its implementation.

■ The Marketing Helm

Many text books refer to implementation as a single step at the end of the planning process. There are two problems with this:

- Implementation continues in parallel with the other steps. The previous year's marketing plan continues to be implemented at the same time that the new plan is being developed.

- Secondly, implementation is not a single gigantic step that cannot be broken down. Indeed, it must be divided into smaller steps so we can plan and monitor our implementation progress.

The Marketing Helm breaks implementation down into four smaller steps that we will call the implementation phases. These have been developed from decades of our own experience implementing marketing plans, from our experience of implementing other (non-marketing) programs and from incorporating the best change management principles.

These phases are critical because they help you reduce the risks of failure and increase the commitment to implementation. The phases are:

Implementation phase 1: Plan

The key term here is think ahead. It is about anticipating the threats and having good plans ready to deal with them. To do this, we actually need two plans:

1 The marketing plan. This documents the *market* strategy and generally has an *external* focus. It needs to answer the following questions: *What* market conditions will we be facing? *Where* shall we compete? *How* shall we compete? *When* shall we compete?

2 The change plan. This documents the *change* strategy and generally has an *internal* focus. It needs to answer the following related questions: *What* implementation conditions will we be facing? *Where* shall we implement? *How* shall we implement? *When* shall we implement?

Marketers tend to be well-practiced in writing a marketing plan but not good at writing the change plan that goes with it. They may know the beautiful blue ocean where we need to sail to but have not planned how to convince the crew that it is worth the effort!

There is more on this in Chapter 4.

Implementationphase 2: Pilot

Whereas the last phase was about thinking, this is about action. But we need to walk before we can run. We need to act small first with a carefully planned pilot exercise.

A pilot can take many forms. At the simple end it can be an online marketing test to see if there is any interest in the new product/solution you are developing. At the other end it can be a lengthy series of interactions with targeted users to evaluate all aspects of the strategy.

The main purpose of the pilot is to help ensure you get the formula right on a small scale, similar to a laboratory test, before taking the plunge into massive implementation work.

There is more on this in Chapter 5.

Implementation phase 3: Rollout

In this phase, we can incorporate the lessons learned from the pilot to scale up the implementation effort and deploy our solution across the entire marketplace.

This still needs careful planning and monitoring. Our pilot will only have covered a fraction of the target market and may have involved an incomplete solution. The feedback may also have forced us to change some key aspects of the solution, the target audience and how we reach them. So we need to think carefully about the roadmap that will take us from insignificance to dominance (even if this is dominance of our chosen niche). Do we need to have the final product tested and ready before we market it or are there some aspects that can be added later? Do we start locally then expand internationally or should we start with an international segment then roll-out to an adjacent international segment?

Each rollout will be different but the key is to set a navigable path to success and to track your progress against it.

There is more on this in Chapter 6.

Implementation phase 4: Refine

Finally, we need to refine the solution so it is integrated into the DNA of the businesses involved in delivering it. The key term here is *think back*. We have reverted our focus from action back to thinking. We need to reflect on the implementation program and:

- Plug any final threats to its success. This will ensure that implementation does not slip back when we are not looking, plus
- Ensure that the key learnings from this implementation journey are carried forward to the plan phase for the next implementation journey.

There is more on this in Chapter 7.

The central test

In the middle of the Helm is the word 'test.' This is to demonstrate that at every stage of our journey we will be looking to test our progress. Continuous testing will allow us to both track our position through the current phase and to determine whether we are ready to pass on to the next phase.

Testing can also be done in any phase at any time:

- *Forward testing* may be done in a future phase to see if we are ready to attack it. This is similar to how a military campaign will send out advanced scouts to test defenses before the main force is sent in.
- *Retro-testing* may also be done in past phases to make sure that they are secure. We need to be sure that there is not a rear-guard attack on our implementation as we move our forces towards the end objectives.

There is more on this in Chapter 8.

The dynamic Helm

The Helm model is not a stage gate process (i.e. one where the project must pass through a series of filters on its route to completion). It is more dynamic than that. Although we need to be clear about which phase we are in and whether we can transition our forces to the next phase, we can also make little quick journeys around the Helm.

At Parker, before the main Winmap program was implemented, there was a quick cycle through all the phases of the Helm with a smaller implementation exercise. This was hugely valuable in planning how to implement the much larger Winmap program.

At European e-Cards (see Part 4), continuous testing is now part of the culture and has led to a smarter, more dynamic way of doing marketing. If the tests do not deliver the results they had anticipated, they will try another pilot exercise or even go back and re-plan.

So a typical implementation path will look like Figure 2.5.

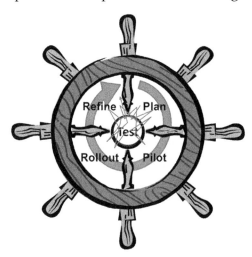

Figure 2.5: A typical dynamic implementation journey

We should see the Helm then as more of a dynamic steering wheel than a rigid step-by-step process. It can be turned clockwise or counter-clockwise dependent on events. Like any journey, some turns will be planned in, but others will have to be performed in response to unanticipated events.

So long as we are progressing overall through the implementation journey well (on course, on time and on budget) then we will allow ourselves unplanned deviations to cope with the ever changing conditions of a dynamic world.

■ Using all the tools together

The most powerful approach is to use the Helm, Matrix and Diagnostic together. The RC Diagnostic gives you your current position. The RC Matrix gives you your map and the Helm helps you steer from your current position to safety.

Moreover, there are many routes that you can take to get your implementation back on course. Figure 2.6 shows the three main ones.

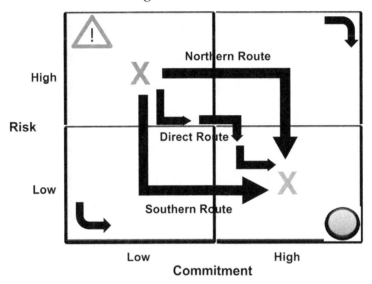

Figure 2.6: Three routes to getting back on course

Let us assume that the Diagnostic puts your implementation program in the worst possible position, i.e. in the top left 'Danger' box of the Risk–Commitment Matrix. To be here, you must have an overall NO GO on both risk and commitment. There are three possible strategies to get you safely from here to the bottom right 'On Course' box:

1 *Take the northern route:* This is the commitment-first route. It involves selling the marketing plan to key stakeholders, then using their skills and experience to drive down the commercial risks. It can be seen as a top-down implementation strategy.

2 *Take the southern route:* This is the risk-first route. It involves changing the plan and/or its implementation path to reduce the risks of failure, then selling a less risky plan to the stakeholders. It can be seen as a bottom-up implementation strategy.

3 *The direct route:* This is risk–commitment corrections route. It involves making a continuous series of smaller left and right turns, gradually

building confidence and apostles as you simultaneously reduce the commercial risks. It is like a sailing boat tacking left and right while sailing against the wind.

We cannot tell you which one is the best route for your implementation program. Each program is different and there are too many variables for us to be prescriptive. Indeed, we have witnessed organizations follow all three routes successfully.

However, we would advise you to consider the direct route first. Despite its name, it may not be any quicker than the other routes. However, taking lots of small steps along the way is generally safer than taking two giant leaps. The constant feedback from these steps and their testing, means you will maintain a much clearer understanding of your true position. Taking small steps means you can also try lots of small countermeasures along the way. If one fails, you have not lost much ground. This means you can afford to be more entrepreneurial, innovative and dynamic about your implementation path. You can steer your plan left and right with small turns to see how it responds to all the forces blowing around you. Taking lots of small turns will also improve your skills in using the toolset together.

■ Working smarter with the Navigation System

Using the Navigation System as a portfolio tool

So far, we have talked about the marketing plan as if it were a single object progressing through turbulent waters. While it is very useful to have a summary of how well our plan is progressing, we must also realize that many plans will have multiple programs that are being implemented concurrently.

In this case, we simply need to drop down a level or two and use the Marketing Navigation System to track specific aspects (e.g., programs or campaigns) within the overall plan. In this case, there will be a one-page Dashboard for each program. Programs can then be analyzed, tracked and managed separately.

We would also recommend that instead of an 'X' you use a 'bubble' whose size represents the relative value of the implementation prize. The larger the bubble, the larger its relative value compared to other programs. The value can be represented in different ways, for example: sales, profits or net present value (NPV).

The RC Matrix can then be used to visualize instantly both the relative size/importance of these programs and whether they are on course or not. This then becomes a very useful implementation portfolio chart (see Figure 2.7).

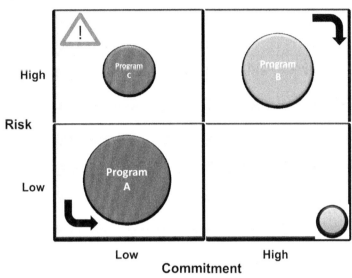

Figure 2.7: The RC Matrix portfolio

This shows a number of useful things:

1 The degree to which each program is on course for successful implementation

2 The nature of the threat ('commitment' issue or 'commercial risk' issue)

3 The size of the prize

The risk vs. reward ratio

Figure 2.7 suggests the following actions:

1 Fix the commitment issues in program A. Understand the NO GO issues here and work out a testable plan to improve it. This has the largest prize so needs to be given top priority.

2 Reduce the risks of failure in program B. Understand what the NO GO risks are and focus on sorting them out. This is the second priority.

3 Address the concerns of program C. This does not have a large prize so how can we simply and efficiently get this program back on course? If the effort is not worth the reward, then consider re-specifying the program, delaying it until conditions are more favorable, or killing it so that the business can focus better on the other programs.

This brings us to a further implication. We can also use the RC Matrix portfolio to help us choose the best options for implementation.

Program C will be linked to an aspect of the marketing plan (e.g., the development of a new product). If we know that there are high risks of failure and that support will be low, then it will be more difficult to implement. 'Implementability' can then be added as an additional attractiveness factor to our regular portfolio analysis (such as the directional policy matrix) to help you choose the best opportunities for the future.

Going beyond GO, NO GO

In plotting your position on the RC Matrix we have kept things deliberately simple up to this point. By using our GO, NO GO Diagnostic, your program can only be in one of four positions. This simplicity means you can quickly and continuously sense your position and respond accordingly.

However, instead of a simple Yes/No conclusion, you can modify the Diagnostic to give you a score instead. This score can either be:

■ Inserted directly into the Diagnostic based on the degree to which the failure threat passed or failed the test (e.g., 1 = Failed badly, 2 = Just failed, 3 = Just passed, 4 = Passed comfortably). The scores can then be summed to get an overall score for both commitment and risk. This will give you a plot on both axes.

■ Carried over directly from an FMEA analysis on each failure threat. This is done by using the FMEA total points from multiplying (or adding) probability of occurrence, impact on the program and invisibility. We would recommend you use testing as part of your FMEA analysis to ensure you score each failure threat correctly.

By doing this, you can get a more accurate understanding of how far into each quadrant of the RC Matrix your program is and a more granular feel for how your program is progressing.

In Part 2 we will show you how to create your own Marketing Navigation System.

Over-performance

Before we conclude this chapter, we should mention that marketing plans can over-perform as well as under-perform. In simple terms, plans can deliver a higher quality solution that was expected, do it earlier than planned and/or do it for less than was budgeted.

2

This happened to one of the authors when he was the marketing director of a global drinks retailer:

"One summer there was unusually warm weather for about three months and the company just could not meet demand. So, in a typical portfolio analysis, the strategic marketing plan was checked to see which were the key target markets and who were the key customers within them. Because these were the customers who would ensure the long term future of the company it was decided that, whatever happened, the company would meet their demand in full and on time. Whilst the non-key customers were not deliberately let down, it was made clear to them that the company could only deliver when stocks were available. Fortunately, all the competitors were in a similar situation, but they had rationed all their customers the same across the board. This had a lasting negative impact on their major customers and the company became their supplier of choice when times reverted to normal. Soon, all the targets in the plan were being beaten!"

In most cases, over-performing would be seen as a great success and not something to concern us in our navigational plans. However, we should offer a cautionary note. Over-performing can cause problems. For example:

- Implementing too fast can cause problems up and down the supply chain. Distributors and retailers may not have sufficient stocks, IT systems may not be ready and enough training may not have been done.

- Achieving higher than expected quality may mean higher than necessary costs. If the customer does not value the additional features, why spend money adding them in? A classic case of over-engineering.

The lesson is this: in considering your threats, give a little thought also to the most probable threats of over-performance and the impact they would have on the business.

Conclusion

Marketers are not traditionally schooled in good implementation practices. To help fill this gap, we have imported proven good practice from a variety of disciplines to provide a straightforward but powerful implementation management system. Moreover, the key tools within this system can be brought together on a single sheet of paper. If required, they can be expanded upon to provide greater accuracy and course diagnosis.

Used properly, this system will help you navigate your marketing plans to implementation success.

References

Covey, S.R. (2004) *The Seven Habits of Highly Effective People*, Simon & Schuster Ltd

Isaacson, Walter (2012) 'The real leadership lessons of Steve Jobs', *Harvard Business Review*, April

Further Tools: Segment SWOT Analysis

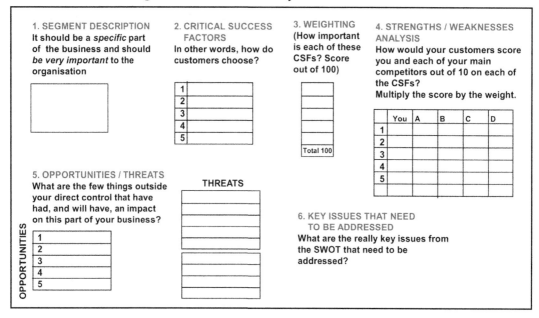

Figure 2.8: Segment SWOT analysis.

Further reading

McDonald, M. (2007) *Marketing Plans, How to Prepare Them, How to Use Them,* Butterworth-Heinemann. For a more comprehensive SWOT analysis see Form 5, p. 533 of this book.

Additional frameworks for creating excellent marketing plans are also discussed in the next chapter.

3 The essential elements of an excellent marketing plan

by Professor Malcolm McDonald

Summary

Before we explain how to use the Marketing Navigation System, we need to check if you have a good marketing plan ready to implement. This chapter looks at the key elements of marketing plans and how to prepare them. Those readers totally familiar with and experienced in preparing excellent strategic and tactical marketing plans can go directly to Chapter 4.

In order to explore the complexities of developing a strategic marketing plan, this chapter is written in four sections.

- The first section summarizes the contents of a world-class SMP and sets out the criteria for judging its effectiveness.

- The second describes the strategic marketing planning process itself and the key steps within it. It also deals with implementation issues and barriers to marketing planning.

- The third section provides guidelines for the marketer which will ensure that the input to the marketing plan is customer focused and considers the strategic dimension of all of the relationships the organization has with its business environment.

- The fourth section provides a brief overview of a process for assessing whether the strategic marketing plan creates or destroys shareholder value, having taken account of the risks associated with the plan, the time value of money and the cost of capital. It also outlines other metrics for measuring the effectiveness of the marketing strategy.

■ Introduction

Research into the efficacy of formalized marketing planning (Thompson 1962; Leighton 1966; Kollatt et al. 1972; Ansoff 1977; McDonald 1984; Greenley 1984; Piercy 1997; Smith 2003) has shown that marketing planning can make a significant contribution to commercial success. The main effects within organizations are:

- The systematic identification of emerging opportunities and threats
- Preparedness to meet change
- The specification of sustainable competitive advantage
- Improved communication among executives
- Reduction of conflicts between individuals and departments
- The involvement of all levels of management in the planning process
- More appropriate allocation of scarce resources
- Consistency of approach across the organization
- A more market-focused orientation across the organization.

However, although it can bring many benefits, a strategic marketing plan is mainly concerned with competitive advantage – that is to say, establishing, building, defending and maintaining it.

In order to be realistic, it must take into account the organization's existing competitive position, where it wants to be in the future, its capabilities and the competitive environment it faces. This means that the marketing planner must learn to use the various available processes and techniques which help to make sense of external trends, and to understand the organization's traditional ways of responding to these.

However, this poses the problem regarding which are the most relevant and useful tools and techniques, for each has strengths and weaknesses and no individual concept or technique can satisfactorily describe and illuminate the whole picture. As with a jigsaw puzzle, a sense of unity only emerges as the various pieces are connected together.

The links between strategy and performance have been the subject of detailed statistical analysis by the Strategic Planning Institute. The PIMS (Profit Impact of Market Strategy) project identified from 2600 businesses, six major links (Buzzell and Gale, 1987). From this analysis, principles have been derived for the selection of different strategies according to industry type, market conditions and the competitive position of the company.

However, not all observers are prepared to take these conclusions at face value. Like strategy consultants Lubatkin and Pitts (1985), who believe that all businesses are unique, they are suspicious that something as critical as competitive advantage can be the outcome of a few specific formulae. For them, the PIMS perspective is too mechanistic and glosses over the complex managerial and organizational problems which beset most businesses.

What is agreed, however, is that strategic marketing planning presents a useful process by which an organization formulates its strategies, providing it is adapted to the organization and its environment.

■ Section 1 – What should appear in a strategic marketing plan?

Table 3.1: What should appear in a strategic marketing plan

1 Start with a mission statement.

2 Include a financial summary which illustrates graphically revenue and profit for the full planning period. Ideally, explain this according to the Ansoff Matrix – defined later – in terms of revenue and profit from: productivity improvements; existing products in existing markets; new products in existing markets; existing products in new markets; new products in new markets: and if necessary, from acquisitions, joint ventures, licensing and the like.

3 Do a market overview: preferably, draw a market map plotting revenue and volume flows from producers through to end users, with major decision points highlighted. Has the market declined or grown? How does it break down into segments? What is your share of each? Keep it simple. If you do not have the facts, make estimates. Use lifecycles, bar charts and pie charts to make it all crystal clear.

4 Identify the key segments – described later – and do a SWOT analysis for each one: outline the major external influences and their impact on each segment. List the key factors for success. These should be less than five. Give an assessment of the company's differential strengths and weaknesses compared with those of its competitors. Score yourself and your competitors out of 10 and then multiply each score by a weighting factor for each critical success factor (e.g., CSF 1 = 60, CSF 2 = 25, CSF 3 = 10, CSF 4 = 5).

5 Make a brief statement about the key issues that have to be addressed in the planning period.

6 Summarize the SWOTs using a portfolio matrix in order to illustrate the important relationships between your key products and markets. Key segments should be plotted on a vertical axis according to the potential for growth in your profits over the next three years from each and on the horizontal axis according to your company's relative strengths in each – which of course come from the segment SWOT analyses (see the Segment SWOT template at the end of Chapter 2).

7 List your assumptions.

8 Set objectives and strategies.

9 Summarize your resource requirements for the planning period in the form of a budget.

Consequently, too much detail should be avoided. Its major function is to determine where the company is, where it wants to go and how it can get there. It lies at the heart of a company's sales-generating activities, such as the timing of the cash flow. This strategic marketing plan should be distributed only to those who need it, but it can only be an aid to effective management. It cannot be a substitute for it.

It will be obvious from Table 3.1 that not only does budget setting become much easier and more realistic, but the resulting budgets are more likely to reflect what the whole company wants to achieve, rather than just one department.

The problem of designing a dynamic system for setting budgets is a major challenge to the marketing and financial directors of all companies. The most satisfactory approach would be for a marketing director to justify all marketing expenditure from a zero base each year against the tasks to be accomplished. If these procedures are followed, a hierarchy of objectives is built in such a way that every item of budgeted expenditure can be related directly back to the initial financial objectives.

For example, if sales promotion is a major means of achieving an objective, when a sales promotion item appears in the program, it has a specific purpose which can be related back to a major objective. Thus every item of expenditure is fully accounted for.

Marketing expense can be considered to be all costs that are incurred after the product leaves the 'factory', apart from those involved in physical distribution. When it comes to pricing, any form of discounting that reduces the expected gross income – such as promotional or quantity discounts, overrides, sales commission and unpaid invoices – should be given the most careful attention as marketing expenses. Most obvious marketing expenses will occur, however, under the heading of promotion, in the form of advertising, sales salaries and expenses, sales promotion and direct mail costs.

The important point about the measurable effects of marketing activity is that anticipated levels should result from careful analysis of what is required to take the company towards its goals, while the most careful attention should be paid to gathering all items of expenditure under appropriate headings. The healthiest way of treating these issues is through zero-based budgeting.

We have just described the strategic marketing plan and what it should contain. The tactical marketing plan layout and content should be similar, but the detail is much greater, as it is for one year only.

Strategic marketing plan quality

An overall checklist to help judge the quality of the total plan. The checklist in Figure 3.1 was prepared for IBM to help them to evaluate the quality of the plans emerging from the process. It is universally applicable.

How good is your strategic marketing plan?

Score out of 10

Market structure and segmentation

- Is there a clear and unambiguous defintion of the market we are interested in serving?
- Is it clearly mapped, showing product/service flows, volumes/values in total, our shares and critical conclusions for our organisation?
- Are the segments clearly described and quantified? These must be groups of customers with the same or similar needs, not sectors.
- Are the real needs of these segments properly quantified with the relative importance of these needs clearly identified?

Differentiation

- Is there a clear and quantified analysis of how well our company satisfies these needs compared to competitors?
- Are the opportunities and threats clearly identified by segment?

Scope

- Are all the segments classified according to their relative potential for growth in profits over the next three years and according to the company's relative competititve position in each?

- Are the objectives consistent with their position in the portfolio? (volume, value, market share, profit)
- Are the strategies (including products, services and solutions) consistent with the objectives?
- Are the measurement metrics proposed relevant to the objectives and strategies?
- Are the key issues for action for all departments clearly spelled out as key issues to be addressed?

Value capture

- Do the objectives and strategies add up to the profit goals required by the company?
- Does the budget follow on logically and clearly from all the above, or is it merely an add-on?

Figure 3.1: IBM's marketing plan evaluation checklist

Table 3.2: A more detailed plan component critique:

Mission/ purpose

Level 1: Clearly spells out role, business definition, distinctive competence and indications for the future

Level 2: Spells out most of this, but has some omissions

Level 3: Spells out some of this, but has some major omissions

Level 4: Some very general statements that could apply to any organization

Level 5: So brief or vapid as to be meaningless, (e.g., 'people company', 'delight customers', etc.)

Financial summary

Level 1: Very specific summary of what the revenue and profit will be over the planning period, spelled out in terms of: Productivity, Market growth, Market share growth, New products, New markets, New products in new markets

Level 2: A clear summary of what the revenue and profit will be, but there are some gaps in the detail of where they are emanating from

Level 3: A clear summary of what the revenue and profit will be, but with little or no detail of where they are emanating from

Level 4: Some forecasts and budgets with some indication of where they are emanating from

Level 5: Some forecasts and budgets, unrelated to any source

Market summary/ overview

Level 1: A quantified market map, with key decision-making junctions highlighted. Specific conclusions drawn. Proper, needs-based segments described.

Level 2: A quantified market map, but no clear conclusions drawn

Level 3: Some general discussions of the market and how it works. Segments are SECTORS, or a priori descriptors, such as socio-economics

Level 4: Little evidence of market understanding, how it works and what the key parts of the market are

Level 5: No evidence of any kind that the organization understands what the market is, how it works and what the key segments are

SWOT analyses of key segments

Level 1: Critical success factors, by segment, weighted according to their relative importance, scored relative to competitors. External opportunities and threats related to specific segments. Conclusions for action drawn from the analysis

Level 2: Critical success factors duly weighted and scored relative to competitors, are not anchored in proper segments. Actions are too general

Level 3: Critical success factors are not quantified and weighted, but are reasonably useful as a comment on the overall strengths, weaknesses, opportunities and threats facing the business

Level 4: Some effort made to describe strengths and weaknesses, opportunities and threats, but these are not properly anchored in the specifics of the market. Likewise, opportunities and threats are not anchored in the specifics of the business

Level 5: Little other than generalized comments about the organization's strengths and weaknesses, totally unrelated to segments. No actionable conclusions drawn.

'Portfolio' summary of the SWOTs

Level 1: Segments classified according to their potential for profit growth over the planning period and the organization's strengths relative to competitors (see SW from SWOT analyses above). Meaningful conclusions drawn

Level 2: Sectors (not segments) classified according to attractiveness and relative strengths. These are likely to be equally applicable to competitors.

Level 3: Some general conclusions drawn about the commercial situation facing the organization, loosely linked to the previous analysis

Level 4: Some summary comments drawn about the commercial situation facing the organization, but not linked to the previous analysis

Level 5: No summary of the previous analysis. No conclusions drawn

Marketing objectives and strategies

Level 1: A 'pictorial' (DPM) analysis showing revenue and profit by segment over the planning period. Quantified marketing objectives: value, volume, market share, profit by segment, with quantified strategies for the four Ps fully costed with responsibilities

Level 2: Quantified marketing objectives, but some are not really marketing objectives (see level 1). Marketing strategies look believable, but are not classified according to the relative impact of each

Level 3: Some effort to relate the forecasts and budgets to previous analysis, but objectives are not strictly marketing objectives and strategies are not tied in tightly with the objectives

Level 4: Forecasts and budgets for major products for markets, only loosely related to previous analysis

Level 5: Forecasts and budgets for most products, but unrelated to any previous analysis, probably merely forecasts related to what was achieved in previous years

Budgets for the planning period

Level 1: Budgets wholly believable based on the previous analysis

Level 2: Budget not wholly tied into the previous analysis

Level 3: Budget only partly tied into previous analysis

Level 4: Detailed budget, but difficult to tie into the previous analysis

Level 5: Forecasts and budgets totally unrelated to any previous analysis

Positioning marketing planning within marketing

Smith's PhD thesis (2003) proved a direct link between organizational success and marketing strategies that conform to what previous scholars have agreed constitutes strategy quality, which was shown to be independent of variables such as size, sector, market conditions and so on.

This thesis linked superior performance to strategies with the following qualities:

1 Homogenous market segment definition
2 Segment specific propositions
3 Strategy uniqueness
4 Strength leverage and weakness minimization
5 Creation of internal and external synergies
6 Provision of tactical guidance
7 Alignment to objectives
8 Alignment to market trends
9 Appropriate resourcing
10 Clear basis of competition.

Let us first, however, position strategic marketing planning firmly within the context of marketing itself.

Marketing is a process for:

- defining markets;
- quantifying the needs of the customer groups (segments) within these markets;
- determining the value propositions to meet these needs;
- communicating these value propositions to all those people in the organization responsible for delivering them and getting their buy-in to their role;
- playing an appropriate part in delivering these value propositions to the chosen market segments; monitoring the value actually delivered.

For this process to be effective, organizations need to be consumer/customer-driven.

A map of this process is shown in Figure3.2. This process is clearly cyclical, in that monitoring the value delivered will update the organization's understanding of the value that is required by its customers. The cycle is predominantly an annual one, with a marketing plan documenting the output from the 'understand value' and 'determine value proposition' processes, but equally changes throughout the year may involve fast iterations around the cycle to respond to particular opportunities or problems.

It is well known that not all of the value proposition delivering processes will be under the control of the marketing department, whose role varies considerably between organizations.

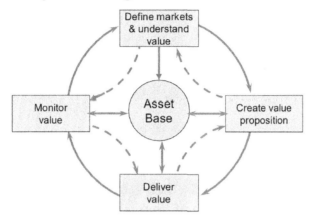

Figure 3.2: Map of the marketing process

The marketing department is likely to be responsible for the first two processes, 'Understand value' and 'Determine value proposition', although even these need to involve numerous functions, albeit coordinated by specialist marketing personnel. The 'Deliver value' process is the role of the whole company, including, for example, product development, manufacturing, purchasing, sales promotion, direct mail, distribution, sales and customer service. The marketing department will also be responsible for monitoring the effectiveness of the value delivered.

The various choices made during this marketing process are constrained and informed not just by the outside world, but also by the organization's asset base. Whereas an efficient new factory with much spare capacity might underpin a growth strategy in a particular market, a factory running at full capacity would cause more reflection on whether price should be used to control demand, unless the potential demand warranted further capital investment. As well as physical assets, choices may be influenced by financial, human resources, brand and information technology assets, to name just a few.

Thus, it can be seen that the first two boxes are concerned with strategic marketing planning processes (in other words, developing market strategies), whilst the third and fourth boxes are concerned with the actual delivery in the market of what was planned and then measuring the effect.

This book is predominantly about how to deliver a strategic marketing plan but delivery and planning are not isolated activities. Figure 3.2 emphasizes the importance of:

- Being excellent at the other processes in order for implementation to succeed

- Ensuring that delivery of the plan and monitoring its value reinforces the whole planning process.

Input to the strategic marketing planning process will commonly include:

- The corporate mission and objectives, which will determine which particular markets are of interest

- External data such as market research

- Internal data which flow from ongoing operations.

Also, it is necessary to define the markets the organization is in, or wishes to be in, and how these divide into segments of customers with similar needs. The importance of doing this correctly was emphasized earlier in the reference to Smith's 2003 PhD thesis. The choice of markets will be influenced by the corporate objectives as well as the asset base. Information will be collected about the markets, such as the market's size and growth, with estimates for the future.

The map is inherently cross-functional. 'Deliver value proposition', for example, involves every aspect of the organization, from new product development through inbound logistics and production to outbound logistics and customer service.

The map represents best practice, not common practice. Many aspects of the map are not explicitly addressed by well-embedded processes, even in sophisticated companies.

Also, the map is changing. One-to-one communications and principles of relationship marketing demand a radically different sales process from that traditionally practiced. Hence exploiting new media such as the Internet requires a substantial shift in thinking, not just changes to IT and hard processes. An example is illuminating. Marketing managers at one company related to us their early experience with a website which was enabling them to reach new customers considerably more cost-effectively than their traditional sales force. When the website was first launched, potential customers were finding the company on the Web, deciding the products were appropriate on the basis of the website, and sending an e-mail to ask to buy. So far so good. But stuck in a traditional model of the sales process, the company would allocate the 'lead' to a salesperson, who would phone up and make an appointment perhaps three weeks' hence. The customer would by now probably have moved on to another online supplier who could sell the product today, but those that remained were subjected to a sales pitch which was totally unnecessary, the customer having already decided to buy. Those that were not put off would proceed to be registered as able to buy over the Web, but the company had lost the opportunity to improve its margins by using the sales force more judiciously. In time the company realized its mistake: unlike those prospects which the company identified and contacted, which might indeed need 'selling' to, many new Web customers were initiating the dialogue themselves, and simply required the company to respond effectively and rapidly. The sales force was increasingly freed up to concentrate on major clients and on relationship building.

Having put marketing planning into the context of marketing and other corporate functions, we can now turn specifically to the marketing planning process, how it should be done and what the barriers are to doing it effectively.

■ Section 2 – The marketing planning process

Most managers accept that some kind of procedure for marketing planning is necessary. Accordingly they need a system which will help them to think in a structured way and also make explicit their intuitive economic models of the business. Unfortunately, very few companies have planning systems which possess these characteristics. However, those that do tend to follow a similar pattern of steps.

Figure 3.3 illustrates the several stages that have to be gone through in order to arrive at a marketing plan. This illustrates the difference between the process of marketing planning and the actual plan itself, which is the output of the process, which is discussed later in this chapter

Each of the process stages illustrated in Figure 3.3 will be discussed in more detail in this chapter. The dotted lines joining up stages 5–8 are meant to indicate the reality of the planning process, in that it is likely that each of these steps will have to be gone through more than once before final programs can be written.

How formal should this process be?

Although research has shown these marketing planning steps to be universally applicable, the degree to which each of the separate steps in the diagram needs to be formalized depends to a large extent on the size and nature of the company. For example, an undiversified company generally uses less formalized procedures, since top management tends to have greater functional knowledge and expertise than subordinates, and because the lack of diversity of operations enables direct control to be exercised over most of the key determinants of success. Thus, situation reviews, the setting of marketing objectives, and so on, are not always made explicit in writing, although these steps have to be gone through.

In contrast, in a diversified company, it is usually not possible for top management to have greater functional knowledge and expertise than subordinate management, hence planning tends to be more formalized in order to provide a consistent discipline for those who have to make the decisions throughout the organization.

Either way, there is now a substantial body of evidence to show that formalized planning procedures generally result in greater profitability and stability in the long term and also help to reduce friction and operational difficulties within organizations.

Bailey, Johnson and Daniel's (2000) typology of the different styles of planning went some way to throwing light on the actual degree of formalization of marketing planning processes, although Smith's 2003 thesis reduced these to three – visionary processes, rational processes and incremental processes, with most successful companies using some combination of all three.

Where marketing planning has failed, it has generally been because companies have placed too much emphasis on the procedures themselves and the resulting forecasts, rather than on generating information useful to and consumable by management. But more about reasons for failure later. For now, let us look at the marketing planning process in more detail, starting with the mission statement.

Figure 3.3: The ten steps of the strategic marketing planning process

Step 1: Mission statement

Figure 3.3 shows that a strategic marketing plan should begin with a mission or purpose statement. This is perhaps the most difficult aspect of marketing planning for managers to master, because it is largely philosophical and qualitative in nature. Many organizations find their different departments, and sometimes even different groups in the same department, pulling in different directions, often with disastrous results, simply because the organization hasn't defined the boundaries of the business and the way it wishes to do business.

Here, we can see two levels of mission. One is a corporate mission statement, the other is a lower level, or purpose statement. But there is yet another level, as shown in the following summary:

■ Type 1: 'Motherhood' – usually found inside annual reports designed to 'stroke' shareholders. Otherwise of no practical use.

■ Type 2: The real thing. A meaningful statement, unique to the organization concerned, which 'impacts' on the behavior of the executives at all levels.

■ Type 3: This is a 'purpose' statement (or lower level mission statement). It is appropriate at the strategic business unit, departmental or product group level of the organization.

The following is an example of a meaningless, vapid, motherhood-type mission statement, which most companies seem to have. They achieve nothing and it is difficult to understand why these pointless statements are so popular. Employees mock them and they rarely say anything likely to give direction to the organization. We have entitled this example 'The generic mission statement' and they are to be avoided.

The Generic Mission Statement

Our organization's primary mission is to protect and increase the value of its owners' investments while efficiently and fairly serving the needs of its customers.

[…insert organization name…] seeks to accomplish this in a manner that contributes to the development and growth of its employees, and to the goals of countries and communities in which it operates.

The following should appear in a mission or purpose statement, which should normally run to no more than one page:

1 Role or contribution
- Profit (specify), or
- Service, or
- Opportunity seeker.

2 Business definition – define the business, preferably in terms of the benefits you provide or the needs you satisfy, rather than in terms of what you make.

3 Distinctive competences – these are the essential skills/capabilities resources that underpin whatever success has been achieved to date. Competence can consist of one particular item or the possession of a number of skills compared with competitors. If. However, you could equally well put a competitor's name to these distinctive competences, then they are not distinctive competences.

4 Indications for the future
- What the firm will do
- What the firm might do
- What the firm will never do.

Step 2: Setting corporate objectives

Corporate objectives usually contain at least the following elements:

- The desired level of profitability
- Business boundaries
  - ☐ What kind of products will be sold to what kinds of markets (marketing)
  - ☐ What kinds of facilities will be developed (operations, R&D, information systems, distribution, etc.)
  - ☐ The size and character of the labor force (personnel)
  - ☐ Funding (finance).
- Other corporate objectives, such as social responsibility, corporate image, stock market image, employer image, etc.

Such a corporate plan, containing projected profit and loss accounts and balance sheets, being the result of the process described above, is more likely to provide long-term stability for a company than plans based on a more intuitive process and containing forecasts which tend to be little more than extrapolations of previous trends. This process is further summarized in Figure 3.4.

Figure 3.4

Step 3: The marketing audit

Any plan will only be as good as the information on which it is based, and the marketing audit is the means by which information for planning is organized. There is no reason why marketing cannot be audited in the same way as accounts, in spite of its more innovative, subjective nature. A marketing audit is a systematic appraisal of all the external and internal factors that have affected a company's commercial performance over a defined period.

Given the growing turbulence of the business environment and the shorter product lifecycles that have resulted, no one would deny the need to stop at least once a year at a particular point in the planning cycle to try to form a reasoned view of how all the many external and internal factors have influenced performance.

Sometimes, of course, a company will conduct a marketing audit because it is in financial trouble. At times like these, management often attempts to treat the wrong symptoms, most frequently by reorganizing the company. But such measures are unlikely to be effective if there are more fundamental problems which have not been identified. Of course, if the company survived for long enough, it might eventually solve its problems through a process of elimination. Essentially, though, the argument is that the problems have first to be properly defined. The audit is a means of helping to define them.

Two kinds of variable

Any company carrying out an audit will be faced with two kinds of variable. There is the kind over which the company has no direct control, for example economic and market factors. Second, there are those over which the company has complete control, the operational variables, which are usually the firm's internal resources. This division suggests that the best way to structure an audit is in two parts, external and internal. Table 3.3 shows areas which should be investigated under both headings. Each should be examined with a view to building up an information base relevant to the company's performance.

Many people mistakenly believe that the marketing audit should be some kind of final attempt to define a company's marketing problems, or, at best, something done by an independent body from time to time to ensure that a company is on the right track. However, many highly successful companies, as well as using normal information and control procedures and marketing research throughout the year, start their planning cycle each year with a formal, audit-type process, of everything that has had an important influence on marketing activities. Certainly, in many leading consumer goods companies, the annual self-audit approach is a tried and tested discipline.

Table 3.3: Conducting an audit

External audit	Internal audit
Business and economic environment	Own company
Economic political, fiscal, legal, social, cultural	Sales (total, by geographical location, by industrial
Technological	type, by customer, by product)
Intra-company	Market shares
The market: Total market, size, growth and trends	Profit margins, costs
(value volume)	Marketing information research
	Marketing mix variables,
Market	Product management, operations and resources
Characteristics, developments and trends	Key strengths and weaknesses
Products, prices, physical distribution,	
channels	
Customers, consumers, communication, industry	
practices	
Price, distribution, promotion,	
Competition	
Major competitors	
Size	
Market share coverage	
Market standing and reputation	
Production capabilities	
Distribution policies	
Marketing methods	
Extent of diversification	
Personnel issues	
International links	
Profitability	

The market overview

A key part of the marketing audit is an overview of the market. This should appear prominently in the actual strategic marketing plan and spell out clearly:

- What the market is
- How it works
- What the key decision making points are
- What the segments are.

Market definition is fundamental to success and must be made in terms of need sets rather than in product/service terms. Thus, Gestetner failed by defining its markets as 'duplicators' and IBM almost failed by defining its market as 'main frames'. More recently Kodak failed because it defined its market as 'films'. Accordingly, a pension is a product, not a market, as many other products can satisfy the same or similar needs. The following lists hypothetical markets in the financial services sector.

Some market definitions (personal market)

Market	Need (online)
Emergency cash ('rainy day')	Cash to cover an undesired and unexpected event, often the loss of/damage to property.
Futuer event planning	Schemes to protect and grow money for anticipated and unanticipated events (e.g., car replacement/ repairs, education, weddings, funeral health care).
Asset purchase	Cash to buy assets they require (e.g., car purchase, house purchase, once-in-a-lifetime holiday).
Welfare contingency	The ability to maintain a desirred standard of living (for self and/or dependants) in times of unplanned cessation of income.
Retirement income	The ability to maintain a desired standard of living (for self and/or dependants) after stopping work.
Wealth care and building	The care and growth of assets (with various risk and liquidity levels)
Day-to-day money management	The ability to store and readily access cash for day-to-day requirements.
Financial protection & security from motor vehicle incidents	Currently known as car insurance

Figures 3.5 and 3.6 show the marketing books market in the UK. The first shows the market 'mapped' solely as marketing books. The second shows the market mapped in terms of the broader market definition of marketing knowledge promulgation, from which it can be seen that new competitors and distribution channels come into play. Thinking and planning like this certainly had a dramatic effect on the marketing strategy of the major publisher involved.

Figure 3.7 is a generic market map, which shows how a market works from suppliers to users and, like a balance sheet, it must 'balance', in the sense that if five million radiators are made or imported, five million must be distributed, five million must be installed and the decision about which radiators are to be installed must be made by someone. It is the purpose of the market map to spell all this out quantitatively.

It is at key decision points that market segmentation should take place. A segment is a group of customers or consumers that share the same (or similar) needs. This step is crucial, for it is upon the key segments from the market map that SWOT analyses should be completed.

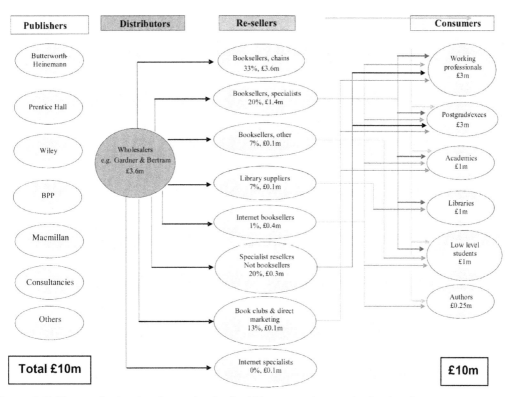

Figure 3.5: The marketing books market in the UK, mapped as marketing books.

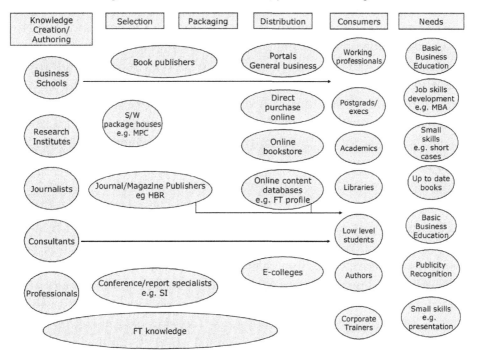

Figure 3.6: The marketing books market in the UK, mapped as marketing knowledge promulgation.

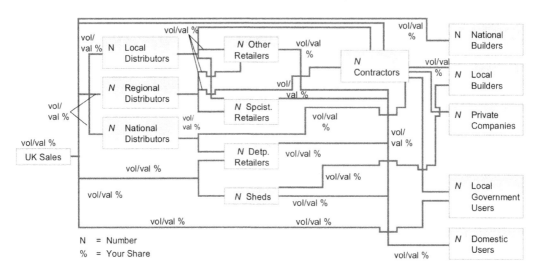

Figure 3.7: Generic market map

Step 4: SWOT analyses

The only remaining question is what happens to the results of the audit? Some companies consume valuable resources carrying out audits that bring very little by way of actionable results.

Indeed, there is always the danger that, at the audit stage, insufficient attention is paid to the need to concentrate on analysis that determines which trends and developments will actually affect the company. Whilst the checklist demonstrates the completeness of logic and analysis, the people carrying out the audit should discipline themselves to omit from their audits all the information that is not central to the company's marketing problems. Thus, inclusion of research reports, or over-detailed sales performance histories by product which lead to no logical actions whatever, only serve to rob the audit of focus and reduce its relevance.

Since the objective of the audit is to indicate what a company's marketing objectives and strategies should be, it follows that it would be helpful if some format could be found for organizing the major findings.

One useful way of doing this is in the form of a number of SWOT analyses. A SWOT is a summary of the audit under the headings, internal *strengths* and *weaknesses* as they relate to external *opportunities* and *threats*. A SWOT should be conducted for each segment that is considered to be important in the company's future. These analyses should, if possible, contain a few paragraphs of commentary focusing on key factors only. They should highlight internal differential strengths and weaknesses versus competitors and key external opportunities and threats. A summary of reasons for good or bad performance should be included. They should be interesting to read, contain concise statements, include only relevant and important data, and give greater emphasis to creative analysis.

To summarize, carrying out a regular and thorough marketing audit in a structured manner will go a long way towards giving a company a knowledge of the business, trends in the market, and where value is added by competitors, as the basis for setting objectives and strategies.

Step 5: Assumptions

Let us now return to the preparation of the marketing plan. If we refer again to the marketing planning process, and have completed our marketing audit and SWOT analyses, assumptions now have to be written.

There are certain key determinants of success in all companies about which assumptions have to be made before the planning process can proceed. It is really a question of standardizing the planning environment. For example, it would be no good receiving plans from two product managers, one of whom believed the market was going to increase by 10%, while the other believed the market was going to decline by 10%.

Examples of assumptions might be:

'*With respect to the company's industrial climate, it is assumed that:*

1. *Industrial overcapacity will increase from 105% to 115% as new industrial plants come into operation.*
2. *Competition will force price levels down by 10% across the board.*
3. *A new product in the field of x will be introduced by our major competitor before the end of the second quarter.*'

Assumptions should be few in number, and if a plan is possible irrespective of the assumptions made, then the assumptions are unnecessary.

Step 6: Marketing objectives and strategies

The next step in marketing planning is the writing of marketing objectives and strategies, the key the whole process.

An *objective* is what you want to achieve. A *strategy* is how you plan to achieve your objectives. Thus, there can be objectives and strategies at all levels in marketing. For example, there can be advertising objectives and strategies, and pricing objectives and strategies.

However, the important point to remember about marketing objectives is that they are about products and markets only. Common sense will confirm that it is only by selling something to someone that the company's financial goals can be achieved, and that advertising, pricing, service levels and so on are the means (or strategies) by which we might succeed in doing this. Thus, pricing objectives, sales promotion objectives, advertising objectives and the like should not be confused with marketing objectives.

Marketing objectives are simply about one, or more, of the following:

- Existing products for existing markets
- New products for existing markets
- Existing products for new markets
- New products for new markets.

They should be capable of measurement, otherwise they are not objectives. Directional terms such as 'maximize', 'minimize', 'penetrate', 'increase', etc. are only acceptable if quantitative measurement can be attached to them. Measurement should be in terms of some, or all, of the following: sales volume; sales value; market share; profit; percentage penetration of outlets (for example, to have 30 per cent of all retail outlets stocking our product by year 3).

Marketing strategies are the means by which marketing objectives will be achieved and generally are concerned with the four Ps, as follows:

- **Product:** The general policies for product deletions, modifications, additions, design, branding, positioning, packaging, etc.
- **Price:** The general pricing policies to be followed by product groups in market segments.
- **Place:** The general policies for channels and customer service levels
- **Promotion:** The general policies for communicating with customers under the relevant headings, such as advertising, sales force, sales promotion, public relations, exhibitions, direct mail, etc.

Steps 7–8: Estimate expected results and identify alternative plans and mixes

Having completed this major planning task, it is normal at this stage to employ judgment, analogous experience, field tests, and so on, to test out the feasibility of the objectives and strategies in terms of market share, costs, profits, and so on. It is also normally at this stage that alternative plans and mixes are considered, if necessary.

Step 9: The budget

In a strategic marketing plan, these strategies would normally be costed out approximately and, if not practicable, alternative strategies would be proposed and costed out until a satisfactory solution could be reached.

This would then become the budget. In most cases, there would be a budget for the full three years of the strategic marketing plan, but there would also be a very detailed budget for the first year of the plan which would be included in the one-year operational plan.

It will be obvious from all of this that the setting of budgets becomes not only much easier, but the resulting budgets are more likely to be realistic and related to what the whole company wants to achieve, rather than just one functional department.

The problem of designing a dynamic system for budget setting, rather than the 'tablets of stone' approach, which is more common, is a major challenge to the marketing and financial directors of all companies.

As stated earlier, the most satisfactory approach would be for a marketing director to justify all marketing expenditure from a zero base each year against the tasks he or she wishes to accomplish. A little thought will confirm that this is exactly the approach recommended in this chapter. If these procedures are followed, a hierarchy of objectives is built up in such a way that every item of budgeted expenditure can be related directly back to the initial corporate financial objectives. For example, if sales promotion is a major means of achieving an objective in a particular market, when sales promotional items appear in the program, each one has a specific purpose which can be related back to a major objective.

Doing it this way not only ensures that every item of expenditure is fully accounted for as part of a rational, objective and task approach, but also that when changes have to be made during the period to which the plan relates, these changes can be made is such a way that the least damage is caused to the company's long-term objectives.

There is, of course, no textbook answer to problems relating to questions such as whether packaging should be a marketing or a production expense, and whether some distribution costs could be considered to be marketing costs. For example, insistence on high service levels results in high inventory carrying costs. Only common sense will reveal workable solutions to issues such as these.

Under price, however, any form of discounting that reduces the expected gross income, such as promotional discounts, quantity discounts, royalty rebates, and so on, as well as sales commission and unpaid invoices, should be given the mot careful attention as incremental marketing expenses.

Most obvious incremental marketing expenses will occur, however, under the heading promotion, in the form of advertising, sales salaries and expenses, sales promotional expenditure, direct mail costs, and so on. The important point about the measurable effects of marketing activity is that anticipated levels should be the result of the most careful analysis of what is required to take the company towards its goals, while the most careful attention should be paid to gathering all items of expenditure under appropriate headings. The healthiest way of treating these issues is a zero-bases budgeting approach.

Step 10: First year detailed implementation program

In a one-year tactical plan, the general marketing strategies would be developed into specific sub-objectives, each supported by more detailed strategy and action statements.

- A company organized according to functions might have an advertising plan, a sales promotion plan a pricing plan, and so on.
- A product-based company might have a product plan, with objectives, strategies and tactics for price, place and promotion as necessary.
- A market or geographically based company might have a market plan, with objectives, strategies and tactics for the four Ps as necessary.
- A company with a few major customers might have customer plans.

Any combination of the above might be suitable, depending on circumstances.

A written strategic marketing plan is the backdrop against which operational decisions are taken. Consequently, as we discussed at the start of this chapter, too much detail should be avoided. Its major function is to determine where the company is, where it wants to go and how it can get there. It should be distributed on a 'need to know' basis only. It should be used as an aid to effective management. It cannot be a substitute for it.

Marketing planning implementation

Many companies with financial difficulties have recognized the need for a more structured approach to planning their marketing and have opted for the kind of standardized, formalized procedures written about so much in textbooks. Yet, these rarely bring any benefits and often bring marketing planning itself into disrepute.

It is quite clear that any attempt at the introduction of formalized marketing planning requires a change in a company's approach to managing its business. It is also clear that unless a company recognizes these implications, and plans to seek ways of coping with them, formalized strategic planning will be ineffective.

Research (McDonald 1982) has shown that the implications are principally as follows:

1 Any closed-loop planning system (but especially one that is essentially a forecasting and budgeting system) will lead to dull and ineffective marketing. Therefore, there has to be some mechanism for preventing inertia from setting in through the over-bureaucratization of the system.

2 Planning undertaken at the functional level of marketing, in the absence of a means of integration with other functional areas of the business at general management level, will be largely ineffective.

3 The separation of responsibility for operational and strategic planning will lead to a divergence of the short-term thrust of a business at the operational level from the long-term objectives of the enterprise as a whole. This will encourage preoccupation with short-term results at operational level, which normally makes the firm less effective in the longer term.

4 Unless the chief executive understands and takes an active role in strategic marketing planning, it will never be an effective system.

5 A period of up to three years is necessary (especially in large firms) for the successful introduction of an effective strategic marketing planning system.

The same PhD (McDonald, 1982) also found that the principal barriers to implementing marketing planning are:

1 Weak support from the chief executive and top management.

2 Lack of a plan for planning.

3 Lack of line management support due to any of the following, either singly or in combination:

 - Hostility
 - Lack of skills
 - Lack of information
 - Lack of resources
 - Inadequate organizational structure.

4 Confusion over planning terms.

5 Numbers in lieu of written objectives and strategies.

6 Too much detail, too far ahead.

7 Once-a-year ritual.

8 Separation of operational planning from strategic planning.

9 Failure to integrate marketing planning into total corporate planning system.

10 Delegation of planning to a planner.

How the marketing planning process works

As a basic principle, strategic marketing planning should take place as near to the marketplace as possible in the first instance, but such plans should then be reviewed at higher levels within an organization to see what issues may have been overlooked.

It has been suggested that each manager in the organization should complete an audit and SWOT analysis on his or her own area of responsibility. The only way that this can work in practice is by means of a hierarchy of audits. The principle is simply demonstrated in Figure 3.8. This figure illustrates the principle of auditing at different levels within an organization. The marketing audit format will be universally applicable. It is only the detail that varies from level to level and from company to company within the same group.

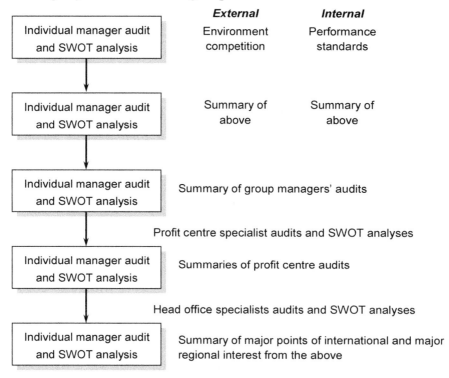

Figure 3.8: Hierarchy of audits

Figure 3.9 illustrates the total corporate strategic and planning process. This time, however, a time element is added, and the relationship between strategic planning briefings, long-term corporate plans and short-term operational plans is clarified. It is important to note that there are two 'open-loop' points on this last diagram. These are the key times in the planning process when a subordinate's views and findings should be subjected to the closest examination by his or her superior. It is by taking these opportunities that marketing planning can be transformed into the critical and creative process it is supposed to be rather than the dull, repetitive ritual it so often turns out to be.

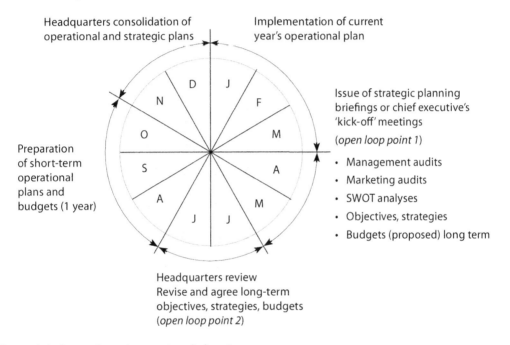

Figure 3.9: Strategic and operational planning

Since in anything but the smallest of undiversified companies it is not possible for top management to set detailed objectives for operating units, it is suggested that at this stage in the planning process strategic guidelines should be issued. One way of doing this is in the form of a strategic planning letter. Another is by means of a personal briefing by the chief executive at 'kick-off' meetings. As in the case of the audit, these guidelines would proceed from the broad to the specific, and would become more detailed as they progressed through the company towards operating units.

These guidelines would be under the headings of financial, manpower and organization, operations and, of course, marketing.

Under marketing, for example, at the highest level in a large group, top management may ask for particular attention to be paid to issues such as the technical impact of microprocessors on electromechanical component equipment, leadership and innovation strategies, vulnerability to attack from the flood of Japanese, Korean and Third World products, and so on. At operating company level, it is possible to be more explicit about target markets, product development, and the like.

The marketing planning process – conclusions

In concluding this section, we must stress that there can be no such thing as an off-the-peg marketing planning system and anyone who offers one must be viewed with great suspicion. In the end, strategic marketing planning success comes from an endless willingness to learn and to adapt the system to the people and the circumstances of the firm. It also comes from a deep understanding about the nature of marketing planning, which is something that, in the final analysis, cannot be taught.

However, strategic marketing planning demands that the organization recognizes the challenges that face it and their effect on its potential for future success. It must learn to focus on customers and their needs at all times and explore every avenue which may provide it with a differential advantage over its competitors.

The next section looks at some guidelines which lead to effective marketing planning.

■ Section 3 – Guidelines for effective marketing planning

Although innovation remains a major ingredient in commercial success, there are nevertheless other challenges which companies must overcome if they wish to become competitive marketers. While their impact may vary from company to company, challenges such as the pace of change, the maturity of markets and the implications of globalization need to be given serious consideration. Some of the more obvious challenges are shown in Table 3.5.

To overcome these challenges the following guidelines are recommended to help the marketer to focus on effective marketing strategies.

Table 3.4: Change and the challenge to marketing

Nature of change	Marketing challenges
Pace of change	
• Compressed time horizons	Ability to exploit markets more rapidly
• Shorter product life cycles	More effective new product development
• Transient customer preferences	Flexibility in approach to markets
	Accuracy in demand forecasting
	Ability to optimize price-setting
Process thinking	
• Move to flexible manufacturing and control systems	Dealing with micro-segmentation
	Finding ways to shift from single focus to the forging of long-term relationships
• Materials substitution	
• Developments in microelectronics and robotization	Creating greater customer commitment
• Quality focus transaction	
Market maturity	
• Over-capacity	
• Low margins	
• Lack of growth	
• Stronger competition	Adding value leading to differentiation
• Trading down	New market creation and stimulation
• Cost-cutting	
Customer's expertise and power	
• More demanding,	Finding ways of getting closer to the customer,
• Higher expectations	Managing the complexities of multiple market channels
• More knowledgeable	Concentration of buying power,
• More sophisticated buyer behavior	
Internationalization of business	
• More competitors	Restructuring of domestic operations to compete internationally
• Stronger competition	Becoming customer-focused in larger and more disparate markets
• Lower margins	
• More customer choice	
• Larger markets	
• More disparate customer needs	

Twelve guidelines for effective marketing

1   Understand the sources of competitive advantage

Guideline 1 (Figure 3.10) shows a universally recognized list of sources of competitive advantage (Porter, 1980). For small firms, these are more likely to be the ones listed on the left. It is clearly possible to focus on highly specialized niches with special skills and to develop very customer-focused relationships not possible for large organizations. Flexibility is also likely to be a potential source of competitive advantage.

What all firms should seek to avoid wherever possible is competing with an undifferentiated product or service in too broad a market.

The author frequently has to spell out to the self-employed consultants who seek his advice that without something different to offer (that is required by the market, of course!), they will continue to struggle and will have to rely on the crumbs that fall from the table of others.

This leads on to the second point.

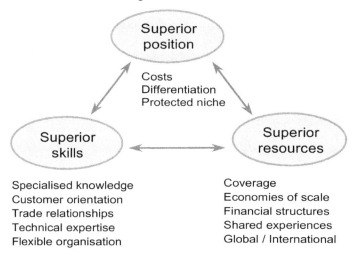

Figure 3.10 Guideline 1: understand the sources of competitive advantage

2   Understand differentiation

Guideline 2 takes this point a little further and spells out the main sources of differentiation. The fifth of these in particular, superior service, is likely to be the main source of competitive advantage and firms should work relentlessly towards the differential advantage that these will bring.

Understand differentiation

- Superior product quality
- Innovative product features
- Unique product or service
- Srong brand name
- Superior service (speed, responsiveness, ability to solve problems)
- Wide distribution coverage

It is essential to be committed to innovation. Continuously strive to serve customer needs better.

3   Understand the environment

Guideline 3 spells out what is meant by the word 'Environment'.

Although this one will be the least appealing to many organizations, nonetheless, there is now an overwhelming body of evidence to show that it is failure to monitor the hostile environmental changes that is the biggest cause of failure in both large and small companies. Had anyone predicted the demise of IBM five years ago, they would have been derided. Yet it was IBM's failure to observe the changes taking place about them that caused its current problems.

Clearly, 'Marketing' has a key role to play in the process. This means devoting at least some of the key executives' time and resources to monitoring formally the changes taking place about them. If they do not know how to go about doing this, get in a good consultant to start them off and they can then continue to do it themselves.

Understand the environment (opportunities and threats)

Macro environment

■ Political/regulatory

■ Economic

■ Technological

■ Societal

Market/industry environment

■ market size and potential

■ Customer behavior

■ Segmentation

■ Suppliers

■ Channels

■ Industry practices

■ Industry profitability.

Carry out a formal marketing audit

This leads on naturally to the next point.

4   Understand competitors

Guideline 4 is merely an extension of the marketing audit. Suffice it to say that if any organization, big or small, doesn't know as much about its close competitors as it knows about itself, it should not be surprised if it fails to stay ahead.

Again, if anyone is unsure how to go about this, use a consultant initially, although the author's advice is to use a modicum of common sense and sweet reasonableness in this process, stopping short, of course, of industrial espionage!

Closely connected with this is a final piece of information in this process we have referred to as a marketing audit.

Understand competitors

- Direct competitors
- Potential competitors
- Substitute products
- Forward integration by suppliers
- Backward integration by customers
- Competitors' profitability
- Competitors' strengths and weaknesses.

Develop a structured competitor monitoring process. Include the results in the marketing audit.

5   Understand your own strengths and weaknesses

Guideline 5 sets out potential sources of differentiation for your own organization. It represents a fairly comprehensive audit of the asset bases. Along with the other two sections of the Marketing Audit (The Environment and Competitors), it is important to make a written summary of your conclusions from all of this.

If you cannot summarize on a couple of sheets of paper the sources of your own competitive advantage, it has not been done properly. If this is the case, the chances are that you are relying on luck. Alas, luck has a habit of being somewhat fickle!

Strengths and weaknesses

Carry out a formal position audit of your own product/market position in each segment in which you compete. In particular, understand by segment:

- What the qualifying features and benefits are
- What the differential features and benefits are
- How relatively important each of these are
- How well your product or service performs against your competitors on each of these requirements.

6   Understand market segmentation

Guideline 6 looks somewhat technical and esoteric, at first sight. Nonetheless, market segmentation is one of the key sources of commercial success and needs to be taken seriously by all organizations, as the days of the easy marketability of products and services have long since disappeared for all but a lucky few. The secret of success, of course, is to change the offer in accordance with changing needs and not to offer exactly the same product or service to everyone – the most frequent, production-oriented mistake of large organizations.

Closely connected with this is the next point.

Market segmentation

- Not all customers in a broadly-defined market have the same needs.

- Positioning is easy. Market segmentation is difficult. Positioning problems stem from poor segmentation.

- Select a segment and serve it. Do not straddle segments and sit between them.

  - Understand how your market works (market structure)
  - List what is bought (including where, when, how, applications)
  - List who buys (demographics, psychographics)
  - List why they buy (needs, benefits sought)
  - Search for groups with similar needs.

7   Understand the dynamics of product/market evolution

Whilst at first sight Guideline 7 looks as if it applies principally to large companies, few will need reminding of the short-lived nature of many retailing concepts, such as the boutiques of the late 1980s. Those who clung doggedly onto a concept that had had its day lived to regret it.

8   Understand your portfolio of products and markets

Guideline 8 suggests plotting either products/services, or markets (or, in some cases, customers) on a vertical axis in order of the potential of each for you to achieve your personal and commercial objectives as, clearly, they can't all be equal. Organizations will obviously have greater or lesser strengths in serving each of these 'markets'. For each location on the four box matrix, put a circle, the size of which represents current sales. This will give a reasonably accurate 'picture' of your business at a glance and will indicate whether or not it is a well balanced portfolio. Too much in any one box is dangerous.

Understand your portfolio of products and markets

You cannot be all things to all people. A deep understanding of portfolio analysis will enable you to set appropriate objectives and allocate resources effectively. Portfolio logic arrays competitive position against market attractiveness in a matrix form.

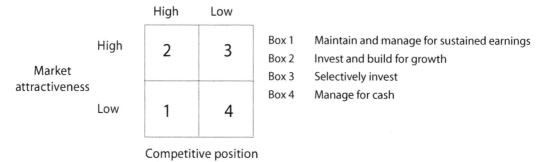

Figure 3.11

Follow the guidelines given and there is no reason why any firm should not have a healthy and growing business.

9   Set clear strategic priorities and stick to them

Guideline 9 suggests writing down the results of your earlier endeavors in summary form (a marketing/business plan).

Set clear strategic priorities

- Focus your best resources on the best opportunities for achieving continuous growth in sales and profits.
- This means having a written strategic marketing plan for three years containing:
  - ☐ A mission statement
  - ☐ A financial summary
  - ☐ A market overview
  - ☐ SWOT analyses on key segments
  - ☐ A portfolio summary
  - ☐ Assumptions
  - ☐ Marketing objectives and strategies
  - ☐ A budget
- This strategic plan can then be converted into a detailed one-year plan.
- To do this, an agreed marketing planning process will be necessary.
- Focus on key performance indicators with an unrelenting discipline.

While it is not the intention of the author to stifle creativity by suggesting that any firm should get into a bureaucratic form of planning, it remains a fact that those individuals and organizations who can make explicit their intended sources of revenue and profits, tend to thrive and prosper in the long term. This implies something more sophisticated than forecasts and budgets. Commercial history has demonstrated that any fool can spell out the financial results they wish to achieve. But it takes intellect to spell out how they are to be achieved. This implies setting clear strategic priorities and sticking to them.

10   Understand customer orientation

Guideline 10 will be familiar to all successful firms. BS 5750, ISO 9001 and the like, whilst useful for those with operations such as production processes, have little to do with real quality, which, of course, can only be seen through the eyes of the customer. It is obvious that making anything perfectly that no one buys is somewhat of a pointless exercise.

Understand customer orientation

- Develop customer orientation in all functions. Ensure that every function understand that they are there to serve the customer not their own narrow functional interests.

- This must be driven from the board downwards.

- Where possible, organize in cross-functional teams around customer groups and core processes

- Make customers the arbiter of quality.

While it is, perhaps, easier for small companies than for large companies to check out customer satisfaction, this should nonetheless be done continuously, for it is clearly the only real arbiter of quality.

11   Be professional

Guideline 11 sets out some of the marketing skills essential to continuous success. Professional management skills, particularly in marketing, are becoming the hallmark of commercial success. There are countless professional development skills courses available to all firms. Alas, too many directors consider themselves too busy to attend, which is extremely short sighted. Entrepreneurial skills, combined with hard-edged management skills, will see any firm through.

Be professional

Particularly in marketing, it is essential to have professional marketing skills, which implies formal training in the underlying concepts, tools and techniques of marketing. In particular, the following are core:

- Market research
- Gap analysis
- Market segmentation/positioning
- Product life cycle analysis
- Portfolio management
- The four Ps
  - Product management
  - Pricing
  - Place (customer service, channel management)
  - Promotion (selling, sales force management, advertising, sales promotion).

12   Give leadership

Guideline 12 sets out the final factor for success.

Give leadership

- Do not let doom and gloom pervade your thinking
- The hostile environment offers many opportunities for companies with toughness and insight
- Lead your team strongly
- Do not accept poor performance in the most critical positions.

Charismatic leadership, however, without the eleven other pillars of success, will be to no avail. Few will need reminding of the charisma of Maxwell, Halpen, Saunders and countless others during the past decade. Charisma, however, without something to sell that the market values, will ultimately be pointless. It is, nonetheless, still an important ingredient in success.

Effective planning – conclusions

Lest readers should think that the twelve factors for success are a figment of the imagination, there is much recent research to suggest otherwise. The four ingredients listed in Figure 9 are common to all commercially successful organizations, irrespective of their national origin.

From this is can be seen that the core product or service on offer has to be excellent.

Secondly, operations have to be efficient and, preferably, state-of-the-art.

Thirdly, the research stresses the need for creativity in leadership and personnel; something frequently discouraged by excessive bureaucracy in large organizations.

Finally, excellent companies practice professional marketing. Inter alia, this means that the organization continuously monitors the environment, the market, competitors and their own performance against customer-driven standards and makes differential offers to its key target segments, whose needs they understand in depth.

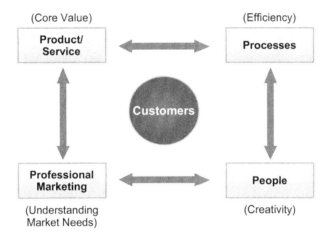

Figure 3.12

■ Section 4 – Do marketing plans contribute to profitability?

Marketing metrics, or accountability, is one of the biggest challenges facing the marketing community today. It is a major theme of research at the Australian Marketing Institute, the Worshipful Company of Marketors, the British Chartered Institute of Marketing, the Chief Marketing Officer, Council of America and at Cranfield School of Management, to name but a few.

The reason is not hard to find, given the pressure that so many Western European and American companies are under because of maturing markets. Certainly, any chief executive officer, on asking their marketing chief what shareholders had received for the millions spent on marketing, on being told that a change in attitude or an improvement in awareness had occurred, they would be justified in replacing them with someone who could be more accountable and responsible. So, in a chapter on marketing planning, it would be remiss not to address this topic.

Three distinct levels for measuring marketing effectiveness

When the author was marketing director of a fast moving consumer goods company 30 years ago, there were many well tried-and-tested models for measuring the effectiveness of marketing promotional expenditure. Indeed, some of these were quite sophisticated and included mathematical models for promotional campaigns, for advertising threshold and wear out levels and the like.

Indeed, it would be surprising if marketing as a discipline did not have its own quantitative models for the massive expenditure of FMCG companies. Over time, these modelss have been transferred to business-to-business and service companies, with the result that, today, any organization spending substantial sums of shareholders' money on promotion should be ashamed of themselves if those responsible could not account for the effectiveness of such expenditure. But, at this level, accountability can only be measured in terms of the kinds of effects that promotional expenditure can achieve, such as awareness, or attitude change, both of which can be measured quantitatively.

But to assert that such expenditure can be measured directly in terms of sales or profits is intellectually indefensible, when there are so many other variables that affect sales, such as product efficacy, packaging, price, the sales force, competitors and countless other variables that, like advertising, have an intermediate impact on sales and profits.

So, the problem with marketing accountability has never been with how to measure the effectiveness of promotional expenditure, for this we have had for many years. No, the problem occurs because marketing isn't just a promotional activity. As was illustrated in Figure 3.4 earlier in this chapter in world class organizations where the customer is at the center of the business model, marketing as a discipline is responsible for defining and understanding markets, for segmenting these markets, for developing value propositions to meet the researched needs of the customers in the segments, for getting buy-in from all those in the organization responsible for delivering this value, for playing their own part in delivering this value and for monitoring whether the promised value is being delivered.

Indeed, this definition of marketing as a function for strategy development as well as for tactical sales delivery, when represented as a map, can be used to clarify the whole problem of how to measure marketing effectiveness (see Figure 3.13).

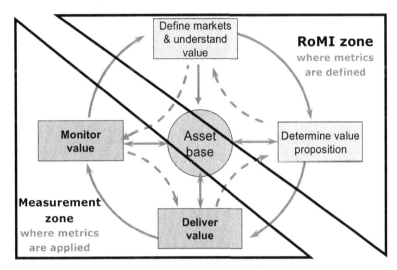

Figure 3.13: Map of the marketing domain with metrics superimposed

Note: RoMI means Return On Marketing Investment

From the map in Figure 3.13, it can be seen that there are three levels of measurement, or metrics.

Level 1 is the most vital of all three, because this is what determines whether or not the marketing strategies for the longer term (usually three to five years) destroy or create shareholder value added. In capital markets, success is measured in terms of shareholder value added, having taken account of the risks associated with the strategies set out in the strategic marketing plan, the time value of money and the cost of capital. This is a totally different measurement from outmoded accounting notions of profit.

It is justified to use the strategic marketing plan for assessing whether shareholder value is being created or destroyed because, as Sean Kelly agrees.

The Customer is simply the fulcrum of the business and everything from production to supply chain, to finance, risk management, personnel management and product development, all adapt to and converge on the business value proposition that is projected to the customer.

(Kelly, 2005)

Thus, corporate assets and their associated competences are only relevant if customer markets value them sufficiently highly that they lead to sustainable competitive advantage, or shareholder value added. This is our justification for evaluating the strategic plan for what is to be sold, to whom and with what projected effect on profits as a route to establishing whether shareholder value will be created or destroyed.

Once the hype and jargon is cleared away, all marketing plans say the same thing: 'We're going to do these things in this market and make this much profit'. Digging deeper, we can discern three fundamental assertions that lie at the root of all marketing plans:

- The market we are going for is this big.

- Our strategy will achieve this much share

- That share will result in this much profit.

It is these three assertions that give rise to the three components of business risk:

- *Market risk*: the risk that the market is not as big as you think it will be.

- *Share risk*: the risk that your strategy will not deliver the share it promises.

- *Profit risk*: the risk that you will not make the margins you promised.

It is comparatively easy to envisage how each of these can be broken down into sub components of risk, which can be assessed using the basic tools of marketing such as Ansoff's Matrix, product lifecycle analysis, market segmentation robustness, offer specificity and so on.

Cumulatively, these three component risks add up to business risk. If all three are certain, then there is no risk and the plan will deliver what it promises. To the extent that there is some uncertainty in one or more areas, the plan is risky and the promised returns must be higher to compensate for the risk. If we could objectively assess business risk, using data in a specific and systematic way, it would help us to create shareholder value in two ways. Firstly, it would allow us to identify the main areas of risk in our strategy and act to reduce that risk. Secondly, it would give us a tool to sell our strategy to investors, demonstrating in detail that our plan is well-thought out and creates shareholder value. The challenge lies in accurately assessing each of those three areas of risk.

The process for doing this has been labeled 'Marketing due diligence' based on years of research at Cranfield School of Management. In short, marketing due diligence is a process which assessed the probability of a marketing plan delivering its promises. It then adjusts the promised profit to reflect that probability and calculates if, for the firm's cost of capital, the plan would create or destroy shareholder value.

Level 3 is the level of micro promotional measurement we have described above.

Level 2. There is another level, however, that few academics or practitioners have addressed to date. We shall describe it briefly here, although once the process of marketing due diligence has been applied to the long-range marketing strategy, it remains central to the issue of marketing metrics and marketing effectiveness. Further, however, let us destroy once and for all one of the great myths of measurement – marketing return on investment. This implies 'return' divided by 'investment' and, for marketing expenditure such as promotional spend, it is an intellectually puerile notion. It's a bit like demanding a financial justification for the wings of an aircraft! (See the points we make above). Also, as McGovern et al. (2004), say:

> *Measuring marketing performance isn't like measuring factory output – a fact that many non-marketing executives don't grasp. In the controlled environment of a manufacturing plant, it's simple to account for what goes in one end and what comes out the other and then determine productivity. But the output of marketing can be measured only long after it has left the plant.*

Neither is the budget and all the energy employed in measuring it a proxy for measuring marketing effectiveness. Indeed, as Simon Caulkin (2005) says:

> *90% of USA and European firms think budgets are cumbersome and unreliable, providing neither predictability nor control.*

- *They are backward-looking and inflexible. Instead of focusing managers' time on the customers, the real source of income, they focus their attention on satisfying the boss, i.e. the budget becomes the purpose.*
- *Cheating is endemic is all budget regimes. The result is fear, inefficiency, sub-optimization and waste.*
- *In companies like Enron, the pressure to make the numbers was so great that managers didn't just doctor a few numbers, they broke the law.*
- *People with targets and jobs dependent on meeting them will probably meet the targets, even if they have to destroy the enterprise to do it.*

So, once the marketing due diligence is completed, we can turn our attention to what needs to be measured in the one year plan.

Figure 3.14 shows the Ansoff Matrix. Each of the cells in each box (cells will consists of products for segments) are planning units, in the sense of objectives which are set for each for volume, value and profit for the first year of the strategic plan.

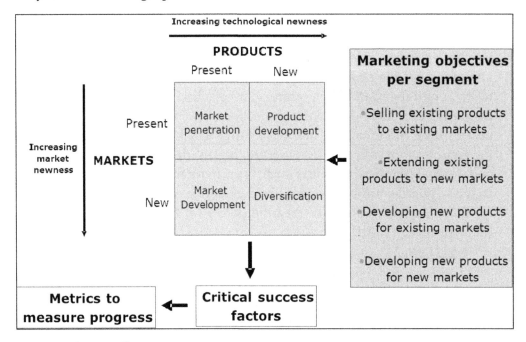

Figure 3.14: The Ansoff Matrix

For each of the products for segment cells, having set objectives, the task is then to determine strategies for achieving them. These strategies, or critical success factors (CSFs), will be weighted according to their relative importance to the customers in the segment.

Critical Success Factors	Weighting factor	Your organisation	Competitor A	Competitor B	Competitor c
CSF 1					
CSF 2					
CSF 3					
CSF 4					
Total weighted score (score × weight)	100				

Strategies to improve competitive position/ achieve objectives over time (4Ps)
Metrics (each CSF) to measure performance over time in achieveing goals

Figure 3.15 Critical success factors: In each segment, defined by the segment

It is unlikely that the marketing function will be directly responsible for what needs to be done to improve a CSF. For example, issues like product efficacy, after sales service, channel management and sometimes even price and the sales force, are often controlled by other functions, so marketing needs to get buy-in from these functions to the need to improve the CSF scores. There will be other responses that will need to be measured such as productivity factors and hygiene factors, but to keep it simple, we have only shown customer-based critical success factors here.

Figure 3.16 shows another level of detail, i.e. .

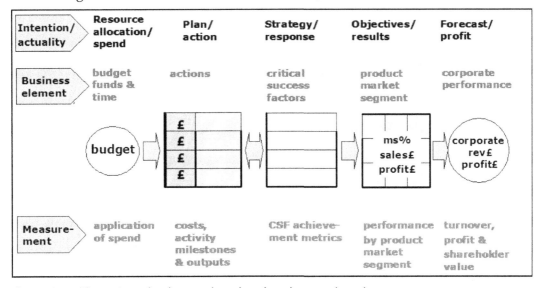

Figure 3.16: The actions that have to be taken, by whom and at what cost.

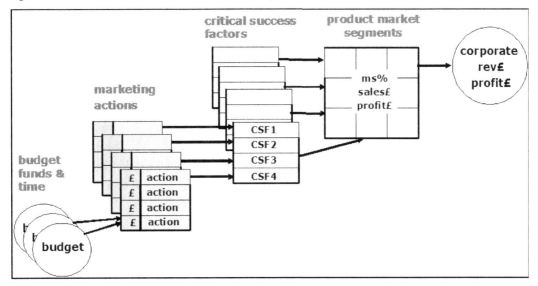

Figure 3.17: How these actions multiply for each box of the Ansoff Matrix.

Thus, it can be seen how the expenditure on marketing and other functional actions to improve CSFs can be linked to marketing objectives and, ultimately, to profitability and it becomes clear exactly what must be measured and why. It also obviates the absurd assumption that a particular marketing action can be linked directly to profitability. It can only be linked to other weighted CSFs which, if improved, should lead to the achievement of volumes, value and, ultimately, profits.

We stress, however, that the corporate revenue and profits shown in the right of Figures 3.16 and 3.17 are not the same as shareholder value added, which takes account of the risks involved in the strategies, the time value of money and the cost of capital.

■ Conclusions

Compliant marketing plans, in the sense of being theoretically sound, that do not make a measurable contribution to achieving an organization's objectives, are really not worth all the effort in putting them together.

This section outlined three levels of marketing measurement, the most important of which is whether the plan achieves shareholder value, having taken account of the risks associated with the strategies outlined in the plan, the time value of money and the cost of capital.

Summary and conclusions

In conclusion, we must stress that there can be no such thing as an off-the-peg marketing planning system. In the end, strategic marketing planning success comes from an endless willingness to learn and to adapt the system to the people and the circumstances of the organization. It also comes from a deep understanding about the nature of marketing planning.

However, strategic marketing planning demands that the organization recognizes the challenges that face it and their effect on its potential for future success. It must learn to focus on customers and their needs at all times and explore every avenue which may provide it with a differential advantage over its competitors.

Strategic marketing planning, when sensibly institutionalized and driven by an organization's top management, can make a significant contribution to the creation of sustainable competitive advantage. It is, however, important to distinguish between the process of marketing planning and the output. Indeed, much of the benefit will accrue from the process of analysis and debate amongst relevant managers and directors rather than from the written document itself.

Ten guidelines were provided which have been shown to be significant contributors to determining an organization's competitiveness.

Finally, some processes were outlined for measuring the effectiveness of marketing planning. Clearly, a theoretically-compliant plan that does not contribute measurably to an organization's objectives cannot be worth the effort.

3

References

Ansoff, H.I. (1977) 'The state and practice of planning systems', *Sloan Management Review*, **18** (2), 1–24.

Bailey, A., Johnson, G. and Daniel, K. (2000) 'Validation of a multi-dimensional measure of strategic development process', *British Journal of Management*, **11** (2), 151–162.

Buzzell, R.D. and Gale, B.T. (1987) *The PIMS Principles: Linking Strategy to Performance*, New York: Free Press.

Caulkin, S. (2005) 'Escape from the budget straightjackets', *Management Today*, January, 47–49.

Greenley, G. (1984) 'An exposition into empirical research into marketing planning', *Journal of Marketing Management* **3** (1), 83–102.

Kelly, S. (2005) *Customer Intelligence*, Wiley.

Kollatt, D.J., Blackwell, R.D. and Robeson, J.F. (1972) *Strategic Marketing*, New York: Holt, Rinehart & Winston.

Leighton, D.S.R. (1966) *International Marketing: Text and Cases*, New York: McGraw-Hill.

Lubatkin, M. and Pitts, M. (1985) 'The PIMS and the policy perspective: a rebuttal', *Journal of Business Strategy*, Summer, 85–92.

McDonald, M. (1982) 'The theory and practice of industrial marketing planning', PHD thesis, Cranfield Institute of Technology.

McDonald, M.H.B. (1984) 'The theory and practice of marketing planning for industrial goods in international markets', PhD thesis, Cranfield Institute of Technology.

McGovern, G., Court, D., Quelch, A. and Crawford, B. (2004) 'Bringing customers into the boardroom', *Harvard Business Review*, Nov, pp. 70-80

Piercy, N.F. (1997) *Market-led Strategic Change – Transforming the Process of Going to Market*, 3rd edn, Oxford: Butterworth-Heinemann.

Porter, M. (1980) *Competitive Strategy: Techniques for Analysing Industries and Competitors*, New York: Free Press.

Smith, B.D. (2003) 'The effectiveness of marketing strategy making in medical markets', PhD thesis, Cranfield University.

Thompson, S. (1962) 'How companies plan', *AMA Research Study no.54*, Chicago: AMA.

Further reading

Brown, S. (1996) 'Art or science?: fifty years of marketing debate', *Journal of Marketing Management*, **12**, 243–267.

This fascinating and highly readable paper discusses the eternal debate about whether marketing is more art than science. Readers should never lose sight of the need for strategic marketing plans and the process that produces them needs to be creative as well as diagnostic.

Burns, P. (1994) 'Growth in the 1990s: winner and losers', *Special Report 12*, 31 European Enterprise Centre, Cranfield School of Management.

Leppard, J. and McDonald, M. (1987) 'A reappraisal of the role of marketing planning', *Journal of Marketing Management*, **3** (2) 159–171.

This throws a considerable amount of light onto why marketing planning is rarely done. It examines the organization's context in which planning takes place and gives a fascinating insight into how corporate culture and politics often prevent the marketing concept from taking hold.

McDonald, M. (1994) *Marketing – the Challenge of Change*, Chartered Institute of Marketing.

McDonald, M. (1996) 'Strategic marketing planning: theory; practice; and research agendas', *Journal of Marketing Management*, **12** (1–3), 5–27.

This summarizes the whole domain of marketing planning, from its early days to the current debate about its contribution. It also explores forms other than the more rational/scientific one described in this chapter.

McDonald, M. (1999) *Marketing Plans: How to Prepare Them; How to Use Them*, 4th edition, Butterworth-Heinemann, Oxford.

The standard text on marketing planning in universities and organizations around the world. It is practical, but based on sound theoretical concepts.

Saunders, J. and Wong, V. (1993) 'Business orientations and corporate success', *Journal of Strategic Marketing*, **1** (1), 20–40.

Part 2

Using the Marketing Navigation System

Case examples

Throughout this part of the book we will be referring to real case examples of marketing implementation programs.

From the Parker Hannifin Corporation we will be referring to both their *Winmap* and *OEM System* cases. The first is a good example of applying the principles of Marketing Navigation to a large marketing implementation program. The second is a good example of applying the Marketing Navigation System to a significant sales project.

The other cases have been written up from interviews by the authors with the people at the very heart of their implementation program. These cases are described in detail in Part 4 of this book.

4 How to plan your implementation journey

The great thing about not planning is that failure comes as a complete surprise and is not preceded by long periods of worry and depression.

John Perton, Boston College

Summary

In this chapter we:

- Explain how to complete the first phase of implementation
- Dig down to find the causes of implementation failure
- Show the importance of doing a root cause analysis
- Discuss the importance of developing a change plan
- Reveal how you can improve your implementation chances straight away.

■ Introduction

This is the first phase of the implementation journey. In this phase you will need to understand what your marketing strategy (and plan) is seeking to achieve and then plan a route to get you there. This is done by being crystal clear about your marketing brief, diagnosing your current implementation issues, anticipating implementation problems ahead and planning your best route to success. This implementation plan is a vital additional element of an excellent marketing plan. Good work today will save many a weary night later.

Key principles

- The marketing plan must be ready for implementation
- Do the implementation diagnostics
- Write a change plan
- Test this in a variety of ways
- Move firmly to the next phase only when ready.

Jigsaw Web Design provides a range of web design, search engine optimization, seminars and web hosting services in the UK. In the case below, Savannah Richards, their Senior Manager, tells the story of one client that tried to implement a new website without a strategic marketing plan.

4

Implementing with a bad plan: A start-up business

In June 2011 I received a phone call from someone (we will call her 'Jane') saying she was interested in using us to create a new website for them. We soon met and she explained that she was an entrepreneur and wanted to create a new social media business. In order for this business to compete more effectively we suggested two modifications: First, that we make online discounts a central part of the website. Second, that we allow advertising on the site to boost the revenues. Although the idea was somewhat sketchy, we used our own standard Web Design Brief to itemize the key requirements for the site.

Once she had approved the brief, we then got to work building the website and looking for potential advertisers.

By August the site had been built, an initial batch of advertisers had been added and it had gone live.

But not for long! After a few months, she decided that she needed to go back a step and write a strategic plan for the business. The project was then put on hold and the website removed from public view until a contact of hers (whom we will call 'Peter') had written the plan.

Peter duly completed this in October. Jane, Peter and our team then sat down to go through the plan and its implications for the website.

The plan was just ten pages of waffle! It called for a new website template but did not give any specifics on what the requirements were. It was a long essay talking about how people use the internet and some descriptions of other online campaigns. Much of it looked like it had been copied from the Internet. There were no objectives, targets, timetables, strategies, actions or anything concrete!

The meeting was pretty inconclusive and by the end of it, Jane said, 'We need to come at this from a different angle. We'll pull our team together and come up with a new website brief.'

Peter was sent off to improve his plan. Jane also then contacted a separate marketing company for their help in getting the strategy right. Unfortunately, this was a PR Agency that had few real skills in strategy development.

We all met again in December. Peter went through his new presentation. This again was not a marketing plan but 26 slides on understanding online usage. It was full of desk research that he had done. It did have some interesting graphs but again had no strategy to implement. Then the PR Agency went through their ideas of all the media vehicles that could be used. But again we had no overall strategy to work with.

Shortly after the meeting, Jane dismissed Peter from the project.

The Agency is now Jane's main strategic advisor on the project. They are both excellent at coming up with new creative ideas but most of these are difficult for us to put into practice. I get the feeling that many of her advisors on the project are not thinking about giving her a good return on her investment. They are just thinking about how they can keep using up her budget.

She really needs to form a competent team to develop the strategy and marketing plan so we can simply get the website up and working well for her.

Jane gets very excited about new ideas and will move from one idea to another quickly. She simply gets taken in by what people say. She is a terrific networker and is forever asking us to meet person after person. She is very entrepreneurial but has really poor follow-through.

The net result of all this is that we end up spending a lot of time designing one element of the website and then being told that something else is now the priority. You can pile everything in but you do not know what is working. It is much better to try something, test it and get it working properly rather than always to be trying something new.

How to plan your implementation course

As Savannah's story demonstrates, much time and money can be wasted on implementing strategies that have not been properly thought through. Many programs fail even before they start because they have not been planned properly.So, the first step must be about planning your journey ahead. As the old saying goes, 'failing to plan means planning to fail.'

■ Step 1: Is your marketing plan ready for implementation?

Do I need a marketi ng plan?

There is an assumption in Step 1 that you already have a marketing plan. Can you proceed to implementation without one? The answer is yes but your chances of success will already be much undermined. How do we know this?

Firstly, as we saw in Chapter 3, there is much research evidence to show that marketing plans do indeed make a significant difference to commercial success.

Secondly, no plan means no clarity. Prior to implementation, you need to be clear about what it is that you wish to implement and why. Any business is likely to have dozens of market segments, several product lines, lots of competitors, shifting customer needs, changing macro forces, changing industry structures and changing internal issues, etc. The company's current position, desired position, mission, objectives, strategies and tactics will need explaining. Where you are now, where you need to get to, how you will get there, how it will help you achieve sustainable competitive advantage and increased shareholder value all need to be thought through and communicated clearly. These are complex but vital issues and best written down in a plan.

Having a good marketing plan will reduce the risks of implementation failure.

Do I have a clear vision and strategy?

The plan is important because it creates the business case for change. It provides a good technical and financial proposal for doing things differently. This will help win the minds of stakeholders. But will people get excited about it? How motivated will staff be about those marketing phrases? You may have gained their logical acceptance to the strategy but to help really motivate them to implement it you need to get them excited. This means translating the technical and financial ideas into an emotional case for change. To do this, you should add one or two simple diagrams illustrating the strategy and make clear statements like, 'Here we are and if we do not change our business we will be in dire difficulties. We need to get over here to be safe. The only way for us to move here is if we do the following things.'

Box 4.1

When Steve Jobs arrived back at Apple in 1997, it was a business in trouble. No doubt there were many detailed plans for him to look through. 'After a few weeks of product review sessions, he'd finally had enough. 'Stop!' he shouted. 'This is crazy.' He grabbed a Magic Marker, padded in his bare feet to the whiteboard, and drew a two-by-two grid. 'Here's what we need,' he declared. Atop the two columns he wrote 'Consumer' and 'Pro.' He labeled the two rows 'Desktop' and 'Portable.' Their job, he told his team members, was to focus on four great products, one for each quadrant. All other products should be cancelled.'

'The real leadership lessons of Steve Jobs', Walter Isaacson, *Harvard Business Review*, April 2012

Translating the plan into a clear vision and strategy will improve the level of commitment to implementation.

I have a good plan, what now?

In Chapter 3, we provided clear guidelines to help you find out if you had a good marketing plan. If you think you have a good plan you now need to check something else.

How many of the key stakeholders who will be involved in implementing the plan were also involved in developing it? Are there any key stakeholders who have not been involved at all? If the answer is yes, then they may not have bought into it and you may need to change your plan in order to win their support.

This idea of co-creation is important. The more stakeholders feel they have helped to shape the plan, the more buy-in you will get to it. In other words, change is happening with them and not to them. The most difficult plans to implement are the ones that have been written solely by one or two people in the marketing function and then 'sold' to others.

Co-creating the plan with key stakeholders will improve the level of commitment to implementation.

So, a good plan that has been developed in the right way and translated into a compelling argument for change will have higher commitment and lower risks.

■ Step 2: Do the implementation diagnostics

Why does implementation typically succeed or fail in your organization?

Next, you need to consider the business environment in which the plan is to be implemented. For example, does your business have a history of good or bad implementation programs?

If it is a bad history, then think about doing some simple Root Cause Analysis to uncover the underlying problem. Root Cause Analysis is a standard tool used in engineering to root out defects. The basic principle is very simple: Ask 'Why has this happened?' five times. By the time you have answered the fifth question, you should be at the bottom of things. Box 4.2 shows an example of this in use in a vehicle manufacturer.

We have used this approach to identify the typical causes of marketing plan implementation failure (see Figure 4.1). This is a very useful template for your own diagnostics and a good checklist of failure threats.

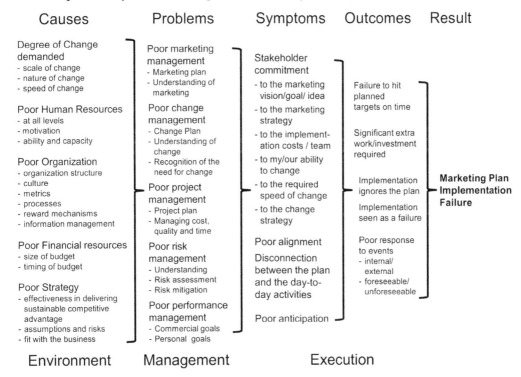

Figure 4.1: Causes of implementation failure

Box 4.2 Root cause analysis – a powerful and sophisticated tool

Root cause analysis (Wilson et al., 1993) is a powerful exercise with which marketers should become more familiar. It is used frequently in the manufacturing industry to understand the root cause of failure with a product. It follows seven steps:

1. **Define the problem.** You must clearly define the problem right at the start. 'Failure to implement last year's marketing plan' is too broad. 'Failure to secure the targeted sales of Product X by year-end' is a much better definition of the problem and will help you find the root cause more easily. A problem in implementation could either be an outcome, symptom or cause for which you wish to find and address the root cause.

2. **Protect the customer.** Even though you have not dug down into the root cause yet, you need immediately to assess the impact of this problem on your customers and ensure they are protected. What is the customer impact and what emergency procedures do you need to enact immediately before your investigations are complete?

3. **Brainstorm the possible causes of the problem.** Use all the normal rules of brainstorming to ensure all possible causes are covered. We recommend you use Professor Ishikawa's 'Fishbone' tool that separates the possible causes into six main categories: manpower, machines, methods, materials, measurements and environment. Alternatively, use Figure 4.1 in this chapter. This will help you cover all the bases.

4. **Gather data to identify the actual or probable cause(s).** Use the Pareto principle to find the 20% of causes that drive 80% of the problem. For example, in one exercise undertaken, just three faults were found to cause 80% of the low power problems of a diesel engine. Addressing these faults became an important priority in fixing the overall problem.

5. **Ask 'Why?' five times** to work your way down to the root cause of the problem. You are really asking, 'Why does this happen?' and when you have answered it, ask the question again and again repeatedly. It was developed by Sakichi Toyoda, the founder of Toyota and has been used by them (and thousands of other companies) for decades as a key tool of quality control. You may need to ask the question more than five times to get to the real root cause.

6. **Take countermeasures to address the root cause.** This may include re-training, new procedures, new key performance indicators, better IT systems, clearer roles and responsibilities etc.

7. **Monitor, standardize and learn.** Monitor the problem back down to the root cause to ensure that it is under control; standardize the procedures and activities to ensure that a high level of consistency is maintained; learn the lessons from the experience and apply those lessons elsewhere.

Throughout the exercise, it is important that you:

- Are open-minded about the cause of the problem (e.g., even if the CEO was not really committed to the plan, consider if it may have stalled for other reasons)

- Do not make assumptions about the problem or answer (e.g., the answer may not be to throw more resources or money at the execution problem)

- Use data, facts and experts as much as possible (e.g., even if sales did not improve, what was the size of the new opportunities uncovered?)

- Get the right team to go through the process.

Problem Resolution Document				PRD Number	Vehicle Manufacturing Inc.		
				PRD0012			
Problem name	Raised by	Peter Holden	PRD Raised by	John Smith	PRD Closed by		Owner
Coat defect on conical pad	Department	Engineering					John Smith
	Date	May 10, 2010	Department	Quality Assurance	Department		
	Process	Build	Date	May 10, 2010	Date		
1 Problem statement	Part delivered to stores and customer as good						
2 Definition of problem			4 Establish possible causes				
• Part was defective when it arrived from the supplier • Part has gone through process and delivered to stores as good							
3 Customer protection			5 Establish probable causes				
			Why 1	Why 2	Why 3	Why 4	Why 5
Stock to be checked ASAP			Part received by customer as good	Part was not laser etched properly	Part was overlooked on visual inspection	Operator may have been distracted or lost concentration	Operator error. Only two people trained. No set rest time for visual and not distraction free
6 Establish corrective/counter measures			7 Implement corrective/counter measures			8 Are counter measures effective?	
1.Process to be changed to have laser etch operation before visual inspection. Parts to be marked at this stage from known supplier parts 2.Manning level insufficient 3.Visual time to be set to a maximum of 30 minutes with 10 minutes rest 4.Distraction zone/awareness that operator is inspecting			1.Update SOP and change routing – ensure all are aware of change	DONE			
			2.Review resource level	PH			
			3.Set optimum time and rest periods – use of clock/alarm	DONE			
			4.Critical inspection in progress ; 'Do Not Disturb' sign to be installed immediately	DONE			

Figure 4.2: A root cause analysis of a defect on a car

In Figure 4.2, a major vehicle manufacturer used root cause analysis to understand why a defective part was sold to their customers. They used a

> one-page 'problem resolution document' (PRD) to define the problem and systematically drill down to the actual root cause. Note how they followed the steps above and asked 'Why' five times to identify the root causes as a combination of insufficient trained resources and rest times.

Understanding the past will help you identify the future threats to your plan.

Assess the commitment levels

(a) Understand commitment

Before you assess commitment, you need to understand what it means.

We often talk about commitment as if there are only two possibilities: we either have it or we don't. Many programs that we have worked on have been implemented successfully without it. Conversely, we have seen many programs fail with it! A key problem is that people think they have commitment when, in fact, they don't.

The confusion lies with the fact that *commitment is a point on a continuum of buy-in* (see Figure 4.3).

The Commitment Continuum

Negative Buy-in   Positive Buy-in

Disengagement   Hostility   Opposition   Disapproval   Disinterest   Indifference   Interest   Approval   Support   Commitment   Entanglement

Figure 4.3: The commitment continuum

Just as you have a range of feelings for most things in life, stakeholders also have a range of buy-in levels to an implementation program. *Commitment* lies towards the *positive buy-in* end, and its counterpart, *hostility* towards the *negative buy-in* end. In between these lie a range of points including *indifference* in the middle.

A common mistake that many people make is mistaking approval or support for commitment. Simply because your plan has been approved by the leadership team does not mean they are committed to it. They may simply think it is a worthwhile exercise and should be handed down to somebody else to get on and implement. Neither does it mean it is a top priority for them. There may be many other programs that they support more than yours. Some of these may even get their personal commitment.

You will probably also find that amongst the stakeholders the normal change rules apply in that a few will be clustered around the support end and a few clustered around the opposition end. But in the middle will be the majority of indifferent stakeholders who could be persuaded to go one way or the other. A common key tactic of change management is to not worry about the opposition too much but to focus your attention on your supporters so that they can influence the majority of indifferent stakeholders to support it in the future.

There are also two extreme positions worth mentioning. Better than commitment is entanglement (Wilson et al., 1993). Here, stakeholders demonstrate their full buy-in to the program by personally getting closely entangled in its implementation. This means they invest a significant percentage of their own time (not just their firm's money) in being closely involved in meetings, communications, discussions and key decisions during the whole implementation journey. This can be seen in the Austro, IEB, Kennametal and MEDIC cases in Part 4 of this book.

At the other end, beyond the cold point of hostility, lies the freezing point of disengagement. This is worse than hostility because there is no engagement at all. While there is still a chance that you can turn around a hostile enemy, there is little chance that you can do so with someone that refuses even to engage in the argument. Your best chance here may be to influence this person by proxy (a third party supporter) or plan in program wins that will help melt the ice.

(b) Identify the key stakeholders and assess their commitment

We now need to identify our stakeholders. For this, we should look to the tools of key account management (KAM). KAM professionals have spent many years refining their thinking on how to develop strong supplier–customer relationships with complex organizations. Indeed, the sales from some key accounts are worth more than entire countries to these suppliers. For example, Procter & Gamble's Wal-Mart account is so large it has over 250 people fully dedicated to planning and implementing joint improvement programs just with that one account!

There are many tools in the KAM community for identifying stakeholders and assessing their support for the supplier. One of these is the 'relationship map'. This can be imported and adapted for our purposes.

First, you need to think about the customers. In key account management, this means all the stakeholders in a large account who influence the decision to use the products and services of a particular supplier (including opinion-formers about whether the supplier is good or not). Here, this means all the stakeholders who influence the decision to use your proposed solution in the marketing plan (including opinion-formers about whether the implementation is good or not).

To begin with, list the names of these implementation stakeholders. This includes anyone who has a pivotal role in making the implementation happen. It should also include people who are not personally involved in the program but who carry much influence on whether it is perceived to be successful or not. Under their name, state their title and degree of influence on the outcome (see Figure 4.4).

		Implementation Stakeholders			3rd Party Influencers
Implement-ation Relationship Map	Name:	Alice	Brian	Chris	Davina
	Title:	Vice President	Director	Manager	Consultant
	Influence on Outcome:	Very High	High	High	High
	Level of Buy-in	Opposed	Indifferent	Supportive	Committed
Our Program Team (Change Agents)	John		X		
	Leslie			X	X
	Mike	X			

Figure 4.4: The implementation relationship map

Then state their level of buy-in to the implementation (using the labels on the commitment continuum above). You can also use different shades of colors to show different levels of buy-in.

If required, you can add more details including their function, business unit and location. You can also show how many steps they are away from the CEO. This is their reporting rank. The CEO will be given a score of zero, the C-Suite that reports to him will be given a score of one, the Presidents that report to the C-Suite will be given a score of two, etc.

For the top influencers (like Alice in our example) go further by listing any relevant unmet needs they may have. These can either be commercial needs (like achieving above target super-profits) or personal needs (like spending more time with the family). These will be useful in helping you increase their commitment by linking successful implementation to achieving these unmet needs.

Next, on the other axis, list the names of the program team (change agents) who are driving the implementation work. You can add further details (as above) to these names if required.

Then consider any third parties who have a strong influence on success. These may include customer senior executives, consultants, friends of the C-Suite, technical advisors, business partners or other 'apostles' of change that you have nurtured etc.

These two axes form your implementation relationship map.

Color code any cells where there is a good, routine or bad relationship between stakeholders and the team. If there is no relationship, then you can leave the cell blank. Then put an X or a number 1 in each cell where you wish to adopt 1:1 marking. You should ensure that every stakeholder is marked by at least one member of the team. This is just like man-to-man marking in sports teams.

In the simple example in Figure 4.4 above, John has a good relationship with Brian, a routine relationship with Chris and no relationship with either Alice or Davina. As for Leslie, people either love or hate her! Unfortunately, our senior and very high influencer, Alice, has a bad relationship with her (as does Brian). However, Davina loves her. So, a good relationship strategy to improve buy-in might be to have Mike meet with Alice, John meet with Brian and see if we can use Davina's influence on them both.

This exercise will help you:

1 Identify the key stakeholders clearly

2 Show their level of buy-in to implementation

3 Show where you can use good relationships to develop or maintain their buy-in

4 Identify key gaps where there is a poor or zero relationship with a stakeholder

5 Develop an effective coverage model for your team – focusing on the key stakeholders

6 Efficiently spread the team's resources over the stakeholder population

7 Provide role clarity to the team ensuring they are responsible for specific stakeholder buy-in.

Using a Relationship Map will help you do a first-class commitment and relationship audit. This will be key to helping you formulate your plan to increase commitment.

(c) Complete an FMEA on commitment

You should now have a good feel for the commitment issues around your plan. To help you prioritize the key risks here, you should complete a simple FMEA exercise on commitment (see Figure 4.5).

	Risk - Commitment Diagnostic (FMEA)								
Marketing Plan growth idea: **Wind Energy Program**								Date: **June 15 2012**	
FMEA assessment owner: **Helga Schmidt**								Revision Number: **2.9**	
				With current controls					Action Ref: (see Actions Summary)
Ref:	**Risk Area**	**Risk Descripton (Failure Mode)**	**Effect if this failure happens (Failure Effect)**	Severity of Impact	Probability	Escape Detection?	Risk Total (RPN)	% of Max (1000 pts)	
				Low = 1 High = 10	Low = 0 High = 10	Low = 1 High = 10	Low = 1 High = 1000		
	Commitment								
C1	Alice	Secretly tells her salespeople not to cooperate with the new BU	We will need to develop our own relationships with key customer prospects	8	8	9	576	57.6%	A1
C2	Brian	Is persuaded by Alice to resist implementation	Poor quality engineers will be chosen by Brian for the new BU (i.e available rather than the best)	7	7	8	392	39.2%	A2
C3	Davina	Has no influence over Alice	Will need to find alternative route to Alice in case Mike fails	7	5	2	70	7.0%	A3

Figure 4.5: An FMEA on commitment

To do this, list all the stakeholders who are negative towards implementation from the relationship map exercise. Then describe the risk, its effect on implementation should it occur and score it for impact, probability of occurring and whether it will escape your detection (its invisibility).

Then multiply the scores together to make a risk total (or risk priority number). The highest scores will indicate the top issues for you to manage.

Undertaking an FMEA will help ensure sure you correctly identify the top commitment issues in implementing your plan

(d) Complete the 'top commitment issues' box of the Dashboard

You can now use the FMEA to help complete the top commitment issues box of the Navigation Dashboard.

Start by thinking with the end in mind. What is the desired state that you are looking to achieve? Then use the FMEA and the relationship map to identify the key stakeholders and their possible threats to achieving that state.

Next, think about the test that you need to perform to determine whether that is a real threat or not. Then update the current status and decide if each one is a GO or NO GO issue.

Assess the commercial risks to implementation:

Consider the degree of change demanded by the plan

We can think about change in three dimensions: scale, speed, and complexity. To help visualize this we have developed the change cube (see Figure 4.6).

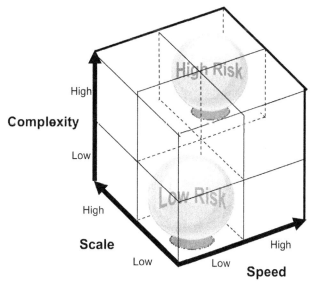

Figure 4.6: The change cube

Scale relates to the risks associated with the geographic, functional and business unit change required. A plan that requires switching the advertising supplier for a UK business unit has few implementation risks to the global corporation. A plan that requires a new global account management program will touch many business units and functions worldwide. This has much greater implementation risks.

Speed relates to how fast the implementation must happen compared to the speed that the organization can normally change. IT companies can normally change a lot faster than government organizations.

Complexity relates to the type of change. Switching data sources is far less risky to implement than introducing a cultural change initiative. The table shows the different types of change and their approximate level of risk.

Table 4.1: Types of change and their complexity/risk

Type of change	Example(s)	Complexity and risk
Data/material	Implementing direct feedback from customers rather than from the sales force to understand why we lost proposals	Low
Procedural	Implementing a new competitor intelligence gathering process	
Definitional	Redefining marketing from being low level 'promotional support' to 'a key process that drives long-term shareholder value'	
Behavioral	Introducing a customer engagement program that requires all key executives to spend time with our top customers	
Attitudinal	Launching a new scorecard that will get greater balance between future long-term growth and past sales	
Organizational	Setting up a new customer-facing business unit to replace the duplication in current business units	
Cultural	Developing from a product-driven business to a market-driven business	High

So the least risky plan to implement is one that demands small scale, simple change within a comfortable time period. The most risky is one that demands global and complex change quickly.

You can afford to have a light but professional touch in the front of this cube (where the low risk ball is positioned). However, the nature of the change at Lafarge and IEB (see Part 4) meant they did not have this luxury. Their plans were necessarily high risk and firmly at the top back part of the cube. They understood that this was the most challenging place to be and injected a heavy dose of implementation professionalism to keep their programs on course.

Review your plan and see if you can reduce the degree of change that it demands of the organization.

Consider how risky your strategy is

Some strategies involve incremental change, others involve revolutionary change. The greater the change demanded, the greater the risks. Revolutionary change usually requires more planning and problems often occur when marketers underestimate the impact of their strategy on the organization and their plan becomes impotent.

A great tool for understanding the risk involved in your strategy is the Ansoff Matrix (see Figure 4.7).

We do not aim to teach its use here as it can be found in many strategy books. However, the important thing for you is that the degree of risk increases from top left to bottom right. A new *market penetration strategy* involves changing how you market our existing products/services to your existing markets. These products and customers are known and the strategy should have relatively low risks surrounding its implementation.

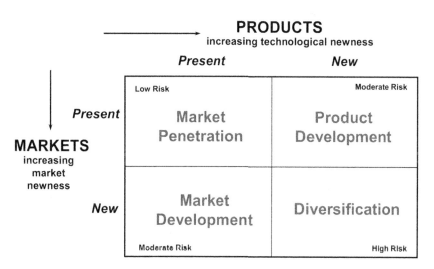

Figure 4.7: The Ansoff Matrix

Selling your existing products into new markets (e.g., exporting them to new developing nations or finding new market segments for them) through a market development strategy is riskier to implement. You have to get to know those new customers, possibly compete with new competitors and develop new ways to reach them. Similarly, developing new products successfully for our existing markets through a *product development strategy* is more risky than a simple *penetration strategy*. According to Cincinnati research agency AcuPOLL, 'Many estimates place new product failure rates at 75–90%. While some of these failures can undoubtedly be traced to poorly thought out and researched ideas, many failures are simply the result of poor execution' (Gordon, 2011)

However, a new *diversification strategy* that calls on us to develop new products/services and then sell them successfully into new markets is the riskiest affair of all. It requires implementation of a new product development program and a new market development program within the same planning horizon. Many companies try to short-cut this route by pursuing an acquisition program. However, acquisitions are themselves a relatively risky undertaking (Harschberger, 2009).

Worse, Ansoff (1987) also describes how many companies try to follow multiple strategies at the same time. Different strategies require different competencies and different types of companies. A marketing plan that calls for simultaneous implementation of multiple strategies runs the risk of failing on all fronts.

Review the strategies in your plan and see if you can reduce their demands on the organization.

Do some strategy due diligence

In *Marketing Due Diligence* the authors divide strategy risk into three main areas (Table 4.2; McDonald et al., 2006):

- **Market risk** – the risk that the market may not be as big as promised in the plan
- **Market share risk** – the risk that the strategy may not deliver the share promised in the plan
- **Shareholder value risk** – the risk that the strategy may not deliver the profits promised in the plan.

Each of these three risk areas should be reviewed in detail and the risks added to the Commercial Risk section of the FMEA (see below).

Table 4.2

Strategy risk profiles

Market risk	
Product category existence	The marketing strategy has a higher probability of success if the product category is well established
Segment existence	If the target segment is well established
Sales volumes	If the sales volumes are well supported by evidence
Forecast growth	If the forecast growth is in line with historical trends
Pricing assumptions	If the pricing levels are conservative relative to current pricing levels

Market share risk	
Target market definition	The marketing strategy has a higher probability of success if the target is defined in terms of homogeneous segments and is characterized by utilizable data
Proposition specification	If the proposition delivered to each segment is different from that delivered to other segments and addresses the needs which characterized the target segment
SWOT alignment	If the strengths and weaknesses of the organization are independently assessed and the choice of target and proposition leverages strengths and minimizes weaknesses
Strategy uniqueness	If choice of target and proposition is different from that of major competitors
Anticipation of market change	If changes in the external microenvironment and macroenvironment are identified and their implications allowed for

Shareholder value risk	
Profit pool	The marketing strategy has a higher probability of success if the targeted profit pool is high and growing

Profit sources	If the source of new business is growth in the existing profit pool
Competitor impact	If the profit impact on competitors is small and distributed
Internal gross margin Assumptions	If the internal gross margin assumptions are conservative relative to current products
Assumptions of other costs	If assumptions regarding other costs, including marketing support, are higher than existing costs

Consider other commercial risks

Your root cause analysis above should have identified some other commercial risks to consider. In addition to the strategy and change risks mentioned above, these could include:

- **Funding risks.** This could be either that the program is underfunded in total, or the budget is fine but you see a problem in the flow of funds to the program (e.g., it will be cash starved at the start).

- **Technology risks.** Your implementation is dependent on a particular new technology either in the solution itself (e.g., new software) or as part of the support infrastructure (e.g., SAP implementation).

- **Environment risks.** This covers the whole implementation environment and includes all organizational and human resource issues.

Consider downside risks

Any particular risk can have different scenarios: currency exchange rates can move a little or a lot, competitors can respond softly or strongly to your price changes, etc. For the most important risks, you should define a downside (pessimistic) scenario, the triggers that define it and the countermeasures to respond to it.

One of the authors of this book held a senior position in the drinks industry. After an unusually cold summer led to a lower seasonal demand for drinks, the sales and marketing team was instructed to do a serious downside risk assessment on the one-year plan every year as a matter of course. For example, even though the major assumptions were triple-checked, the team knew what the consequences would be to sales and profits if the lower assumption happened. They then had to spell out what actions they would take to ensure that the forecast profits were achieved. However, under no circumstances were any of them allowed not to achieve the profit they had committed to in the one-year plan, barring a catastrophe like the factory burning down! They also had to spell out how they would check whether the stated assumptions were indeed happening (i.e. how they would measure and test those assumptions).

This way, the team NEVER failed to make the profits it had promised to the parent corporation and the company tended to be left alone.

Complete an FMEA on commercial risks

You should now have a good feel for the commercial risks to your plan. To help you prioritize them, you should complete a simple FMEA exercise on commercial risks (see Figure 4.8).

				With current controls					
Risk - Commitment Diagnostic (FMEA)									

Marketing Plan growth idea: **Wind Energy Program**   Date: **June 15 2012**
FMEA assessment owner: **Helga Schmidt**   Revision Number: **2.9**

Ref:	Risk Area	Risk Descripton (Failure Mode)	Effect if this failure happens (Failure Effect)	Severity of Impact Low = 1 High = 10	Probability Low = 0 High = 10	Escape Detection? Low = 1 High = 10	Risk Total (RPN) Low = 1 High = 100	% of Max (1000 pts)	Action Ref: (see Actions Summary)
	Commercial Risk								
R1	Size of Potential	Overestimated market-size by more than 50%	Significant reduction in market potential	9	3	5	135	13.5%	A4
R4	Share of Potential	Competitor enters exclusive agreement with our top account	Loss of $15m of sales over three years	8	4	6	192	19.2%	A5
R5	Profit	Bought-in costs rise by >10%	Fall in profit margins of 5% (after improved efficiencies)	7	6	1	42	4.2%	A6
R6	Speed of Change	Government ends subsidy scheme	Significant drop in end-customer demand	9	5	2	90	9.0%	A7

Figure 4.8: Commercial risks captured in an FMEA

In Figure 4.8, the top risk is R4, where a competitor enters an exclusive long-term agreement with the top account. This has a slightly lower impact than R1, over-estimating the market size by more than 50%, but has a higher probability of occurring and will be more difficult to detect until it happens.

Undertaking an FMEA will help ensure sure you correctly identify the key risks in implementing your plan

Complete the 'top risk issues' box of the Dashboard

You can now use the FMEA to help complete the *Top commitment issues* box of the Navigation Dashboard.

Start by thinking with the end in mind. What is the desired state that you are seeking to achieve? Then use the FMEA and your strategy diagnostics to identify the key threats to achieving that state.

Next think about the tests that you need to perform to determine whether that is a real threat or not. Then update the current status and decide if each one is a GO or NO GO issue.

Plot your position on the risk–commitment matrix

You can now apply your conclusions to the risk–commitment diagnostic to plot your position on the risk–commitment matrix and see whether you are on or off course.

■ Step 3: Develop a change plan

The diagnostics that you have done in Step 2 should now enable you to write a clear plan for how you wish to implement your plan.

Write a clear program specification

4

The first step here is to write a clear specification for how you wish to implement the plan. This is often known as the project/program specification or the terms of reference. In our experience, many implementation programs fail because they were not specified clearly in the first place. Poor specification leads to unclear expectations, poor focus, scope creep, role ambiguity, drifting, stress and failure!

Box 4.3 gives an example of a program specification. We have kept the examples brief so you can get a feel quickly. You should adapt and expand these for your own program.

Box 4.3 Program specification example

- **Background:** Write here why the program is needed and why now. *e.g., We are losing bids because our competitors act as one supplier better than us. This is costing us $m every year and will only get worse. We therefore launched a strategic account management (SAM) program in Q1. We have completed the first two steps. We now need to take the third and final step of Phase 1 which is to launch a pilot program with a few selected strategic accounts. This will help to demonstrate how true SAM should be undertaken and the benefits that such an approach provides.*

- **Summary:** Write here a short summary of the program to be undertaken. *e.g., This program covers the third step in designing and implementing a model for effective SAM. The work to be done covers the development of three initial strategic account plans.*

- **Deliverables:** List here what the program will deliver to the business when it is complete. These may be hard and soft deliverables, but try and be specific.

For example: In undertaking this work, the business unit will achieve significant benefits including:

- ☐ three business development plans for three strategic accounts
- ☐ a set of account teams with clearly defined ownership of the issues and relationships
- ☐ etc.

■ **Scope**: Write here what will be IN the scope of the program and what will be OUT of scope. This will help to ensure there is no scope-drift once the program is underway. *e.g., This program is focused on developing a SAM model for the <u>XYZ business unit only.</u> The SAM Model will NOT consider compensation and remuneration as this will be covered in a later program. Neither will it cover our various joint ventures around the world.*

■ **Approach and timing**: Write here the major steps that will be undertaken within the program and their timing. Keep things at a high level and try to use diagrams where possible. This will help to explain the work that will be undertaken by the program team and how the program will achieve its deliverables. If necessary, break down each step into its key tasks. For complex programs, you may want to add in a program plan. Add in key milestones where you would like to review progress. *e.g., Our proposed approach follows the ABC methodology for designing and implementing strategic account management programs which has been developed over many years and repeated deployments. The methodology follows six basic steps.*

■ **Key resources**: Describe here the key resources allocated to the program. This may include people, program rooms, budgets, etc. You can also write here how the program team(s) will be structured and the purpose of each program team. *e.g., We propose a program core team that reports into a program steering group. The purpose of the core team is to do the work and make key recommendations. The purpose of the steering group is to act on those recommendations and ensure the program remains on track. These will be composed of the following specific people...*

■ **Program management and reviews:** Write here who will be responsible for managing the program an d how it will be reviewed. *e.g., The program manager will be [name] (see core team above). The core team will meet every week to review progress and agree upcoming tasks. The program manager will meet with [name] from the steering group every month. The full core team will meet with the full steering group every quarter.*

Not only is a program specification a good planning exercise to go through, it should also help you apply early stage change principles defined by Kotter (1996), i.e.

- Establishing a sense of urgency
- Creating the guiding coalition
- Developing a vision and strategy
- Communicating the change vision.

The best teams that we have worked with spend a lot of time developing their program specification and then use it frequently to communicate how implementation will be done, when it will be done, why it is being done, who will do it, who is guiding it and what benefits we will all get out of it.

Include a roadmap

One of the most important diagrams for you to include in your program specification is an implementation roadmap. This lays out in one simple diagram how you propose to implement the various components of your plan or program.

The best way to understand a roadmap is to see an example. Here we will use the Parker Winmap Program as our example (see *Planning the implementation of Winmap* at the end of this chapter).

For the Parker Winmap program, the roadmap showed the key activities and milestones for each fiscal year of implementation (see Figure 4.9). This roadmap was carefully developed at the start of the program using the Helm model as a guide. Despite all the unexpected events that occurred during implementation, the roadmap was robust enough that it did not need much adjustment and remained virtually the same through to the end of implementation.

In Figure 4.10, we show how the Helm model was converted to a roadmap to implement a key account management program in a European real estate business. This was a complex program involving change across many different dimensions. These dimensions were captured on the left-hand side and each had its own separate work stream. This was useful in that people could see how the dimensions would be implemented over time. So, for example, if anyone wanted to know about compensation or training, they could just follow that work stream and quickly see what would be tackled and by when.

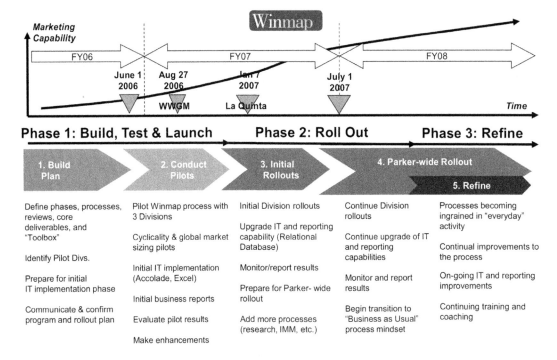

Figure 4.9: The Winmap roadmap

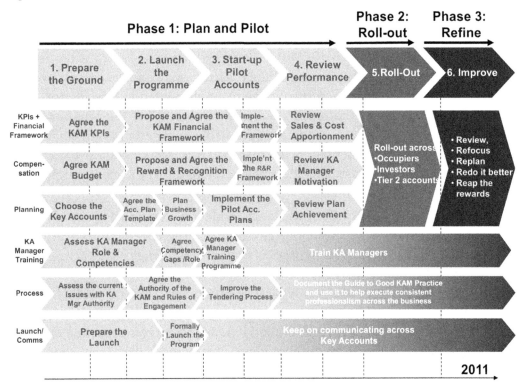

Figure 4.10: KAM program roadmap

A roadmap is important because it:

■ Provides a clear implementation strategy for the program(s) in the marketing plan. Just like your marketing strategy, if it is well planned, it will give you a robust route to your destination, although you may need to make tactical adjustments along the way.

■ Illustrates many of the details in the specification. People can understand and remember images much better than text.

■ Shows the complexity of implementation. People can appreciate the amount of work involved and the dependencies between tasks.

■ Is much easier to comprehend than a complex Gantt chart.

■ Manages expectations. People can see what will be delivered and by when. They know that their first experience of the solution may in fact be a test exercise, not the final version.

Box 4.4 Winmap's guiding coalition

Pulling together the right team and organizing them in the right way was crucial for Winmap. A team structure was sketched out that identified the key people involved in doing, supporting and in reviewing the work to be done (see Figure 4.11).

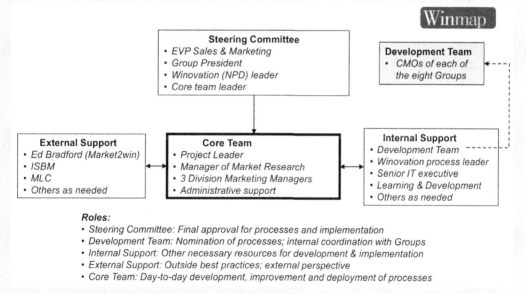

Figure 4.11: Winmap implementation team structure

The people doing the work of developing the strategic marketing process were located in the core team. They were either full-time or had this project as a key priority. Not only did they have a technical role in coming up with the solution itself, but they also had a key soft role as ambassadors for the project internally.

The core team also gained ad hoc internal support from different functions and processes, plus external support from outside experts.

Their recommendations were reviewed by the development team made up of the marketing leaders of each group. They were responsible for final approval of the recommended solution and for overcoming any major obstacles that could not be solved by the core team themselves.

Once the core team had approval to develop a solution blueprint, they began sharing their vision more broadly with the corporation. The first step was to initiate close collaboration with each of the group's sales and marketing vice presidents (the group CMOs). Each of these CMOs was the top marketer in their group and had strong views on the issue. They also were important because they would be in the best position to explain how they were doing strategic marketing currently and have a major influence on its implementation success (or otherwise) in their particular group. These CMOs were pulled together into a development team sitting outside the core team + steering group structure.

The team also worked closely with other key individuals who would influence the outcome. For example, one of these managed the corporate planning process and another managed the Winovation process. Of course, these were not all the key stakeholders. The core team delayed reaching out to other stakeholders until consensus had been reached with the development team.

The development team ensured that each of the groups was heard and had a major input to the solution. The CMOs knew that change was happening through them, rather than to them. This helped to achieve good support from the marketing leadership of the whole corporation and was critical to winning over key stakeholders later.

■ Step 4: Use the plans to improve your position immediately

We mentioned earlier that your Risk-Commitment Diagnostic will either show you are on course or (more likely) off course. Dependent on your current position, you will need to plan what mix of risk-reduction and commitment-improvement will get you back on course. Do you intend to follow a risk-reduction first approach, a commitment-improvement first approach, or a 'tacking' approach of both?

If you are in the commitment alert box, then this would suggest that you should fix this issue first. Or, if you are in the risk alert box it should be best to fix the risk issues first.

The good news is that now you have done the hard work of planning your implementation program, you can use that work immediately to get you on course.

To improve commitment

- Follow up the actions on the Dashboard resulting from the Commitment Diagnostic. These will be targeted at closing the most important commitment gaps with specific stakeholders.

- Use the relationship map to identify:
  - How you can use senior supporters of implementation to influence others
  - How you can strengthen your program team by adding people who already have strong relationships with opponents.

- Use the program specification to:
  - Help people gain an appreciation of the *need for change* and its urgency
  - Understand where you are going and how you are going to get there
  - Strengthen the steering group to ensure the program has more authority and credibility across the organization. Consider the merits of adding opponents to the steering group on the basis that (a) they may be more committed if they feel they have an influence on implementation, and (b) you should keep your friends close and your enemies closer!

- Use the commitment continuum to ensure you know exactly where each stakeholder sits. It is better to be very cautious than overly optimistic. Identify any key stakeholders with potential for 'entanglement' and plan how to engage with them.

- If you have time, consider creating a separate development team of influential pioneers who are keen to help you implement the strategy and who can influence the key stakeholders.

- *Listen* to people's concerns. Active listening is a key skill at this stage.

4

- Build confidence in implementation by demonstrating that:
  - ☐ You are personally committed to the success of your plan
  - ☐ Implementation will be managed in a professional manner
  - ☐ You have the right stuff to get this done (see Box 4.5, Great people are as important as a great plan).

Box 4.5 Great people are as important as a great plan

R&D guys are not always the best presenters', says Craig Maxwell, Vice President, Technology & Innovation at Parker. 'They may have a world-beating idea, but they can often bore the pants off a senior audience when they present it. I wondered how I could train these guys to be better presenters. I realized that what they were really doing was pitching their idea for funding. Where do you find really tough funding panels? In the investor community. So I set up a number of presentations to real outside investors and had the R&D guys pitch their ideas to them. Before the pitch, I gave them a lot of help with simplifying their messages, removing all the jargon and converting it to a quick ROI presentation. Investors typically look at the person, as much as the product before committing any funding. This has proved really helpful in upgrading the quality of pitches internally within Parker – and led to some great funding opportunities beyond our internal resources.

To reduce the risks:

- Follow up the actions on the Dashboard resulting from the Risk Diagnostic. These will be targeted at reducing and countering the most serious commercial risks in your plan.
- Improve your market strategy
  - ☐ Focus more on one Ansoff strategy rather than all four with no prioritization.
  - ☐ Reduce your dependence on acquisitions and other diversification strategies.
  - ☐ Simplify the strategy to avoid massive, global complex change.
  - ☐ Take the market strategy test at the end of this chapter, make adjustments and re-test. Repeat until you have a good score.
- Improve your implementation plan
  - ☐ Use root cause analysis to learn from past implementation experience.

☐ Remember the old saying that 'any fool can learn from their own mistakes but a wise person learns from the mistakes of others.' Get outside experience into your implementation thinking. This can be done by reading, benchmarking, researching, training, buying-in expertise (e.g., consultants) or hiring/promoting expertise.

☐ Create and add a professional change plan to the marketing plan. This will include the necessary implementation program specifications and a clear roadmap.

☐ Make sure the implementation plan is designed for the implementation environment in your organization. Make sure the balance of cost, quality and speed is right. Understand the specific leadership gaps that the organization has and plan accordingly. Plan to use a pilot exercise to both reduce the risks and build commitment.

☐ Ensure the funding is sufficient and phased appropriately over the time period,

☐ Ensure the implementation teams are staffed with the best people, not simply the available people,

☐ Take the marketing plan test at the end of this chapter. Re-do and re-test until you get a good score.

■ Step 5: Confirm your readiness for the next phase

The best way to confirm whether your marketing plan (and its change plan) is ready for the next phase is to subject it to a number of stress tests. These include:

■ Sharing drafts of it with trusted allies following the Japanese principle of *'nemawashi'* which is all about doing the groundwork by testing your ideas in lots of 1:1 conversations. The idea is that if all the groundwork has been done informally then formal approval should be a straightforward rubber-stamping exercise.

■ Undertaking a small-scale trial run. This is different to a pilot in that it may involve a completely different solution. However, like the sailors looking for the Northwest Passage, the objective is not to deliver one ship but to find a new route that can be used repeatedly in the future (see *LASER: The first implementation test at Parker*, p 118).

■ Doing some scenario planning either manually or war-gaming with a simulator (see Chapter 8).

If the boundary conditions at the end of this chapter have been met, then you are ready to proceed to the next phase of the journey.

LASER: The first implementation test at Parker

Back in July 2003, a new VP Strategic Business Development was appointed with the task of helping the corporation improve its marketing capabilities. There was limited understanding of strategic marketing, but there was a broad recognition across the groups that too many new products were failing to be launched successfully. It was thought that better marketing might be the answer to this problem.

A key issue that had come to light in one of the groups (which we will call the 'TechX' Group) was that they were competing hard in just too many markets and that this lack of focus was affecting their products. When this was discussed internally, it became apparent that they did not have an agreed way of choosing their best markets.

At this point in many companies, there would have been one of two scenarios:

Hire an external consultant to come and do it for them. The problem here is that the consultant will either write a report (which probably will not get implemented) or will facilitate a few meetings using their methodology (which invariably does not fit the organization's particular issues).

Tell someone internally (hopefully with a sales and marketing background) to work it out. The problem here is that the appointed person probably has 101 other things to do already and is keen only to get something produced and handed over quickly so they can continue with their regular job.

Not here. The VP gathered a few interested people around him to agree how they could develop and implement a new way of targeting the best markets of the future. These included the TechX CMO, a senior engineer from the TechX Group and an external consultant. These were the original core team. All were part-time, but all were very keen to develop a better approach.

The VP and his small team began their preparations by agreeing on the terms of reference for the project. This included the business needs, the project deliverables, the key milestones, the costs and the team resources. The team resources included a core team of talented people who would identify good practice and 'Parkerize' it. Additionally the Group Marketing Vice President (TechX Group CMO) agreed to review the core team's work to ensure it was workable and would fit the business needs.

Furthermore, rather than design and deploy it across the whole Group all at once, the team planned an initial pilot in the US followed by a similar pilot in Europe. They figured that once they had proved the concept in two regions, the other TechX regions would be more interested in coming on board. They therefore also kept the European TechX Group marketing manager closely involved with what they were doing in the US so he could start thinking immediately about how it might work in Europe.

So the small team sat down to develop the solution. They used the 'Directional Policy Matrix' (DPM) model from strategic marketing which delivered a very powerful 'bubble chart' to show the best and worst markets. After a couple of months, the process of doing a DPM had been finalized, rebranded as 'LASER' and was ready for deployment in the first pilot. One-day workshops were then undertaken in the US with all the relevant TechX sales and marketing managers. The workshops concentrated on teaching them about the process (rather than getting them to agree the target markets straight away). The idea was that they would then take that process back to their base and keep applying it until they came to an agreed outcome.

At the end of the workshops they asked the attendees for feedback. They also followed up with them individually a few days later to test how motivated they were to continue the exercise. The feedback was great and they generally felt that they had learned a lot from the day and would definitely use it in their business planning process.

The feedback also helped the team make some modifications to both the process and the workshop itself. These were incorporated and the solution improved before it was taken to Europe. Most of these modifications involved simplification and clarification. They also trimmed back the required attendees for the workshop to ensure that only the key stakeholders were present. In Europe, they were also able to share the American views of the state of various markets before choosing the best local markets. Again, the feedback was good and the process was retained within the European business units.

Shortly after the European workshops finished, the TechX Group CMO mandated that this was the default process for market prioritization and that all TechX business units must follow it as part of the regular annual business planning cycle. This big act of confidence was key to getting the process in place globally across this group.

The first set of Parker LASER charts were produced by the TechX Group in 2004 and presented to their leadership team for review.

The TechX Group then started to present them to the other groups as part of the corporation's business planning process. This led to enquiries from other groups to deploy the same process with them and a series of additional workshops was undertaken to do this.

Today, this simple but powerful market targeting process has been incorporated into the business planning process of many groups in the corporation.

This first exercise in implementing a market targeting process was very useful in establishing a general route to good implementation at Parker.

Planning the implementation of Winmap

This first exercise in implementing LASER was very useful in establishing a general route to good implementation at Parker. Encouraged by this success, the team then cast its mind to a much more ambitious goal: The implementation of the corporation's Win Strategy across the whole organization (see Figure 4.12).

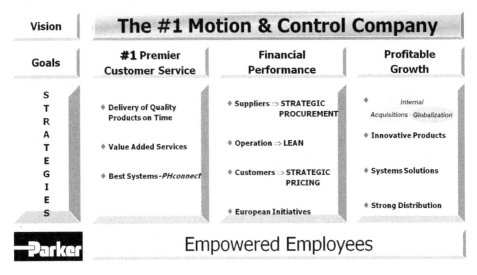

Figure 4.12: The Parker 'Win' framework

Donald E. Washkewicz, the Parker CEO, developed the Win Strategy shortly after he was appointed CEO. The Win Strategy is 'built on long established Parker goals of premier customer service, financial performance, and profitable growth; is a disciplined and consistent business strategy that has transformed the company and improved operations worldwide since it was initiated in 2001. Designed as an instrument of operational change, the Win Strategy is a powerful document adopted by all locations worldwide.' (see *About Us* at www.parker.com)

Since its inception, it has remained the primary blueprint for change in the company.

The team wanted to develop help implement this strategy by developing a more market-driven organization. At the time, there was no clear brief on what this actually was so they sat down to visualize what a good marketing-driven company should look like. One key area was the development of strategic marketing in the business. They discussed many aspects of this including how strategic marketing differs from regular marketing, the outputs and process of strategic marketing, the skills required to do it, the format of a strategic marketing plan, etc.

One diagram in particular that they developed was instrumental in explaining how strategic marketing differs to regular marketing by focusing on the big strategic questions that all business units face (see Figure 4.13).

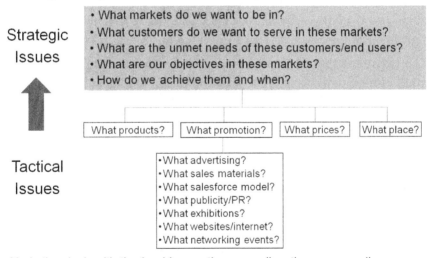

Figure 4.13: An explanation of strategic marketing

From the team's discussions, research and analysis, they also established *15 Principles of What a Good Strategic Marketing Company Looks Like*, i.e. it:

1 Operates to a common high standard of work across all groups globally

2 Follows a clear procedure for doing strategy

3 Has good market analysis and information gathering

4 Connects unmet needs in the market with Parker's capabilities

5 Strategically and intentionally targets selected markets in a proactive manner

6 Balances longer term (e.g., 3 to 5 yrs.) and shorter-term aspects

7 Realizes synergies across divisions and groups

8 Shares knowledge regarding common market efforts across all of Parker

9 Demonstrates commitment to call on and understand customers (down to division level)

10 Grows in niche markets with a full Parker package

11 Is 'market need' driven (not 'competitive pressure' driven)

12 Includes macro trends when formulating strategies

13 Has clear roles defined for marketing, sales and new product commercialization

14 Recognizes/rewards collaboration amongst groups/divisions

15 Has the necessary resources dedicated to marketing.

Against each of these principles they also had further definitions and diagrams that they had sketched out in order to clarify their thinking.

The idea eventually formed that what they needed to implement was a good strategic marketing process that all the business units within the corporation could use to implement the Win Strategy in their own area. A key output of such a process would be a market action plan (map). The program to design and implement such a process therefore was called Winmap.

■ Navigation Dashboard Example

Introduction

In this example (which we will also follow in each of the next three chapters), Parker wished to implement an ambitious plan to sell a completely new technological solution to an original equipment manufacturer (OEM). The solution involved a major new piece of machinery that would form a critical part of the end user's own production line. The solution involved engineering challenges, delivery risks, aftermarket support issues and the coordination of stakeholders across different organizations in multiple countries.

Implementation of this plan was high risk. However, the rewards would be tremendous if implemented successfully.

At the start of the project

Figure 4.14 shows how the project looked when the first Marketing Navigation Dashboard was done at the start of the plan phase.

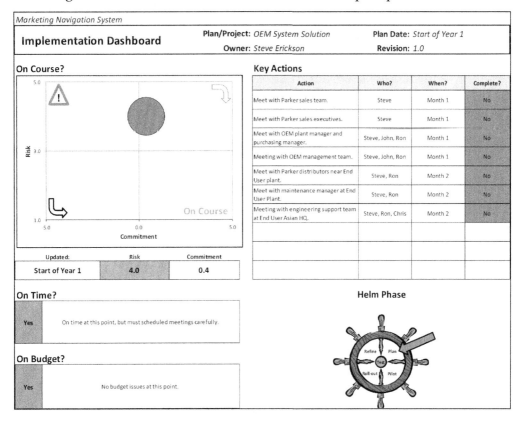

Figure 4.14: Parker OEM System Dashboard – start of plan

There was a high degree of commercial risk and a low level of commitment. Both sets of scores were driven by the fact that this was a new solution being implemented in a new way. Figure 4.15 describes these issues and how they were scored.

The key commercial risks (specifications, pricing and warranty, assistance to OEM and to end user) were all scored high (four out of five), primarily because the details of the solution and its value proposition had yet to be agreed between all the parties. There was also some very strong competition in the market that left little room for error. The plan was unproven and very much still a concept at this stage.

Top Risk Issues

No.	Risk	Desired State	Strategy	Test	Current Status	Rating
R1	Specifications	Meets or exceeds all requirements	Carefully integrate Parker products to optimize the performance of the OEM's equipment.	Confirmation by Parker systems engineer that this can be accomplished.	Pending	4
R2	Pricing & warranty	Competitive at a systems level assuming that will get premium for Parker quality and overall support.	Set pricing and warranty so is competitive at systems level, but more expensive if OEM breaks up into individual component levels.	Confirmation by Sales Team that this is possible.	Pending	4
R3	Engineering assistance for OEM	Parker's engineering assistance level exceeds that of competitors.	Assemble technical team coordinated by Parker KAM.	Verbal agreement to this approach by Parker divisions and sales teams.	Pending	4
R4	Technical assistance at End User plant	End User is comfortable with Parker's ability to provide technical assistance for OEM's equipment in the field.	Jointly develop end user technical assistance plan with Parker distibutors located near End User plant.	Verbal agreement to this approach by Parker distributors covering end user plant.	Pending	4

Score | 4.0

Top Commitment Issues

No.	Desired State	Stakeholders	Strategy	Test	Current Status	Rating
C1	OEM Management committed to Parker solution	General Manager	Build confidence in 1:1 meetings that partnering with Parker is the best way to ensure on time and on budget performance for OEM's equipment.	Informal verbal support expressed	Meeting pending	1
C2	OEM Purchasing committed to Parker solution	Purchasing Manager	Build confidence in 1:1 meetings that a Parker systems solution will provide an overall advantage when volume pricing, system warranties, technical support and logistics are considered.	Informal verbal support expressed	Meeting pending	1
C3	OEM Engineering committed to Parker solution	Engineering Manager	Build confidence in 1:1 meetings that partnering with Parker is the best way to ensure the technical performance of the OEM's equipment.	Informal verbal support expressed	Meeting pending	-1
C4	Parker Sales Team unified and committed to the project	Field sales team (all Groups)	Setup field sales team meeting with all groups to emphasize that everyone has a better chance to succeed if we work closely together as "One Parker."	Informal consensus achieved	Meeting pending	1
C5	Parker Sales Executives committed to the project	Sales VPs from all relevant groups	Build confidence in 1:1 meetings that everyone has a better chance to succeed if we work closely together as "One Parker."	Informal verbal support expressed	Will approach after reach concensus with sales team.	0

Score | 0.4

Figure 4.15: Parker OEM System Diagnostic – start of plan

Although the project scored OK on commitment, this also reflected the fact that many stakeholders were not convinced the new solution would work. The project team knew not to be complacent with this. The commitment score was only just to the right-hand side of the middle vertical line (on the Risk–Commitment Matrix) and certainly not out of the danger zone.

Indeed, with regards to commitment issue, C3, there was a faction within the customer that was committed to the use of a competitor's technology.

One month later

One month into the project and the position was quite different (see Figure 4.16).

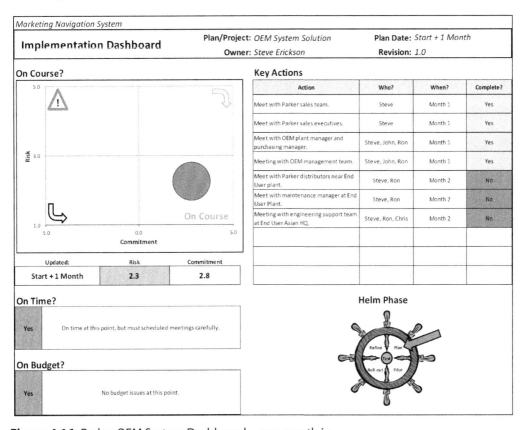

Figure 4.16: Parker OEM System Dashboard – one month in

Confirmation had been given that the solution would meet the specifications and that the pricing & warranty proposition would work. Verbal agreement had also been given to the customer assistance needed (see Figure 4.17). These reassurances that the plan was indeed feasible brought the commercial risk down from an overall score of 4.0 to 2.3.

Top Risk Issues

No.	Risk	Desired State	Strategy	Test	Current Status	Rating
R1	Specifications	Meets or exceeds all requirements	Carefully integrate Parker products to optimize the performance of the OEM's equipment.	Confirmation by Parker systems engineer that this can be accomplished.	Agreed that is possible	2
R2	Pricing & warranty	Competitive at a systems level assuming that will get premium for Parker quality and overall support.	Set pricing and warranty so is competitive at systems level, but more expensive if OEM breaks up into individual component levels.	Confirmation by Sales Team that this is possible.	Agreed that is possible	2
R3	Engineering assistance for OEM	Parker's engineering assistance level exceeds that of competitors.	Assemble technical team coordinated by Parker KAM.	Verbal agreement to this approach by Parker divisions and sales teams.	Agreed to support	2
R4	Technical assistance at End User plant	End User is comfortable with Parker's ability to provide technical assistance for OEM's equipment in the field.	Jointly develop end user technical assistance plan with Parker distibutors located near End User plant.	Verbal agreement to this approach by Parker distributors covering end user plant.	Still pending.	3
					Score	2.3

Top Commitment Issues

No.	Desired State	Stakeholders	Strategy	Test	Current Status	Rating
C1	OEM Management committed to Parker solution	General Manager	Build confidence in 1:1 meetings that partnering with Parker is the best way to ensure on time and on budget performance for OEM's equipment.	Informal verbal support expressed	Expressed strong support.	3
C2	OEM Purchasing committed to Parker solution	Purchasing Manager	Build confidence in 1:1 meetings that a Parker systems solution will provide an overall advantage when volume pricing, system warranties, technical support and logistics are considered.	Informal verbal support expressed	Approves of plan.	2
C3	OEM Engineering committed to Parker solution	Engineering Manager	Build confidence in 1:1 meetings that partnering with Parker is the best way to ensure the technical performance of the OEM's equipment.	Informal verbal support expressed	Willing to move to next step, but still not fully committed.	1
C4	Parker Sales Team unified and committed to the project	Field sales team (all Groups)	Setup field sales team meeting with all groups to emphasize that everyone has a better chance to succeed if we work closely together as "One Parker."	Informal consensus achieved	Sales team strongly support this approach.	4
C5	Parker Sales Executives committed to the project	Sales VPs from all relevant groups	Build confidence in 1:1 meetings that everyone has a better chance to succeed if we work closely together as "One Parker."	Informal verbal support expressed	All are willing to cooperate.	4
					Score	2.8

Figure 4.17: Parker OEM System Diagnostic – one month in

On the commitment axis, the strategy to increase stakeholder buy-in primarily through one-to-one meetings (see the 'Strategy' column in

Figures 4.15 and 4.17) was also working. New relationships with stake-holders needed to be established quickly and this was done successfully with verbal support being given by key individuals and consensus being achieved across the Parker sales team.

This drove the commitment for the project from a risky +0.4 to a much safer +2.8.

Further tools

Market Strategy Test

Source: Strategic Marketing Planning Quality Test, Dr. Brian Smith, Cranfield School of Management

Purpose: To determine whether you have a good market strategy

Note: Rate each aspect on the scale 1 to 5, where 1 = Very poor, 2 = Poor, 3 = OK , 4 = Good, 5= Excellent

By 'future', we mean the relevant planning timescales of your business. This is typically 3–5 years in most businesses but could be shorter in some industries (e.g., IT businesses) and longer in others (e.g., aerospace businesses).

Question	Rating
1.1 Do you have a shared and reliable insight into how our key markets will evolve in the future and the impact on their changing needs upon us?	
1.2 Do you have a shared and accurate insight into the major trends impacting our customers and our industry?	
1.3 Do you have a shared and accurate insight into how our industry will evolve in the future (including our competitors, suppliers, partners, distributors and employees)?	
1.4 Do you have a clear and shared vision of where our future profits will come from (i.e., which product/market segments)?	
1.5 Do you have clear commercial targets (e.g., segment share, segment profitability, value provided and customer satisfaction) for these segments, sequenced over time?	
1.6 Do you have a shared and accurate insight of our position today (including accurate customer perceptions of our relative strengths and weaknesses)?	
1.7 Do you have a clear and widely supported strategy to take us FROM where you are now TO where you need to be in the future (including HOW you are going to beat the competition in getting there)?	
1.8 Have you done a full and proper marketing risk assessment on this strategy (including competitor reactions, weakening assumptions and a threat assessment)?	

Boundary conditions

The conditions to exit the plan phase are:

Condition	Yes/No
You have a clear vision of your goal and a good market strategy to get there	
These are captured in a good marketing plan	
You understand the impact of the strategy on the organization	
You understand the implementation environment	
You have identified the key supporters and opponents of implementation	
You have a good change plan that shows how the strategy will be implemented in your organization	
You have completed a Marketing Navigation Dashboard for this phase	
All sensors on the Dashboard say GO	

If you can answer 'Yes' to all these, then read on!

Conclusions

As in any challenging sea voyage you need to get your vessel, crew and charts in order. You need to double-check where you are going, make sure you have plotted the best route to get there, check that your vessel is seaworthy, check who you can rely on and who may cause you problems along the way, consider the risks (like submerged rocks and the forecasted storms) and, when ready, head out of port. Conducting the proper checks now will help ensure your safe and timely arrival later.

References

Ansoff, I. (1987) *Corporate Strategy*, Penguin, 109.

Gordon, J. (n.d), *Nobody Reads a Concept*, AcuPoll, www.acupoll.com

Harshberger, M. (2009) 'Why do most acquisitions fail to add value?', www.examiner.com, December 15.

Kotter, J.P. (1996) *Leading Change*, Havard Business School

McDonald, M., Smith, K. and Ward, K. (2006) *Marketing Due Diligence, Reconnecting Strategy to Share Price*, Butterworth-Heinemann.

Speare, N. and Wilson, K. (2001) *Successful Global Account Management*, Kogan Page

Wilson, P. F., Dell, L. D., & Anderson, G. F. (1993). *Root cause analysis: A tool for total quality management*. Milwaukee: ASQC Quality Press.

5 Piloting your plan

I may say that this is the greatest factor – the way in which the expedition is equipped – the way in which every difficulty is foreseen, and precautions taken for meeting or avoiding it. Victory awaits him who has everything in order – luck, people call it. Defeat is certain for him who has neglected to take the necessary precautions in time; this is called bad luck.

From *The South Pole*, by Roald Amundsen

Summary

In this chapter we:

- Explain what we mean by a pilot
- Discuss the importance of piloting solutions prior to full implementation
- Explain how to choose a good pilot
- Explain how to run a pilot.

Introduction

You should now have a good marketing plan brimming with growth programs ready for implementation. However complex your plan and its programs, before you commit all the resources required you should conduct a simple pilot test first to ensure that the proposed solution will work with your intended audience. This will give you valuable feedback and confidence before you proceed to full roll out. In this chapter, we explain the steps involved.

Key principles

- Walk before you try to run
- Use lab testing and prototype thinking
- Build the solution dynamically
- Improve your navigation instruments
- Recalibrate as you progress.

Case story: piloting a new idea

In the shallow waters of Gijon harbour, in northern Spain a large yellow fish cuts through the waves. But this swimmer stands apart from the marine life that usually inhabits this port: there's no flesh and blood here, just carbon fibre and metal. This is robo-fish – scientists' latest weapon in the war against pollution. This sea-faring machine works autonomously to hunt down contamination in the water, feeding this information back to the shore.

In Spain, several are undergoing their first trials to see if they make the grade as future marine police. The port at Gijon is being used as a testing environment.

'The idea is that we want to have real-time monitoring of pollution, so that if someone is dumping chemicals or something is leaking, we can get to it straight away, find out what is causing the problem and put a stop to it,' explains Dr. Luke Speller, a senior scientist at the research division of BMT Group, a technology consultancy.

The company is part of the Shoal Consortium, a European Commission-funded group from academia and business that has developed these underwater robots. 'At the moment, in harbours, they take samples about once a month,' says Mr. Speller. 'And in that time, a ship could come into the harbour, leak some chemicals somewhere, then it's gone, all the way up the coastline. The idea is that we will use robot fish, which are in the harbour all of the time, and constantly checking for pollution.'

Ian Dukes from the University of Essex, England – another partner in the consortium – says that nature was an obvious inspiration for their robot. He explains: 'Over millions of years, fish have evolved the ultimate hydrody-namic shape and we have tried to mimic that in the robot. They swim just like fish; they are really quite agile and can change direction quickly, even in shallow water.'

But the researchers say there are other advantages to a fishy design compared with some other autonomous underwater vehicles (AUVs). 'Traditional robots use propellers or thrusters for propulsion,' says Dr. Dukes. 'What we're trying to do is use the fin of a fish to propel ourselves through the water.'

Can robo-fish serve the public well? Tests like this should give some idea. 'The fin does lend itself for a really useful tool in shallow waters especially where there is a lot of debris. We can work in environments that are very weedy, and would usually snag up propellers.' The fish use micro-electrode arrays to sense contaminants. In their current form they can detect phenols and heavy metals such as copper and lead, as well as monitor oxygen levels and salinity.

The team has tried to build in flexibility. Dr. Speller explains: 'We have designed it so you can pull out the chemical sensor unit, and put in different ones for something else, such as sulphates or phosphates, depending on the environment that you are monitoring.'

Once they've sniffed out a problem, the fish use artificial intelligence to hunt down the source of pollution. They can work alone or in a team, communicating with each other using acoustic signals and they can continuously report back to the port.

The trials at Gijon have been designed to put all of this technology to the test to so they can finalize the design of their robots. 'When we have our prototype, then we'll know what needs to be done to make this a complete commercial system. We hope it could happen in the next few years,' said Dr. Speller. 'In the future, what I'd also like to see is not just a single task robot, but robots that can multi-task – robots that can do search and rescue, monitoring for underwater divers, at the same time as tracking pollution.'

Water pollution is an expensive business. The UK's Department for the Environment, Food and Rural Affairs (Defra) has estimated that in England and Wales alone, cost of water pollution in rivers, canals, lakes and coastal waters came to £1.3billion per annum.

But it may be some time before robotic fish become permanent fixtures in our waters. Prototypes currently cost about £20,000 each, although Mr. Speller says costs will drop once more are produced. Battery life is also an obstacle. At the moment, the fish need to be recharged every eight hours.

But, says Richard Harrington from the Marine Conservation Society, if the fish could overcome these barriers they could have a future. 'Ports, harbours and estuaries can be challenging places to routinely monitor for

5

pollutants, often with a lengthy time period between sampling and transport and laboratory time for analysis. A remotely operated device could be
deployed quickly and simply in shallow water environments, enabling a
rapid response for decision making and remedial action to be taken.'

Source: Rebecca Morelle, Science Reporter, BBC News, May 22, 2012

■ What is a pilot?

Prototyping is a familiar concept to most people. As in the robo-fish
example, a prototype is built so that we can test a new product before it
goes into mass production. However, prototyping does more than this:

1 It identifies how the product can be tailored for different environments
   and objectives. Testing the product's flexibility is important.

2 It builds a network of supporters. This can go beyond the business
   itself into a broad coalition of pioneers from both academia and
   business.

3 It builds confidence in the product. The product is tested, improved
   and re-tested in its target environment. This reduces the risks of commercial failure and improves commitment to its success.

4 It provides valuable insights into how the product can be mass produced and mass marketed. Design for Manufacture (DFM) techniques
   can be applied to ensure the product can be produced efficiently.
   Customer feedback can be used to ensure it is mass-marketed
   effectively.

5 It allows the product's manufacturer to get a better forecast of the
   expected return on investment.

6 It allows the manufacturer to make changes at a relatively low cost
   compared with a full product recall.

As marketers we do our own version of prototyping. We may test ideas
with focus groups, test a new product or service, offer it in a small segment first or test changes to our promotion mix to see how customers
respond. We now need to apply these skills to implementing our marketing plan so we can reap the same benefits there.

Scientists do their own version of prototyping. They formulate specific
hypotheses and set up specific tests in laboratory conditions to confirm
or reject each hypothesis. This is a universal process whether it be a new
drug to treat cancer or a new component on a space craft.

Piloting is simply a way of prototyping your implementation strategy in lab conditions. We need to package the strategy into a bite-sized product that we can test effectively to see if it will work when we roll it out on a mass scale later.

■ How to pilot your plan

Step 1: Develop the solution to a testable state

Whatever new products, ideas or initiatives are contained in your marketing plan, you need to get these ready for piloting.

In some cases, you will need to have developed the product (or solution) up to a 99% state of readiness before you can test it with a pilot. This was the case for the implementation of a new telecom offer for English Energy (see Part 4 of this book). A lot of hard work had to be done to get the offer right and the supporting infrastructure in place, before they could run their pilot. However, in many cases, this does not have to be the final, detailed and polished version of the solution. It is quite acceptable to have a few rough edges here and there. For example:

- At Parker, the Winmap templates were simple Excel spreadsheets that could be used in workshops. These would be tidied up later.

- At Austro, they developed their performance scorecard to being only about 80% right so they could knock around with it, test ideas, get feedback quickly and make changes pretty much on the fly. There was not a long period of user needs analysis, software design and programming followed by an eventual go-live date.

- At European e-Cards, they 'continuously ran small tests on chosen segments. This was very powerful in demonstrating both what the IT could do and also in making immediate improvements in performance in these segments. The positive feedback from these tests was critical to the Board in approving the investment for each subsequent phase.'

Also, key elements of the supporting infrastructure should be developed so that they can be tested within the pilot as well. For example, at Parker, they had developed an online Marketing Resource Center to support the process (see the Winmap pilot at the end of this chapter). The success of this was tested by analyzing login data. At Lafarge, an incentive program was defined that would encourage the whole downstream supply chain to sell the new branded product range. This was discussed with a few trusted trading partners before incorporating into the full launch plan.

Step 2: Choose your pilots wisely

You need to select your pilot customers carefully.

For a B2C campaign, the choice of a statistically relevant sample for piloting can get very detailed. There is much written on this and we do not intend to reinvent that wheel here. What we are interested in, however, is how to implement successfully across the organization and marketplace.

The first thing to do is make sure your Navigation Dashboard is up-to-date. If necessary, re-calibrate who the key stakeholders are and re-assess the risks to implementation. From this you will be sure which box on the Risk–Commitment Matrix you are currently positioned in. If you are in the Commitment Alert box, you may want your pilots to have the right stakeholders in them who will be a catalyst for greater commitment across the whole organization. If you are in the Risk Alert box, you may want pilots that enable you to test specific commercial risks. If you are in the Danger box, you will want a combination of both.

You may want your pilots to simply involve the top customers and employees in your portfolio. At Lafarge, they piloted with their top 100 customers and top 15 retail sales teams first before rolling out across all their customers and sales teams (see Part 4). Readers should note that this followed a significant planning phase first.

At Parker, they agreed on seven metrics as part of a rigorous selection process (see the end of this chapter). This allowed them to be very targeted about which business units would be involved at this stage.

At MEDIC (see Part 4 of this book), they agreed on what they wanted their pilot to look like but did not have an opportunity that could meet their requirements. So they waited like a tiger until the right one came along and then pounced on that with all their force, surprising all their competitors in the process.

Either way, the main thing is to be proactive and pragmatic. Do not ask for volunteers or have the pilots chosen for you. If a business unit is a borderline case for selection but is led by an influential executive who is committed to implementing it well, add it in! Make sure you choose the pilots that will give your program the best possible chance of success.

Step 3: Decide how to run the pilot

There is a huge variety of pilot options available to you including:

- **Training**: These are useful when teaching new knowledge and skills. Lafarge ran seminars for their top customers and created their own certified salesperson training program for their top sales teams.

- **Workshops**: These are useful when applying the new product to real problems encountered by the user. Parker ran two-day Winmap launch workshops with its pilot business units to test how the Winmap process worked with real business challenges.

- **Champions**: Both Parker and Lafarge developed product champions for implementation. These became the apostles of change and were key to influencing other stakeholders to increase their buy-in to implementation.

- **Communications**: This is not just about presentations, review meetings and networking. Lafarge developed talk sheets, real-time newsflashes, internal magazines and a list of frequently asked questions to help communicate the program. Parker launched an online Marketing Resource Center as a central repository for strategic marketing intelligence.

The key is to combine these into a pilot program that will test the product in the right way on the right audience.

Step 4: Look for early wins

During the pilot phase, you need to be on the lookout for early successes. These are key to building confidence in the program.

Of course, for a marketing program, what we might like most of all is improved sales, market share, profits and/or customer satisfaction. These are great if you can get them but there are easier successes that can work just as powerfully. These include:

1 Significant improvements to the sales pipeline:

- **New opportunities** that have been uncovered from the pilot or more focus on known opportunities

- **New enquiries or orders** that would not have happened without the pilot. At English Energy, they 'surpassed their initial sign-up target many times over'

- **New trophy accounts** that can be attributed to the program. At MEDIC they won the Andhra Pradesh contract.

- **A better quality pipeline** (e.g., better profit potential).

2 Significant reductions in waste

■ **Stopping wasteful work**. At Parker, the Winmap implementation team was thanked by a divisional general manager who realized he could divert resources from projects elsewhere which have a very small chance of success.

■ **Reduced costs and delivery times**. At an engineering company, one quick win of their marketing plan was to implement simple changes to the way that highly customized products were sold by the sales team. By involving manufacturing earlier in the selling process they avoided selling highly customized products that were disproportionately costly, disruptive and difficult to produce.

These early wins should be shouted from the rooftops (see *Communications* in Step 3 above).

The pilot will also uncover useful hard facts. At Lafarge, these were used to counter opponents of the strategy who said it would not work.

Step 5: Improve the pilot as you go along

If the pilot involves multiple deployment exercises across different user groups (e.g., departments, business units, key accounts or customer groups), then this provides an opportunity to improve your chances of success with each deployment.

At Parker, with each Winmap launch workshop, they:

1 Reduced their commercial risks by improving:

■ The solution: e.g., the tools of Winmap were improved and prioritized

■ The supporting infrastructure: e.g., more information was added to the marketing resource center

■ The piloting process: e.g., the feedback from each workshop helped them improve the deployment of the next workshop: how it was planned, delivered and followed-up

2 Improved buy-in

■ From the general managers and the Winmap champions

■ From the alignment of Winmap with the objectives of the senior executive vice president responsible for sales and marketing, and the CMOs in the Winmap Development Team.

When they started the pilot, they had only a rough idea of what the Winmap process should look like and how it should be delivered. By the end of the pilot, the vision and basics were the same but a lot of the details of how the process would work and how it should be deployed had changed.

Here is another benefit of the pilot: by the end, they had gathered enough feedback to develop a Winmap training manual, complete with real, good, practice examples of how to use the tools in practice.

This is a good example of making many course adjustments along the way (see also Box 5.1).

Box 5.1: How one company has change loop and adjust-as-you-go in its marketing

'Our business has three simple principles for everything we do in marketing:

1. **Think Strategically**. Get the broad picture and implications before taking a decision. This involves thinking 'outside-in' and ensuring we 'begin with the end in mind.'

2. **Focus Sharply**. Choose our activities carefully. Here we must 'segment the challenges' and 'prioritize the mission.'

3. **Move Quickly**. 'Don't wait for perfect information...we move when we think we have 80% of the picture and it's looking positive. Adopt 'adjust as you go.' Monitor results to plan or expectations and adjust accordingly.'

I can think of several projects I have been part of over the years that we just did that. The results were astounding. I also remember instances in my career at other companies where 'additional research' was needed by management in order to 'justify' the project or its investments. However, the team knew we had a 'good enough' plan. We didn't move fast enough and lost opportunities. That's frustrating to all involved.'

Senior marketing executive, global engineering business.

The end goal of delivering a 'world-class strategic marketing process' had not changed nor had the basic roadmap to get there. But each workshop threw up new and unexpected challenges. Some had more staff than were anticipated, some less. Some participants had wildly optimistic expectations of what could be achieved in two days while others appeared not to have been briefed at all. Some parts of the process were really valuable at one workshop, but had little value at another workshop. There were lots of unexpected issues that could not have been anticipated even with a huge planning team on the case.

The lesson is: keep improving every aspect of implementation as you go through the pilot phase.

Step 6: Test and re-test

The pilot phase opens up new opportunities to test implementation in a variety of ways, including:

- **Formal reviews**: e.g., review meetings, presentations, personal appraisals and surveys. At Austro, they conducted a confidential employee survey to test how much buy-in they really had from managers and junior staff.
- **Informal checks**: e.g., networking with key stakeholders. This was done by the core team and the development team. Where necessary, the steering group EVP and senior EVP would have conversations at a senior level.
- **Dynamic implementation testing**: this uses modern technology to provide fast and effective feedback on various marketing tests. We will discuss this further in Chapter 8.

Step 7: Confirm your readiness for the next phase

See 'Boundary conditions' at the end of this chapter.

■ Navigation Dashboard example

Continuing our Parker OEM example from the end of Chapter 4.

At this phase, the project changed from discussion to reality. The engineering and team-working challenges had to be overcome so that a prototype of the solution could be built and tested. While this did not change the headline position of the project (it remained on course, see Figure 5.1), it did mean that risks had to be redefined and tested. In most cases, when this was thought through at the start of the pilot period, the risks remained the same. However, in the case of meeting specifications, this meant the project became more, not less, risky (see R1 on Figure 5.2).

Also, in terms of commitment, the risk around Parker sales executives (C5) was not now a top issue and was replaced by a more urgent issue regarding 'End user global engineering approval' (C6). It was essential that these people at the end-user HQ were bought-in to the solution. At this stage, they were indifferent to it and could be persuaded against it if they were left untouched.

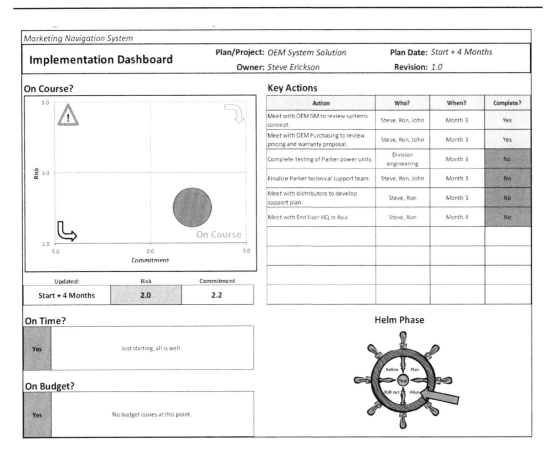

Figure 5.1: Parker OEM System Dashboard – pilot

Top Risk Issues

No.	Risk	Desired State	Strategy	Test	Current Status	Rating
R1	Specifications	Meets or exceeds all requirements	Carefully integrate Parker products to optimize the performance of the OEM's equipment.	Confirmation by Parker systems engineer that this can be accomplished.	Pending	4
R2	Pricing & warranty	Competitive at a systems level assuming that will get premium for Parker quality and overall support.	Set pricing and warranty so is competitive at systems level, but more expensive if OEM breaks up into individual component levels.	Confirmation by Sales Team that this is possible.	Pending	4
R3	Engineering assistance for OEM	Parker's engineering assistance level exceeds that of competitors.	Assemble technical team coordinated by Parker KAM.	Verbal agreement to this approach by Parker divisions and sales teams.	Pending	4
R4	Technical assistance at End User plant	End User is comfortable with Parker's ability to provide technical assistance for OEM's equipment in the field.	Jointly develop end user technical assistance plan with Parker distributors located near End User plant.	Verbal agreement to this approach by Parker distributors covering end user plant.	Pending	4
					Score	4.0

Figure 5.2(a): Parker OEM System pilot – diagnostic: top risk issues

Top Commitment Issues

No.	Desired State	Stakeholders	Strategy	Test	Current Status	Rating
C1	OEM Management committed to Parker solution	General Manager	Build confidence in 1:1 meetings that partnering with Parker is the best way to ensure on time and on budget performance for OEM's equipment.	Informal verbal support expressed	Meeting pending	1
C2	OEM Purchasing committed to Parker solution	Purchasing Manager	Build confidence in 1:1 meetings that a Parker systems solution will provide an overall advantage when volume pricing, system warranties, technical support and logistics are considered.	Informal verbal support expressed	Meeting pending	1
C3	OEM Engineering committed to Parker solution	Engineering Manager	Build confidence in 1:1 meetings that partnering with Parker is the best way to ensure the technical performance of the OEM's equipment.	Informal verbal support expressed	Meeting pending	-1
C4	Parker Sales Team unified and committed to the project	Field sales team (all Groups)	Setup field sales team meeting with all groups to emphasize that everyone has a better chance to succeed if we work closely together as "One Parker."	Informal consensus achieved	Meeting pending	1
C5	Parker Sales Executives committed to the project	Sales VPs from all relevant groups	Build confidence in 1:1 meetings that everyone has a better chance to succeed if we work closely together as "One Parker."	Informal verbal support expressed	Will approach after reach concensus with sales team.	0
					Score	0.4

Figure 5.2 (b): Parker OEM System pilot – diagnostic: Top commitment issues

The Winmap pilot: A significant six months

The final six months of 2006 would be a significant period for Winmap. The roadmap had sketched out an ambitious plan to go from zero users to having Winmap fully tested across multiple divisions.

In August 2006, the senior EVP presented the business development process (BDP) to the entire leadership team at the worldwide general managers' meeting. This included all the group presidents, all the top operating executives and the more than 100 general managers (GMs) of the corporation. One of his key points was that implementation would be led by the GMs and their cross-functional teams, not by anyone at corporate HQ. He stressed that he was not interested in 'taking their turf' but instead helping them to get better at business development themselves.

The Winmap team had their own booth at the meeting and handed out a small brochure summarizing the process. There was a warm reaction to the presentation and a lot of people came to the booth afterwards to find out more about the program.

All the senior executives in the entire corporation were now aware of the program.

In October, a full-time business development director was hired for Winmap so it could have the talented and dedicated resource it needed for implementation. In addition, the development team of group CMOs officially became the 'Winmap Group Champions.' Their role was to lead the implementation of Winmap in their own group.

Starting small

From discussions with these champions, it was agreed that the process should be tested on three to four selected divisions only. These were to be small-scale pilot lab tests undertaken in a controlled and safe environment. The team kept the number deliberately low so that they could give each division a lot of personal support. They would then adjust the solution and the roadmap based on the implementation experience with these.

The team did not risk simply asking for volunteers. That would deliver far too much of a random outcome and the wrong pilots would quickly sail into problematic waters. In order to find the right pilots, the team proactively chose candidates who scored highly on the following criteria:

1 *Likely level of support from management:* they only went for divisions where they knew they had good commitment from the management team.

2 *Location of the division within the Parker structure:* they wanted to cover at least three different Parker groups to give the pilots broader organizational coverage.

3 *Nature of the local issue to be addressed*: they looked for urgent and important challenges that the division needed to address. They also tried to identify different issues in each pilot (in order to test the true capability of the Winmap process). In one case, this was to investigate whether a new product already in the Winovation process actually had good market potential. In another case, it was to identify the best target markets for some of their existing products.

4 *The potential for measurable commercial success:* this could be improved sales, orders, margins, delivery times, product/service quality, developing new capabilities or winning new markets/customers.

5 *The probability of quick wins:* they did not want to finish the pilot without generating a list of attractive opportunities.

6 *The internal credibility of the division and its key executives:* they wanted to ensure that after these pilots were completed they had a pool of

'credible witnesses' that would give renewed momentum to the program across the corporation. They therefore chose divisions and GMs that were highly respected amongst their peers.

7 *Geographical location of the business:* they chose to pilot only in the US where they could keep a close eye on implementation issues.

This was all about reducing the risks of implementation failure. They anticipated that one pilot might fail but, even in that case, at least two would be seen as successful.

Thankfully, there was much enthusiasm from the champions and the team had a harder time deciding which divisions to leave out rather than which to include. After much discussion they agreed upon four pilot divisions.

They then built a standard two-day 'Winmap pilot workshop' that would introduce Winmap to the division and get them started in the right way. They were clear about what a good delegate list looked like. This included the division's general manager, marketing manager, engineering, sales and business development representatives, plus – dependent on the issue being addressed – any necessary subject matter experts and stakeholders from operations and support services (e.g., market and/or product experts, IT support, etc.)

Cross-functional involvement was important. This was not just a marketing process of interest to the internal marketing community. The team wanted to build a broad appreciation of the importance of real strategic marketing to the whole business, spread a common understanding of Winmap across the leadership team and ensure good company-wide buy-in to its localized implementation.

The team did not plan to make much progress in developing strategic marketing leaders at the workshop. They knew that getting everyone on the same page about strategic marketing and the Winmap process would take time and should not be rushed. The key output of the workshop was simply to identify and scope a project that could be 'Winmapped' afterwards.

These workshops were then duly undertaken across the four divisions and the first batch of Winmap projects started. These pilots gave the team a huge amount of feedback on the Winmap process. As a result, the process itself was simplified and clarified. Some tools in the process were de-emphasized while others were promoted. Some were moved backwards in the process and others moved forwards. Almost all of the tools and templates were improved in some way.

The workshops were improved every time they were run. In addition to getting the big things right (like the delegate list, the materials and the timetable) the team also got better at doing the many small things that make a good workshop experience. These include simple things like setting up the meeting room in the right way, getting name tags organized and having proper binders and handouts for the delegates. They also got better at specifying what a good Winmap project would look like as a result. In the end, they developed a 'cook-book' approach to running a Winmap workshop which showed the key ingredients required, how to blend them together and what the final result should look like.

Winmap 2.0

In parallel to these pilots, the team spent the first half of 2007 developing the infrastructure needed.

They used the experience and examples from the workshops to develop a detailed Winmap user manual. This had an introduction from the CEO, included the basics of what it was all about and had detailed instructions – with good practice examples (from their pilots) – of how to use the various tools and templates.

They also worked with IT to launch the online marketing resource center which had an area specifically devoted to Winmap. The center included:

- 'The Winmap Forum' containing the Winmap user manual, FAQs, a template library (toolbox) and Winmap workshop information (e.g., a calendar of workshops)
- Latest market and industry reports of interest to the Parker divisions
- Status reports on each of the pilot Winmap projects.

By June 2007, four Winmap projects were operational with good feedback from all four divisions. This feedback was incorporated into what was called 'Winmap 2.0'. The use of numerical versions was deliberate to demonstrate that the solution will never be complete and will always be improved and upgraded.

The team had now developed their solution and their infrastructure. They had also won over some very credible witnesses and many key stakeholders.

Testing/evaluation

One of the major features of this step was the use of pilots. Piloting was not just about testing ideas formed by the Winmap team. It was also a way of developing important aspects of the solution. The Winmap team deliberately went to these workshops with a rough process in order to get early and powerful feedback on how to shape it properly. The team could have spent longer getting the details right first but this would have slowed down implementation significantly.

Testing was also being done on a continuous basis:

- There were many reviews. *Formal* reviews were undertaken by the Winmap team on a regular basis. For the core team they were typically done weekly and for the development team they were typically done quarterly. Members of the Winmap team would also often attend individual project reviews in the divisions. Formal reviews of the achievement of personal goals were undertaken by line managers as part of the annual appraisal process. For the initial phases, this went right to the top of the corporation. The CEO reviewed the personal goals of the senior EVP and the group presidents reviewed the personal goals of the group CMOs.

- There were also constant *informal* checks via informal networking, constant communications and 1:1 meetings. Furthermore, both EVPs were constantly sensing each of the group president's support for Winmap and the VP strategic marketing was constantly sensing the groups' support for implementation projects.

These reviews informed the team about which frameworks were important and easy to use and which they thought were unimportant or unnecessary. It also gave provided essential feedback on the level of commitment to Winmap within each group.

The team could also track the level of interest in Winmap from the logins to the marketing resource center.

All these evaluation activities reduced the risk of a 'pocket veto' (i.e. someone saying the right things but dragging their feet in reality).

The team was also on the lookout for early wins from putting Winmap into practice. This did not have to be about increased opportunities, orders or sales. In one case, they found an opportunity to save money by stopping further product development. The GM reported back saying, 'Winmap has been very useful in confirming that this project, which has tied up a lot of our resources, will not succeed commercially.'

By the end of this phase, the team was confident that it had reduced the implementation risks, increased the commitment, delivered sufficient short-term wins, proved the process to be capable and had a green light from each group to move forward with them.

All was ready for the global roll-out.

Boundary conditions

If the following boundary conditions have been met, then you are ready to proceed to the next phase of the journey:

The conditions to exit the pilot phase are:

Condition	Yes/ No
You carefully chose a sample of users for your pilot	
You have tested your solution on them	
You have reviewed the results and made the necessary improvements to the solution, its supporting infrastructure and to the implementation plan itself	
Commitment is sufficiently strong across the stakeholders to proceed	
You have completed a Marketing Navigation Dashboard for this phase	
All sensors on the Dashboard say GO	

If you can answer 'Yes' to all these, then read on!

Conclusions

Piloting borrows fundamental principles from science and engineering. The idea of rolling out a new marketing solution without properly testing it first should be as alien to the marketer as it would be to any food, drinks, cosmetics, drugs or aerospace company. Piloting is a major test of the solution under laboratory conditions. The feedback from this helps to improve the solution, the target audience and the strategy for implementation.

Your ship has now passed its essential checks and is ready for the main part of the implementation journey.

Rolling out your plan

Implementation is 1% inspiration and 99% perspiration.

Adapted from Thomas Edison's statement on genius, c.1903

Summary

In this chapter we:

- Cover the six steps required to roll out your marketing plan
- Consider the skills required to do this well
- Show you how to put your existing strategic marketing skills to new uses
- Illustrate how rollout plans and relationship maps can work together.

◼ Introduction

In this phase, we use the results from the pilot to accelerate implementation. This is the major action phase and covers most of the implementation journey. We will make the transition from a few users of our solution(s) to a full market rollout. By the end of this phase, implementation should be around 95% complete.

Key principles

- Use rolling wave planning
- Use strategic marketing thinking to get your rollout strategy right
- Use market maps to plan your rollout
- Use SAM principles to build buy-in
- Adopt continuous improvement
- Use sports thinking to consolidate and progress.

Principles of Play stand the test of time

The common problem with marketing plans is that they get overtaken by events. The planned actions get buried by new actions to cope with unplanned urgent issues. This is a challenge for marketers who must get their plan back on track within the month or the quarter. It is worse for sports coaches whose game plan must cope with very fast change and which has only minutes or hours to succeed. How do they roll out their plan to take control of the game and dominate the field of play? In soccer, good practice is to move from defending home territory well to attacking new territory quickly (and vice versa), using all the players at your disposal. Here, Tony Waiters, President and Technical Director of World of Soccer Ltd., explains how it works.

The Principles of Play

Principles of Play are an essential component of tactical thinking for all soccer players and coaches.

Allen Wade, former Director of Coaching for English Football Association (FA), was the first to formalize the 'Principles' in the late 1960s in the manual, *The FA Guide to Training and Coaching*.

Allen is quick to point out that these 'Principles' were not a personal invention. Others in Continental Europe, in South America and most noticeably, Sir Walter Winterbottom, Alan's predecessor at The FA, had begun the process and clarified the most important 'Principles of Play' before Allen put pen to paper. In his own modest way, Allen only took credit for summarizing them in a comprehensive, but easy-to-understand section, in this visionary coaching book.

So what are the Principles of Play? There are 10 of them. The Five Principles of Attack are countered by the Five Principles of Defence.

Table 6.1: The Principles of Play

ATTACK	DEFENCE
Penetration	Delay
Support	Depth
Width	Concentration (Compaction)
Mobility	Balance
Improvisation/Creativity	Discipline/Patience

- **Attacking Principle No.1 – Penetration**: As soon as the ball is repossessed, the first thought should be, 'Can we score?' If not, is there a forward player in an unmarked or advanced position? The question then is, 'Can we play the ball to him or her'?

- **Defending Principle No.1 – Delay**: The defending team must do everything possible to prevent a quick counter-attack after losing the ball.

- **Attacking Principle No.2 – Support**: To keep possession and to be able to move the ball down the field, the player on the ball needs support. Forward support, back support and side support, will allow the player with the ball, different close supporting options, and put doubts in the minds of the defending players.

- **Defending Principle No.2 – Support in Defense (or Depth)**: As the attacking team seeks to support their 1st Attacker, the defending team, in its cat and mouse persona, supports their 1st Defender – the delaying player.

- **Attacking Principle No.3 – Width**: Stretching the defense is always in the minds of the attacking team. A team can be stretched vertically and laterally.

- **Defending Principle No.3 – Concentration**: If attackers are trying to stretch the defense, it behoves defenders to concentrate themselves in the most vulnerable areas. Concentration and the next defensive principle, balance, work closely together.

- **Attacking Principle No. 4 – Mobility**: Individual speed and the ability to interchange positions are so important in the modern game. As an attacker moves forwards, sideways, or diagonally, with or without the ball, the opposing team has to adjust and this can unbalance the defense and adversely affect the defensive 'shape' and create attacking opportunities.

- **Defending Principle No. 4 – Balance**: If mobility is being used to unbalance teams then that principle of maintaining balance must be exercised to counter the attacking runs. Now the picture is becoming more complex as all players are involved to give the team balance.

Before covering the final two principles of play, we should quickly look at the importance of thinking in 'thirds' of the field, rather than the more conventional halves. In the defending third, the general philosophy is that of caution. The middle third is the battleground for dominance and the build-up area for successful attacks. The final third is where 99% of all goals are scored from.

- **Attacking Principle No. 5 – Improvisation/Creativity**: This is the most exciting principle. Improvisation is not exclusively reserved for the attacking third, but this is where it is most effective. Twists, turns, back-heels, dribbles, volleys, overhead kicks, all kinds of creativity have a place here with only limited risks.

- **Defending Principle No. 5 – Discipline & Patience (Control and Restraint)**: If a defending team has observed all the previous four defending principles, it will find itself, for the moment, in good shape to deal with most, if not all, contingencies.

[Conclusion: Teams must] Transition

The word 'Transition' has become a buzzword in today's game though it has been around the soccer world forever. Good teams have a double persona. They are Dr. Jekyll and Mr. Hyde. They play both ways – immediately [when] they have to. One moment they are free running, expressive and creative. The next moment they are mean, determined and task-oriented.

In this chapter we will see the importance of having a rollout game plan, of defending initial territory won (i.e. not letting it slip back to the previous state) while rolling out the solution to new territories. We will also see that being flexible and willing to move swiftly from defense to offense and vice versa is a great implementation skill.

6

■ How to roll out your plan

Returning to our theme, we are now leaving the safety of the harbor and heading towards the vastness of the ocean. All the planning and prototyping of the previous phases (plan and pilot) can now be used to help us proceed safely. Our final destination, on the other side of that ocean, is known and we have performed all the necessary safety checks. Our instruments have helped us become aware of many threats from many quarters, but we are monitoring them and are confident we can overcome them.

This is a major part of the implementation journey which we have divided into six steps:

Step 1: Finalize the rollout plan

Before we leave the safety of the home waters, we need to return briefly to the plan phase. This is because we need a mini-plan to determine how we are going to do our rollout. We have proven that our solution works on a few trial users, but now we need to scale it up to the total market population.

Get the stages right

The first question to consider is whether to split the implementation into mini-stages. For Winmap, because of the scale of the implementation (covering eight global groups and over 100 divisions), implementation was split into two stages. First, a limited rollout was planned that would engage all eight groups, but not very deeply (e.g., at least one division at each group) and focused mainly in the US. Then, after that was completed, a full rollout was planned that would penetrate deeply into all the divisions and all the regions around the world.

It may be that in your case, as in the Principles of Play above, it makes sense to split implementation into thirds. The first third will defend your program from attack. The second will act as the 'tipping point' for implementation. The final third is where you will press home your advantage.

For complex, more intricate and/or more time-sensitive implementations there could be many more stages to go through. Each stage may even have its own program specification (see Chapter 4). However, the detailed planning of the stages is generally done now, not at the same time that the initial overall implementation plan was written. This is because we are adopting the rolling wave planning principle. This says you should plan the details of implementation later rather than earlier, because more facts are known at that point in the program rather than at the start of the program (see Box 6.1).

Box 6.1: Rolling wave planning

Rolling wave planning is an incremental approach that helps program management focus on more immediate work with a detailed schedule and far term schedules planned at a higher level until the program [manager] better understands the details about the scope, cost and delivery requirements of that effort. As the program progresses and requirements are refined, the program [manager] extends the detailed schedule into the future as a 'rolling wave' of planning. This concept allows program personnel to provide clarity where needed while saving unnecessary time and expense developing plans where details cannot be clearly defined. Rolling wave planning can be especially beneficial to programs where the statement of work (SOW) is likely to change.

Source: *Rolling Wave Planning, Planning & Scheduling Excellence Guide (PASEG)*, Working Draft v1.1b, p111, April 6, 2011, National Defense Industrial Association

Finalize your rollout strategy

As we saw above, the Winmap team decided to get a foothold in each of the eight groups in the US first before rolling out their solution deeply within the US and across the world. But they could have done it differently. They could have completed one group and rolled it out there first, before moving on to the next group. In this case, they would have had an eight-stage rollout plan (one stage for each of the eight groups). Or they could have targeted one region, say EMEA, and implemented there first before rolling out to the other regions. Or they could have followed a hybrid strategy of both.

Why did they develop this particular two-stage plan? One reason was that the US groups were all in easy reach of the Winmap team. They could sense issues quickly and respond quickly. A second reason was that the CMOs and the group presidents of each group were based in the US. Once the US divisions had been launched, it would be easier to gain commitment elsewhere.

So there are many choices to where you do your rollout and when. Your chosen strategy will depend on many factors but ultimately on your current position and how you wish to get (or remain) on course.

As a marketer though, you have another advantage which you can use at this point. You should be good at market strategy. This means you should be good at segmenting your market and developing a market invasion plan. If you have not already done so, take the following steps:

1 Define the scope of the implementation market.

2 Define the main solutions or programs in your marketing plan that you wish to implement.

3 List these across the top of a grid.

4 Divide your market into its various segments. The *external* customers could be predefined as part of an earlier market segmentation exercise. However, the *internal* (and partner) stakeholders and employees may have not have been segmented at all (see McDonald and Dunbar, 2010 for details on segmentation).

5 List these segments down the left-hand side of the grid. This is now your full implementation product-market map.

6 Grey out any product-market cells where implementation is not required in the timeframe.

7 Highlight in green, the product-market cells that you wish to implement in Stage 1 of the rollout. Then copy the map and add further

green cells for target implementations in Stage 2. Continue through all your stages until the entire market map is green. These sequenced maps are your **rollout plan** and show how you wish to invade the entire market by the end of this phase.

An example of a rollout plan is shown in Figure 6.1.

Rollout Stage 1	Alpha Program	Bravo Program	Charlie Program
Business Unit A			
Business Unit B			
Business Unit C			

Rollout Stage 2	Alpha Program	Bravo Program	Charlie Program
Business Unit A			
Business Unit B			
Business Unit C			

Rollout Stage 3	Alpha Program	Bravo Program	Charlie Program
Business Unit A			
Business Unit B			
Business Unit C			

Rollout Stage 4	Alpha Program	Bravo Program	Charlie Program
Business Unit A			
Business Unit B			
Business Unit C			

Figure 6.1: Example rollout plan

Figure 6.1 shows how a four-stage rollout might be planned where:

- Business Unit A has the highest levels of commitment to the three programs in the marketing plan.
- The 'Alpha Program' is the *least* risky program to implement
- The 'Charlie Program' is the *most* risky program to implement
- Business Unit C is the least committed.

Of course, there are many ways to segment both the external and internal market. The above is done simply by business unit. The market could be segmented by territory, buy-in to the marketing plan, capability to change, cost, speed, accessibility, influence, credibility, competition for attention, etc. There are also many different rollout routes. The key is to use your strategic marketing skills to help plan your rollout properly.

The other use for the rollout map is to track implementation progress. You can track the percentage of implementation complete for each segment (as part of your implementation strategy) in the same way as you would if tracking percentage market share in each segment (as part of your marketing strategy). As an example, the rollout maps showing the implementation progress of Winmap across Parker are shown at the end of this chapter (Figures 6.5 and 6.6). Readers should note that this was a single program and so they could use both axes to show two dimensions of the market.

Finalize the relationship strategy

We saw in Chapter 4 how a relationship map can help you identify the key stakeholders and your coverage model for marking them.

The relationship map is more than just a gap-analysis tool. We can also use it to plan our relationship strategy. To see how this works let us return to our simple example above where we have a four-stage rollout of three programs across three business units.

Figures 6.2 and 6.3 shows our relationship strategy to support the rollout plan above.

Rollout Stage 1	Business Unit A			Business Unit B			Business Unit C		
Our team:	Alan (Alpha)	Brenda (Bravo)	Chris (Charlie)	Daphne (Alpha)	Ewan (Bravo)	Franz (Charlie)	Gerhart (All)	Hussam (All)	Ivy (All)
Jack	X								
Kevin		X			X		X		
Linda						X			
Mandy				X				X	
Norris			X						X
Oliver									

Rollout Stage 2	Business Unit A			Business Unit B			Business Unit C		
Our team:	Alan (Alpha)	Brenda (Bravo)	Chris (Charlie)	Daphne (Alpha)	Ewan (Bravo)	Franz (Charlie)	Gerhart (All)	Hussam (All)	Ivy (All)
Jack	X								
Kevin		X			X		X		
Linda						X			
Mandy				X				X	
Norris			X						X
Oliver									

Figure 6.2: Relationship strategy (Stages 1–2)

For simplicity we will assume that there are just three key stakeholders in each business unit and we have an implementation team of six people that we can call upon for support.

In Business Unit A, each stakeholder is concerned with just one of the programs. Alan is concerned only with the Alpha Program, Brenda with the Bravo Program and Chris with the Charlie Program. This could be because each program impacts different business functions (Alpha could be a KAM program that impacts sales; Bravo could be a CRM program that impacts IT; Charlie could be a new product program that impacts operations).

Our rollout plan for Stage 1 focuses on implementing the Alpha Program in Business Unit A. Alan is committed to the Alpha Program's success so (with good navigation) this should get implemented successfully. In this stage we also plan to use Kevin's good relationship with Brenda to build greater commitment from her to the implementation of the Bravo Program.

In Stage 2, we need to implement all three programs in Business Unit A. We will therefore rely upon Kevin to have done his good work with Brenda, supported by good feedback from Alan on how the Alpha Program is going. We will also task Norris with improving his relationship with Chris and making sure Chris is committed to the Charlie Program implementation. At the same time, in Business Unit B, we have tasked Kevin to use his good relationship with Ewan to improve his level of commitment and Linda to work on her relationship with Franz. This will prepare the ground for Stage 3.

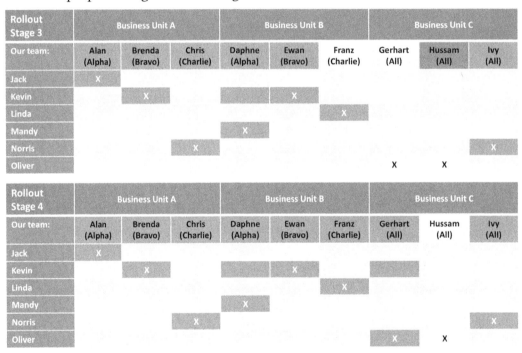

Rollout Stage 3	Business Unit A			Business Unit B			Business Unit C		
Our team:	Alan (Alpha)	Brenda (Bravo)	Chris (Charlie)	Daphne (Alpha)	Ewan (Bravo)	Franz (Charlie)	Gerhart (All)	Hussam (All)	Ivy (All)
Jack	X								
Kevin		X			X				
Linda						X			
Mandy				X					
Norris			X						X
Oliver							X	X	

Rollout Stage 4	Business Unit A			Business Unit B			Business Unit C		
Our team:	Alan (Alpha)	Brenda (Bravo)	Chris (Charlie)	Daphne (Alpha)	Ewan (Bravo)	Franz (Charlie)	Gerhart (All)	Hussam (All)	Ivy (All)
Jack	X								
Kevin		X			X				
Linda						X			
Mandy				X					
Norris			X						X
Oliver							X	X	

Figure 6.3: Relationship Strategy (Stages 3–4)

In Stage 3, we need to get both the Alpha and Bravo Programs implemented in Business Unit B. The good work done by Kevin in Stage 2 should now have paid off and we can do this successfully. Linda's advice to Franz should also have made him at least open to discussions on the Charlie Program by now.

In this stage we also plan to start our preparations for our toughest challenge, Business Unit C. In this business unit we have no one committed to any of the programs and they all work together as a team of stakeholders across all three programs. This is why we sequenced them last in the rollout.

Ivy is at least supportive of the marketing plan so we will task Norris with improving his relationship with her and winning her commitment.

To convert Gerhart and Hussam, we will deploy the Oliver card! Oliver used to work in this business unit and has a lot of credibility there. He is willing to speak with them both to convince them to be more supportive. We will give Oliver relationship responsibility (signified by the X) for them both as well.

In Stage 4, we need to have the marketing plan fully implemented. We will use Linda's continuing advice to Franz to finally implement the Charlie program in Business Unit B. We also plan to have at least two of the stakeholders committed in Business Unit C, they will then be able to out-vote the third stakeholder, who will be effectively neutralized.

In this way, by the end of Stage 4, almost all of the key stakeholders will be committed to the marketing plan and any change blockers neutralized.

For the Winmap program, there was a carefully constructed relationship strategy that supported the overall rollout plan. This strategy mapped out the entire Winmap Team including the Winmap Champions and the key stakeholders found at country, business unit, division and group levels.

Step 2: Ensure the resources are ready to deliver it

Next, we need to ensure we have the right resources in place for a potentially resource-hungry rollout phase. There are two main aspects to think about here.

Funding

First, there is the funding of implementation. This can be divided into two parts: funding for the core programs in the marketing plan and funding for the necessary infrastructure (like IT systems) to support their implementation.

We have already spoken at length about developing the infrastructure to support the programs. We have made the point that key aspects of this can be developed during the pilot phase. Clearly, if you need additional funding beyond what is already planned (either in your marketing plan or other departmental plans) then you need to ensure you get approval for this prior to rollout.

In terms of funding the core programs, you will need to follow whatever approval process your CFO operates. There are many resources (McDonald and Mouncey, 2011) to help you determine the right amount of funding and we do not wish to reiterate them all here. However, we do like the net present value approach and would encourage you to become familiar with its calculations (McDonald, 2007; Doyle, 2008). This method ensures you are thinking not just about the level of funding but also about the timing of cash flows through implementation. Your rollout may require more cash in later stages than in earlier stages, for example.

By running different scenarios (e.g., a fully successful implementation vs. a partially successful implementation) you will also be able to see the cash implications on the business and compare your programs against each other and against other programs requiring funding in the overall business plan. That way, you may be able to convince the C-Suite that diverting a small amount of funds from, say, a risky acquisition program to a safer organic growth program should improve the value of the business altogether.

Skills

Second, there are the skills resources required. This is a soft issue and is often underestimated by marketers. As Larissa Liang, founder of Global Language Partner (GLP) said, 'In implementing my strategy, I thought the biggest issue would be finance. Finance and budgeting are important but not top. Money is just a resource to grow. It is not a determining point for success. Put simply, people have been my greatest implementation issue' (see Part 4).

This also falls into two areas: the skills required to implement the program and the skills required to run the program after implementation. Often we assume that the same set of people will cover both stages. However, quite different skills are required in each stag and these skills differences become acute for complex and challenging implementation programs.

We must separate out the two and not under-resource the first stage. Much can be done with a few good people. Time and again we have seen a few skilled pioneers, committed to changing things, overcome seemingly insurmountable challenges to get programs implemented successfully. Part 4 has many examples where such a small team has beaten the odds.

Step 3: Implement with certainty and flexibility

At English Energy, program leader Ian Helps, mentioned three key factors that contributed to success:

1 **'Clarity of the value proposition**. The value proposition was systematically simplified to make it as clear and compelling as possible. In the end, it was all about 'the same level of service as your existing supplier but at a cheaper price'. Ian underlines the importance of this point, 'In my experience, many product launches fail because of a vague value proposition. Being clear up front about the value being promised is absolutely essential.'

2 **Good plans**. A comprehensive business plan was written that contained the marketing plan and a clear business case for change. Once approved, this was then turned into a detailed project and change plan. One of the first things the team did was to define the implementation steps that would hit the time/cost/quality targets of the project and minimize the risks of implementation failure along the way.

3 **Unbending determination**. The project team also had to convince the executive that the program really was going ahead. 'There is always a natural inertia in doing new things' says Ian. 'Often, it is easier *not* to do something than to do it. To overcome this issue, we were very clear about when the launch date would be and we stuck to it. Even at the eleventh hour there was a big news story in the UK involving a breach of data security in an unrelated industry and we had to investigate our own security systems. However, we just put in the extra hours and confirmed to the executive that all was secure and that the launch date was still good.'

The team was therefore certain about what the customer benefits were to implementation (the value proposition), how they were going to get there (the plan) and the when they were going to arrive (the launch date). This was key to keeping them on course through all the challenges they faced.

As the rollout progresses, implementation will get more complex and you will get more requests to adjust the solution, the plan and the timescales. You will need to keep this certainty in your mind so that you retain constancy of purpose and do not get blown off course towards the rocks of failure.

That is not to say you should be unbending in your tactics. You should be flexible in how you respond to events, but if possible, change your tactics within the original strategy.

At Oxford Learning Labs, their strategy is to exploit the power of online marketing. But in implementing that strategy they discovered that Google Adwords was not working for them. They then successfully changed tactics from selling directly to end-consumers to selling through channel intermediaries. They also changed pricing tactics from a 'free-mium' policy to a free-sample policy.

At Parker, the strategic marketing team had to navigate through the wholly unexpected credit crunch storm. However, rather than let it blow them off course, they turned it to their advantage by adding a critical forecasting tool to the solution. This forecasting tool predicted the drop in sales at one of the groups much better than the group's own sales forecast. Suddenly, the strategic marketing department had a higher level of respect across the leadership team. To get the tool in place, they had to turn the Helm full circle first. They had to plan how it would look, pilot it in Excel with one group, roll it out across all the groups then refine it to make it more accurate. The result though was that the storm was now blowing them faster towards successful implementation!

The vision, strategy and timescales are still the same, but both Oxford Learning Labs and Parker have maneuvered in response to changing conditions in order to get to their end goal. Moreover, they have been prepared to turn the Helm full circle in order to catch a better wind.

This combination of certainty about the journey but willingness to be flexible en-route is essential at this stage.

Step 4: Improve the rollout as you go along

In the pilot phase we discussed the importance of continuous improvement. This principle is also true here. As the rollout progresses, new challenges and opportunities will emerge and additional requirements placed upon the solution. Some of these should be rebuffed or delayed if they risk compromising implementation. But where possible, the easiest and most important ones should be incorporated into the solution.

At Parker they made improvements to Winmap as they rolled it out across the groups. These improvements included:

- A much stronger competitive intelligence process inserted into the process and users trained how to apply it. This improved the way that competitors were identified, analyzed and key actions taken.

- An 'Ansoff Matrix' put on the front end to distinguish the different processes used for marketing existing and new products into existing and new markets.

■ Overhauling the whole process so that it would be simpler to use.

This brings us on to the next point of simultaneously defending the ground you have won but also attacking new ground as well. In other words, you should consolidate gains and produce more change (Kotter, 1996).

At IEB, they had already introduced key account management across five key divisions but Alistair Taylor felt that implementation was not safe. 'I felt things were moving along but the plans were not getting enough senior executive support. I wanted to get the CEO and Executive actively and visibly engaged in reviewing the plans. It was my belief that if a handful were being formally reviewed, with detailed feedback, a powerful message would quickly be spread across the group.' So they then went on both to cement progress and improve the KAM solution by introducing a rigorous and senior level account review process.

Simultaneously defending and attacking is a familiar skill for military strategists. Alexander the Great left behind 'satraps' (or governors) to control territory that he had conquered while he pushed onwards to claim new territory. Victory lies with attacking new territory but good defensive lines are key. Sun Tzu (n.d.) said, 'Invincibility lies in defense but the possibility of victory in attack.'

Perhaps the best analogy though is found on the sports field rather than the battlefield. This is where the best teams swing swiftly from offense to defense and vice versa. The more we can train both our self and our resources to attack segments according to the plan but then also to move swiftly to defend segments under threat, the better.

Allen Wade's 'Principles of play' work well for implementing marketing plans.

Step 5: Test and re-test

Throughout this phase of the journey, there will be a lot of testing. In fact, a full suite of sense-and-respond devices should be carried on board your ship as it traverses this unpredictable ocean. Here is a sample of such devices:

■ Appraisals

■ Feedback meetings

■ External expert input

■ Oral feedback

■ Written surveys

- Project status reports
- Benchmarking
- Customer feedback
- Forecasting
- Online marketing responses
- Employee surveys.

Many examples of these in action can be seen in the Winmap example at the end of this chapter and in the other case examples in Part 4.

Step 6: Confirm your readiness for the next phase

This is a long phase so we should start by listing some of the conditions required to start your rollout. These are that you have:

- Finalized your rollout plan
- Finalized a relationship strategy to support the plan
- Secured sufficient funding to deliver good implementation success
- All the right skills ready to deliver good implementation success, or that any missing skills can reliably be acquired or developed at the right time.

At the end of this phase, if the boundary conditions have been met, you are ready to proceed to the next – and final – phase of the journey.

■ The Winmap rollout

In January 2007, Winmap 2.0 was formally launched at Parker's Annual Executive Planning Meeting at La Quinta, Florida. In a demonstration of solidarity, the EVP and Winovation leader (VP Technology and Innovation) jointly presented the Parker Business Development Process to the assembled senior executives. These executives consisted of the entire C-Suite (including the CEO, the Senior EVP and the Parker Management Committee) and all of its top global operating executives.

The progress that had been made was warmly received and the order was given to roll it out globally. Again, this was formally inserted as a top priority into both the Parker Annual Improvement Plan and the performance goals of the relevant top executives.

Even so, there was no 'Global Big Bang.' The team planned a two-stage rollout consisting of a limited rollout for the remainder of the fiscal year and a full rollout thereafter.

Limited rollout (February–June 2007)

Four divisions (within three global groups) were already using Winmap so the aim was to add another five divisions, one from each of the remaining five groups. Again, the team proactively used their selection criteria and their Winmap champions to help them find good lead divisions with whom to engage. As before, they were not short of interest and ended up with seven divisions in their next batch (making 11 divisions in both batches).

The team then got these lined up, their Winmap roadshow ready and went on a US Winmap tour, launching an improved workshop and process in each division. These focused even more tightly on exposing the divisions to the process rather than on creating the Market Action Plan itself.

The team also continued to strengthen the support they could give to the divisions. They extended the Strategic Marketing Department's services to provide ad hoc research and sales support. They also added searchable metatags to their Marketing Resource Center so that any business unit (whether a pilot or not) could search for relevant market intelligence on specific countries, similar projects, technologies and macroeconomic trends.

By the end of June 2007, the team had received good feedback from all 12 divisions in their pilot program.

They were ready now to really accelerate the implementation of Winmap deeper within the US and right across the global corporation.

Full rollout (July 2007–June 2010)

The rollout plan

The first thing the team had to do was work out was their rollout plan. They had US beachheads established in each of the groups but they needed to get over 100 divisions worldwide using Winmap successfully for the implementation to be complete. So, with their Winmap champions, they sat down to discuss their strategy.

They decided to deepen their hold on North America first with eight parallel implementation exercises across all the groups. Their target was to more than double the usage from 11 divisions to 24 divisions, with three divisions in each group using Winmap. This itself would be a major expansion of the team's workload and would take about a year to complete. However, when completed it would give Winmap a secure position in each of the groups in North America. At the same time, they would be doing four things to aid their global rollout:

- They would seek their first implementation in Europe.

- They would look for additional opportunities for their first global Winmap projects. These would be in targeted global markets where multiple groups were already competing but without the right focus, joint strategy and coordination.

- They would plan how to expand the rollout to all divisions internationally.

- They would plan when to roll out to the Parker sales companies. These are separate business units that are based in each global region and sit outside the group structure.

Implementation of the rollout plan

They had strong interest from North America and the Winmap roadshow spent a lot of time out of the office on tour. By the end of the 2008 fiscal year, they had completed two-day 'Winmap Launch' workshops in 75 divisions. That was, of course, three times their target!

Outside North America, the team implemented a hybrid push-and-pull strategy. They were keen to get footholds in each of the global regions and proactively secured 'lead' divisions there.

In EMEA, they started their first Winmap exercise looking at the European marine market across four different groups. Concentrated efforts were also put into engaging the Latin America and Asia Pacific divisions.

But in addition to this proactive targeting, there was high demand from divisions wanting to be involved in the program. The Winmap team leader was getting calls on a regular basis asking him to schedule a time to run a launch workshop with them.

By 2009, 50% of EMEA, 60% of Asia Pacific and 100% of the Latin America divisions had completed Winmap projects. By 2011, all the global regions and groups had been covered and only one local sales company in Argentina had yet to kick off a Winmap workshop.

Several Winmap projects were started to find multi-group global opportunities. This supported the birth of several new business units. Experience to date had shown that in some cases the best way to get real collaboration between the groups was to create new business units specifically designed to serve a particular market opportunity. These new business units would not be manufacturing the products but would handle all the sales and marketing. In this way, Parker could ensure that it was acting as one company in developing the right products for these markets, integrating them into the right systems and marketing them effectively.

Other accelerated aspects

During this time, the team accelerated other aspects of the implementation:

■ The strategic marketing department was beefed up with the addition of a full-time market researcher and an economist.

The Winmap process itself was also improved:

■ A much stronger competitive intelligence process was inserted into the process and users trained how to apply it. This improved the way that competitors were identified, analyzed and key actions taken.

■ An 'Ansoff Matrix' was put on the front end to distinguish the different processes used for marketing existing and new products into existing and new markets.

■ It was also made much simpler to use.

By June 2010, over 150 divisions around the world had completed the two-day Winmap workshop (see Figure 6.4: Winmap implementation progress). Hundreds of people had been introduced to the process and the rollout was complete. In the vast majority of cases, the divisions subsequently launched their own 'live' Winmap projects with over 230 such projects listed in the Winmap pipeline.

Winmap Rollout Progress

2008	NA	EMEA	AP	LA	Total
Sales Companies	0.0%	0.0%	0.0%	0.0%	0.0%
Group 1	100.0%	100.0%	0.0%	0.0%	100.0%
Group 2	100.0%	75.0%	0.0%	0.0%	66.7%
Group 3	85.7%	25.0%	33.3%	0.0%	53.3%
Group 4	90.0%	100.0%	0.0%	0.0%	75.0%
Group 5	100.0%	100.0%	0.0%	0.0%	72.0%
Group 6	60.0%	0.0%	0.0%	0.0%	50.0%
Group 7	80.0%	80.0%	0.0%	0.0%	72.7%
Group 8	87.5%	100.0%	0.0%	0.0%	71.4%
Total	87.3%	46.2%	3.7%	0.0%	53.3%

2009	NA	EMEA	AP	LA	Total
Sales Companies	50.0%	0.0%	63.6%	100.0%	27.0%
Group 1	100.0%	100.0%	0.0%	0.0%	100.0%
Group 2	100.0%	75.0%	100.0%	100.0%	91.7%
Group 3	85.7%	66.7%	66.7%	100.0%	78.6%
Group 4	90.0%	100.0%	0.0%	100.0%	80.0%
Group 5	100.0%	100.0%	33.3%	100.0%	84.0%
Group 6	50.0%	0.0%	100.0%	0.0%	50.0%
Group 7	80.0%	80.0%	100.0%	100.0%	83.3%
Group 8	100.0%	100.0%	100.0%	100.0%	100.0%
Total	90.3%	49.0%	60.0%	100.0%	70.9%

2010	NA	EMEA	AP	LA	Total
Sales Companies	100.0%	87.0%	90.9%	66.7%	87.2%
Group 1	100.0%	100.0%	0.0%	0.0%	100.0%
Group 2	100.0%	100.0%	100.0%	100.0%	100.0%
Group 3	100.0%	100.0%	100.0%	100.0%	100.0%
Group 4	100.0%	100.0%	100.0%	100.0%	100.0%
Group 5	100.0%	100.0%	100.0%	100.0%	100.0%
Group 6	100.0%	100.0%	100.0%	0.0%	100.0%
Group 7	100.0%	100.0%	100.0%	100.0%	100.0%
Group 8	100.0%	100.0%	100.0%	100.0%	100.0%
Total	100.0%	94.3%	96.7%	88.9%	96.7%

2011	NA	EMEA	AP	LA	Total
Sales Companies	100.0%	95.7%	100.0%	66.7%	94.9%
Group 1	100.0%	100.0%	0.0%	0.0%	100.0%
Group 2	100.0%	100.0%	100.0%	100.0%	100.0%
Group 3	100.0%	100.0%	100.0%	100.0%	100.0%
Group 4	100.0%	100.0%	100.0%	100.0%	100.0%
Group 5	100.0%	100.0%	100.0%	100.0%	100.0%
Group 6	100.0%	100.0%	100.0%	0.0%	100.0%
Group 7	100.0%	100.0%	100.0%	100.0%	100.0%
Group 8	100.0%	100.0%	100.0%	100.0%	100.0%
Total	100.0%	98.1%	100.0%	88.9%	98.7%

Figure 6.4: Winmap implementation progress

In addition to the new opportunities identified, around 10% of projects were deliberately killed by the divisions, as Winmap had identified no viable commercial opportunity. This alone has saved Parker a considerable amount of time and effort.

Winmap, and the continued support of the team, has given the whole corporation a more commercial approach to evaluating opportunities. Managers are now much better at constructing solid business cases for additional resources from their leaders. The leaders are now much better at demanding solid business cases and allocating resources more effectively.

All of this activity has helped transition Winmap from being a tool brought in for special projects to being simply 'the Parker way of doing marketing.' To give a simple example of this, in one division, a new recruit to a senior business development position was told by the general manager, 'Before you do anything, call the Winmap team and get yourself onto one of their training programs. Then you will know how to do business development in Parker.'

Testing/evaluation

In this step, there was both an expansion of current testing/evaluation methods and the deployment of new methods.

The team expanded their use of the following evaluation methods:

- **Pilots**: expanding the number of pilots in the US and test the process in Europe.
- **Feedback meetings**: using Winmap workshops to involve all the divisions in a standard way; and undertaking further presentations/ meetings with stakeholders to evaluate their level of buy-in.
- **External expert input**: using external experts was a common evaluation method. For example:
  - ☐ They hired an additional external consultant who had worked on strategic marketing programs with other large corporations to provide a further fresh evaluation of the process.
  - ☐ They engaged an niche expert on competitive intelligence to evaluate this part of the process specifically.
  - ☐ They also further developed their relationship with knowledge leaders like the Institute for the Study of Business Markets (ISBM). This gave them great access to additional academics and practitioners.

The team also implemented the following additional evaluation methods:

- **Verbal feedback**: at the end of each launch workshop, the Winmap facilitator would ask each delegate what they thought of it and whether it would be useful to their business.

- **Written surveys:** at the end of each launch workshop, delegates were also asked to complete a written survey about Winmap. These were used by the Winmap team to improve the process and workshop format. One thing that came out of this was that some delegates came to the workshops with unrealistic expectations of doubling sales immediately. The team then had to refine the setup process to ensure that expectations were managed better.

- **Project Status Reports:** the IT system was further upgraded to provide better reporting of Winmap projects.

- **Benchmarking**: where useful, members of the team would go on benchmarking visits to other companies to share and evaluate each other's practices. Some of these visits, for example at 3M, proved to be very useful.

- **Improved customer feedback:** A new 'voice of the customer' research module was inserted into the Winmap process and users trained in how to do it. This would check the customer needs identified by the sales force with the actual needs diagnosed by interviewing Parker's customers.

Continuously testing to see how they could improve things was seen as just part of their regular job in getting Winmap implemented.

■ Navigation Dashboard example

Continuing our Parker OEM system example (see the end of Chapter 5):

In this phase, the prototype had already been successfully tested and the project moved into a mass production phase. Although this project was still on course (see Figure 6.5), the reader should not underestimate the challenges involved.

In the pilot phase, if problems were encountered either with people or the solution, there was time to address them. In the rollout phase, there was no time. Between three to five complex machines would need to be produced and shipped by the OEM every week. This brought a new mix of implementation risks to navigate (see Figure 6.6). There needed to be much more assistance/support from Parker planned in to monitor and assist production.

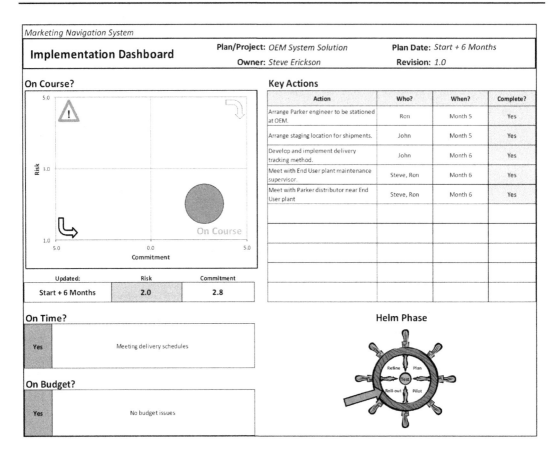

Figure 6.5: Parker OEM System Dashboard – rollout

In terms of commitment, the machines were now arriving at the end user so it was critical that the end user plant maintenance manager was satisfied with Parker's assistance/support. This became a new commitment priority (C7 in Figure 6.6).

Boundary conditions

The conditions to exit the rollout phase are:

Condition	Yes/No
Over 90% of your rollout map is green (signifying implementation is virtually complete)	
The vast majority of key stakeholders say implementation will be a success	
Your relationships are green where they matter	
Powerful opponents of implementation have been won over or their influence is under control	
The solution currently meets or exceeds expectations	
The solution is supported with a good infrastructure	
You have completed a Marketing Navigation Dashboard for this phase	
All sensors on the Dashboard say GO	

If you can answer 'Yes' to all these, then read on!

Top Risk Issues

No.	Risk	Desired State	Strategy	Test	Current Status	Rating
R5	Ongoing support by OEM management team	Consistent, pro-active sales, logistics and technical support.	Locate a Parker engineer at the OEM.	Frequent overall status checks coordinated by the Parker KAM and the Parker engineer located at the OEM.	Continual close coordination required, but basically meeting schedules.	2
R6	Delivery performance (time, accuracy)	Parker shipments consistently accurate and on time.	Deliver "kits" of components matched to the assembly line squence.	Frequent delivery status checks coordinated by the Parker KAM and the Parker engineer located at the OEM.	Continual close coordination required, but basically meeting schedules.	2
R3	Engineering assistance for OEM	Parker's engineering assistance level exceeds that of competitors.	Parker technical team coordinated by a Key Account Manager.	Frequent status checks coordinated by the Parker KAM and the Parker engineer located at the OEM.	Going well	2
R4	Technical assistance at End User plant	End User is comfortable with Parker's ability to provide technical assistance for OEM's	Excellent support by Parker distibutors located near End User plant.	Frequent status checks coordinated by the Parker field sales engineer near the End User plant.	Going well	2

Score: **2.0**

Top Commitment Issues

No.	Desired State	Stakeholders	Strategy	Test	Current Status	Rating
C1	OEM Management committed to Parker solution	General Manager	Build confidence in 1:1 meetings that partnering with Parker is the best way to ensure on time and on budget performance for OEM's equipment.	Continuing commitment voiced in 1:1 meetings.	All positive	4
C2	OEM Purchasing committed to Parker solution	Purchasing Manager	Build confidence in 1:1 meetings that a Parker systems solution will provide an overall advantage when volume pricing, system warranties, technical support and logistics are	Continuing commitment voiced in 1:1 meetings.	Positive feedback; no major problems	3
C3	OEM Engineering committed to Parker solution	Engineering Manager	Build confidence in 1:1 meetings that partnering with Parker is the best way to ensure the technical performance of the OEM's equipment.	Continuing commitment voiced in 1:1 meetings.	Positive feedback; no major problems	3
C4	Parker Sales Team unified and committed to the project	Field sales team (all Groups)	Setup field sales team meeting with all groups to emphasize that everyone has a better chance to succeed if we work closely together as "One Parker."	Continuing to work together well based on individual conversations.	Positive feedback; no major problems	4
C7	End User Plant Maintenance Manager satisfied with Parker support plan.	End User Plant Maintenance Manager	Work closely with Parker distributors to develop and effective and fast technical and logistics support system.	Positive feedback during 1:1 follow up meeting after initial piece of OEM equipment was delivered and installed.	Positive feedback; no major problems	0

Score: **2.8**

Figure 6.6: Parker OEM System Diagnostic – rollout

Conclusions

This phase will probably be the longest and involve the most resources. At the start of this phase we had a working prototype and a small user base. By the end of this phase, the actual solution would have been rolled out across the whole marketplace and a good infrastructure should have been installed to support it. So, in this phase in particular, we will have come across unanticipated threats. These must be dealt with swiftly and decisively when they appear.

To do this will require new skills. Navigating these challenges will require a firm grip on the helm. We will need to keep a close eye on all our navigational instruments in order to sense unplanned threats and keep implementation on course.

References

Doyle, P. (2008) *Value Based Marketing Marketing Strategies for Corporate Growth and Shareholder Value*, 2nd Edn, John Wiley and Sons

Kotter, J.P. (1996) *Leading Change*, Harvard Business School

McDonald, M.. (2007) *Marketing Plans, How to Prepare Them, How to Use Them*, Oxford: Butterworth-Heinemann.

McDonald, M. and Dunbar, I. (2010) *Market Segmentation. How to do it, How to profit from it*, Oxford: Goodfellow Publishers

McDonald, M. and Mouncey, P. (2011) *Marketing Accountability, A New Metrics Model to Measure Marketing Effectiveness*, Kogan Page

Sun Tzu (n.d) *The Art of War*

7 Refining implementation

I have terrible hearing trouble. I have unwittingly helped to invent and refine a type of music that makes its principal proponents deaf.

Pete Townshend, guitarist and songwriter, The Who

Summary

In this chapter we:

- Define what we mean by implementation success
- Explain what we mean by implementation refinement
- Explain how it is different from previous phases
- Explain how to target the most important levers for improved implementation
- Provide some models for understanding the dimensions of refinement
- Define the boundary conditions to complete the implementation journey.

7

■ Introduction

At this stage of the journey we can see our destination. We have covered 95% of our route and simply need to bring our plan safely home. But we should not be over-confident. A common failure of implementation is declaring victory too soon (Kotter, 1996).Too many change leaders think they have implemented their solution when, unseen by them, little has really changed. New CRM tools may lie unused, new behavior reverts back to the bad old ways, new approaches lie abandoned because new behaviors are not rewarded. Indeed, we should think of this part of the journey as being the most challenging. There are so many things to do in order to get our implementation firmly anchored into the business and often with little time. There will be new risks as we enter the harbor.

We must reach port safely and ensure no navigational errors, submerged objects, adverse currents nor wayward ships will sink us as we steer our plan into port.

Key principles

- Embed the changes
- Final 5%. But it could be the small hole that sinks your ship.
- Recognize what drives embedded, successful implementation
- Use the root cause analysis of Appendix 2
- Focus on the drivers of success
- Adopt a continuous improvement philosophy
- Implementation is a process, not a program.

Case story: refining a global phenomenon

The X-Factor has been a global implementation success story. It was piloted in the UK in 2004 and has now been rolled out (in various versions) to 40 countries worldwide from Albania to the USA. Over the last eight years its format has been continuously tested and refined to maintain its appeal. It may be at the end of its (first) implementation cycle now but it has been an incredibly profitable program. Without this continuous refinement, it would not have lasted long in the competitive world of prime-time TV.

Gareth Rees, from the marketing advice website, www.wearethefreeradicals.com explains why you should admire the X-Factor for its marketing, regardless of what you think about its music!

The X-Factor

It's not for me to judge the X-Factor. Whether you love the X-Factor, don't care about the X-Factor, or would rather glue your head to a wasps' nest than watch it, there's a crucial marketing lesson to be learned. Let me hit you with the facts:

- At its peak on Saturday 11th December 2010, the program was watched by 18.8 million people [in the UK]. That's almost 60% of the total audience watching television across all the channels.
- Advertisers, including Sainsbury's, X-Box and Chanel, spent £25million ($39m) on slots during the breaks. Marc Mendoza of the Media Planning

group told the BBC Radio 4 Today program that adverts cost over 1 pence per viewer. A record figure.

- The latest series saw 15,488,019 votes cast. Those who used their land-line or the red button on the TV were charged 35p (about 50 US cents). Those who voted by mobile phones paid even more.

- This translates to almost £6m ($9m) in revenues from votes alone. An undisclosed chunk of this money goes to Simon Cowell's company Syco, a joint venture with Sony. The rest goes to production company Fremantle Media, ITV and Harvest Media – the phone vote operator.

- This year the contestants' performances were made available as paid-for downloads on iTunes which viewers could buy after the show. Again, the money goes to Cowell and ITV. At the time of writing the profits from this are unknown.

That's a lot of money sloshing around. I haven't even included the extra profits raked in by the tabloids when they publish X Factor stories and exclusives.

When it comes down to it, this is the Freemium model in action. It follows 5 classic steps:

7

1. You offer free, compelling content that gathers a large audience. Yes, okay, television isn't strictly free, but in terms of what you get when you own a television, this show isn't on a subscription channel and on [the main UK commercial channel) ITV, so pretty much everyone and anyone can watch it.

2. You engage with your audience. In the X-Factor's case it creates an emotional human drama to get viewers involved with the personal stories behind the contestants. Scandals and leaks are fed to newspapers, posted on Twitter and other social media outlets to stir up hype and discussion.

3. You charge people who are willing to pay for their deeper involvement with the content. While anyone can watch the show for free, millions decide to pay to vote for the outcome. They choose to pay for downloads of the performances they've just watched. They choose to pay for the Christmas single.

4. You test your content on your audience. X-Factor is essentially one long experiment that allows Cowell to see which sorts of acts the public like this year. The very act of voting gives him valuable feedback on acts

which he could potentially launch as a business. Immediately after the 2010 series, he signed up all three finalists to his label.

5. Finally, you up-sell the most dedicated followers to higher priced premium services. Next year people will be able to buy the tour tickets and albums by the winning acts, all of whom are signed by Syco.

These steps can apply to almost any business.

The lesson to be learned

You may hate the music produced by the X-Factor, but it's one hell of a marketing coup. As Mat Osman of the indie band Suede moaned: 'The thing I find incredible is that Simon Cowell gets paid an enormous amount of money to promote his own acts…. It just seems to be the greatest con of all time. He should surely be paying a fortune to put these crappy acts on primetime TV.'

Instead of paying for advertising, Cowell has turned free content into a form of long, slow sales promotion for his business. He's monetized almost every element of the X-Factor. And it's successful because the audience doesn't care whether it's marketing or not. They love it. They're engaged with it. They're willing to spend money on it, even when they don't need to.

■ Why worry about refinement?

In crossing the rollout phase you have implemented almost all your solution. Why not celebrate now? The problem is that making change happen is different to making change stick. You can change lots of things about the solution, the marketing plan and the implementation environment. You may have spent a lot of time and money on communicating the new vision and training people how to use the tools that you have developed. However, if people are not willing or able to change, they won't. As we saw in Chapter 6, this problem was encountered by Larissa Liang at GLP.

The truth is that there will be a lot of lip service paid to the marketing plan. People will say they support it when in fact they don't. They are much further towards the left of the commitment continuum. There are many reasons for this. They may simply be willing to try it out or think that it would be dangerous to express a lack of support. Or they may underestimate the amount of work involved in making the change, they may overestimate their own abilities, or they may misunderstand the change, etc.

The important thing is not to confuse visible change with invisible inertia. Change management thinking often uses the idea of an iceberg. We may see what people are doing and hear what they are saying but there are emotions and expectations happening beneath the waterline that we cannot see. Our new tools and those nodding heads in meetings may lead us to think we are home and dry, when in fact we are heading for some serious icebergs.

In this phase we need to get our marketing programs firmly embedded into the DNA of the business. We need to ensure that it will be almost impossible to disentangle them. Finally, we need to continuously improve them so that they do not become out-of-date and dangerous, like a rusting old oil tanker.

How is this phase different?

We will be looking at many of the areas already explored in previous phases. However, there are four distinct differences here:

1 We will be making the final adjustments to implementation based on our experience of deployment in previous phases. We should be confident that our solution works and so can concentrate on improving it, rather than deploying it.

2 We can work on difficult issues that we either had no time for, or which would have blocked the change had we tackled them earlier. These might include reward mechanisms, changes to the organization structure, fixing IT, etc.

3 The mindset has changed from massive deployment to targeted surgical cures. This means we also move from revolutionary change to more evolutionary change: from upheaval to continuous upgrades.

4 These upgrades may be incremental but could continue for a long time. They are like software updates that continue long after the original software has been launched.

■ How to refine implementation

In order to refine our implementation, we need to understand the levers for improvement. In particular, it is useful to separate out those levers that produce superficial improvements from those that provide deep-rooted change. These are shown in Figure 7.1 (which the alert reader will notice is a positive re-statement of Figure 4.1).

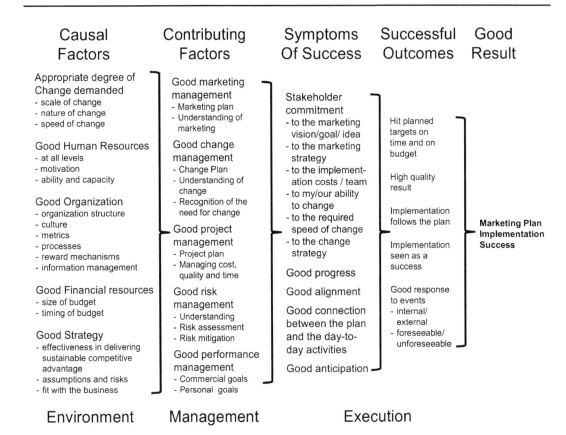

Figure 7.1: The levers for implementation success

On the right-hand side are the common successful outcomes of good implementation. These define the desired state of success. If we are to achieve these we should see the listed symptoms of success. If our business is displaying these symptoms, then successful outcomes should follow. If some symptoms are lacking, like inadequate stakeholder commitment to the marketing strategy, we would be concerned about whether we will achieve a successful outcome. We might address this issue by asking the CEO to tell the stakeholders to get on with implementing the plan.

However, will they agree to it in the boardroom but exercise their 'pocket veto' outside the boardroom to block change? What about next year? Will they need to be hit with the CEO's stick again? What happens if the CEO departs? Here, commitment is fleeting and superficial. We have addressed the symptom of a lack of commitment rather than its underlying causes.

To get to these, we need to ask the question, 'Why are the all the stakeholders not committed?' In doing so, we may find a variety of contributing factors: a poorly written marketing plan, a poor understanding of marketing itself, little recognition of why we need to change, disapproval of the speed of change or the investment required, etc. Once we know these, we can deal with them. We can clarify the marketing plan, adjust the marketing strategy within it, explain how good marketing is vital for the future of the business, change the speed and cost of implementation, etc. Refinements here will have more success than telling the CEO to get more commitment from the C-Suite!

However, we can go even deeper than this to identify the causal factors. We need to ensure the change being demanded is appropriate for the business, that the human resources required to implement the change are motivated and able to do it, that the organizational environment is fertile for implementation, that the financial resources are sufficient and that the strategy is good in the first place.

The more we can refine our understanding of the causal factors, the better we can lay solid foundations for repeated good implementation results.

What does successful implementation look like?

We can now make an important statement about what successful implementation looks like. We have said that implementation can be separated into:

- **Outcomes**: These are the desired outputs from implementation or the implementation desired state.
- Symptoms: These are positive signals that should precede good **outcomes**. They are signs that your implementation is on course and under control.
- **Contributing factors**: These are tactical levers of success and represent good management of implementation programs.
- **Causal factors**: These are strategic levers of success that will transform the environment in which programs are implemented.

We can summarize by saying:

Successful implementation of a marketing plan results from its being perceived by key stakeholders to have delivered its desired outcomes. These outcomes are namely: hitting its planned targets on time and on budget, delivering a high quality result, delivering the marketing plan and responding well to events.

This is more likely to be achieved with strong implementation management and a healthy implementation environment.

Refinement thinking

Although we are thinking about this as the final step in our journey, we should also see refinement as something that is good for the business as a whole. There are many initiatives in business that pick up on this idea under the term 'continuous improvement.' They include initiatives like kaizen (made famous by the Japanese automakers Toyota and Nissan) and Six Sigma (made famous by Motorola, Honeywell and GE).

In these businesses, refinement has not just become something tagged on at the end of a production line. It pervades the culture of the whole company. The more you can do to make refinement (however described) a key part of your culture, the easier you will find it to perform this phase.

Refining the contributing factors

The Contributing Factors for implementation success from Figure 7.1 are repeated in Table 7.1. Each of these areas is a significant management field and there are plenty of resources available to improve your skills and knowledge here. Against each factor we have listed a source of independent support. This is not a definitive list and sources vary by country and by industry. Consequently, you should see these as a starting point; there may be other and more relevant sources closer to you.

Table 7.1: Refining the contributing factors for implementation success

Contributing factor	Source of support
Good marketing management Marketing plan Understanding of marketing	Chartered Institute of Marketing (www.cim.co.uk) Institute for the Study of Business Markets (www.isbm.org) The MAPI Marketing Council (www.mapi.net/councils/marketing-council)
Good change management Change plan Understanding of change Recognition of the need for change	Change Management Institute (www.change-management-institute.com)
Good project management Project plan Management of project cost, quality and time	Project Management Institute (www.pmi.org.uk)
Good risk management Understanding of risk Risk assessment Risk mitigation	The Institute of Risk Management (www.theirm.org)
Good performance management Fit with commercial goals including their key performance Indicators Fit with personal goals of stakeholders	The Performance Management Association (www.performanceportal.org)

If you are weak in any particular area, we would recommend you set improvement in that field as a personal development goal. If appropriate you may wish to share your knowledge with other stakeholders to help ensure a common minimum professional standard.

We will go beyond this though and look in more detail at the deeper causal factors.

Refining the causal factors

As Figure 7.1 showed, there are five different causal factors: The degree of change demanded, the human resources, the organization, the financial resources and the strategy in the marketing plan (CHOFS). Together these define the implementation environment. If they are all good then there are healthy conditions for implementing the plan.

We will look at each of these below.

The degree of change demanded

At Austro, a large amount of change had to happen in a short period of time. This was a high risk implementation strategy but was appropriate given the greater risks of not changing fast enough. Once this step change had been completed, implementation could then settle back into a less risky phase of refined change specified by their new three-year plan.

At IEB, change was seen to have a political dimension and could only travel at the speed the CEO thought appropriate.

Whether your marketing plan calls for a large amount of change across the business or is focused on significant changes in specific areas, you should now have reached the point where the change demanded can be better matched to the ability and capacity of your business to change.

This does not mean that you should let the business ability to change dictate the refinement phase. Indeed, many businesses use stretch targets to ensure their employees do not cruise into complacency (Maister, 1997). Instead, you should actively look for opportunities to adjust the scale, nature or speed of change to ensure your program maintains momentum long into the future. These opportunities can be discovered in quite different areas.

At Lafarge, after the rebranding exercise was rolled out, the team turned its attention to refining the reward mechanism of traders and customers to help ensure the change would endure (see also 'Reward mechanisms' below).

At MEDIC, the team turned its attention to refining how the parent company global policies operated in India. This was a competitive weakness and adjustments here would help win future contracts more easily.

Change needs to be reassessed, realigned and refocused before we can say we are done.

The human resources

In terms of the quality of human resources, both the skill and the will of people can be audited and improved in this phase (Landsberg, 2003, p. 55).

There are many different ways that this can be achieved:

- The final step in the Globalserve International Client Management program was to refine the solution and future-proof the program. Part of this included developing a key account director competency model which was used to 'assess training needs and close skill, knowledge and behavior gaps.'

- Near the end of a significant key account management program at a European real estate business, the leadership team wanted to gauge its success in improving both the motivation for client management excellence and the skills of their client managers. They therefore contracted an independent third party to undertake a confidential survey to research the issue. They found that the project had transformed people's understanding of professional client management and their enthusiasm for it. It also found that the project had helped everyone gauge the skills/competency gaps between where they were and where they needed to be (Bradford, 2010). In this case, the project had improved both the skill and the will of the client manager stakeholders. Moreover, the research had pinpointed specific gaps in skills that could be targeted for additional training and coaching.

In terms of the quantity of human resources, further analysis (e.g., workforce scheduling) can be performed to see if we have the right number of staff available to service anticipated changes in demand. At Parker, Winmap has highlighted the need to improve the number of strategic marketing resources at group level. In addition, a new Winmap certified training program was developed to increase both the quantity and quality of Winmap champions that could be deployed right across the corporation.

Understanding the talent of today and developing the talent of tomorrow is a key refinement activity (Kotter, 1996).

The organization

It is worth remembering that in our survey, organization came up as the most important challenge to implementation success. This is not just about the reporting structure. Structure is just one important component in the overall organizational design or blueprint.

There are many different models for organization design but for our purposes we will consider six key components (see also Peters and Waterman, 1982). If these are operating to support implementation then we can say the organization is implementation-friendly. However, the chances are that most of these areas can be improved in your organization. Refining them should improve your chances of implementation success. The six components of an implementation-friendly organization are shown in Figure 7.2.

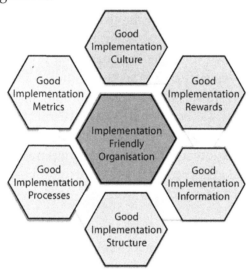

Figure 7.2: The implementation-friendly organization

CRISP-metrics

These can be remembered by the mnemonic: 'Organizations are made from CRISP-metrics'

■ Culture

Here we wish to establish a culture of good implementation. In broad terms this means the norms, standards and behaviors of the organization demonstrate the importance of good implementation. At a recent conference in Dallas Carlos Cardoso, the CEO of Kennametal, explained that he was 'paranoid about implementation. I know I am obsessive about this. I cannot rest until I know that all our great plans are being pursued aggressively and thoroughly.' At Jones Lang LaSalle, their client relationship management program has been refined over the years to the point where it is now simply 'the way we manage our clients' (Bradford *et al.*, 2001). They have also integrated it with other programs to further reinforce behaviors. 'We have introduced Client Relationship Management and a system for individual performance and career management as part of a total performance management program. Total performance management endorses three performance standards which represent non-negotiable minimum standards of behavior – we will serve our clients, support our people and aspire to leadership' (Jones Lang LaSalle, 2012).

■ Reward mechanisms

Incentivizing people to adopt the change does not just mean paying higher salaries. For Lafarge, towards the end of their rebranding program, they looked at a bonus mechanism for traders and customers to buy their new branded products. They created an innovative scheme where scratch cards were handed out based on the volume of product sold. The scheme was backed up with significant prizes and a strong training program. Reward can also be non-monetary. Public recognition by senior executives of people who have put in significant effort to support implementation can be a great motivator. What is important here is to link recognition and reward to people's personal development plans. This is done at Parker for all their key programs through a strategy deployment matrix.

■ Information management

At the end of the implementation journey, the information flows can be tightened up. Better reporting about the solution can be set up. Better communications (e.g., regular updates via online portals) about the progress of the change can be introduced. This is more than just data. It is about improving the way to get the right insights to the right people in the right way at the right time. 'Insights' are important because they are far removed from just 'data.' Data (e.g., our sales, competitors' sales, market size) should be turned into information (e.g., market shares for all competitors), which should be turned into intelligence (e.g., our sales from market growth vs. our sales from winning market share), which should be turned into insight (how much of our sales growth has come from just growing with the market vs. real improved competitiveness). To do this requires good IT but marketers should define the desired state of what insights they want to have (and for whom, when) and then work back to what the IT needs to provide. If required, marketing should have a strong role in defining the IT specifications. For European eCards it was about refining the information in order to get as close as possible to a desired state of real-time granular segments with personalized automated online responses.

■ Structure

The organization's structure can be a significant lever for success or failure. Doing strategic marketing in a decentralized company like CTech is always going to be difficult. Essentially, it does not provide a healthy environment for implementation. Large complex programs (like the development of a new business unit) will already have made significant changes to the organization structure in previous phases. If you are lucky to have a market-driven CEO then one of your programs in the marketing plan might be to sort the structure out! In this phase we are looking to refine the structure so we can embed our implementation better. This can include changes to the reporting structure, the roles, the grades, the career path, the required competencies and the teaming requirements. At Kennametal, they have 'worked hard over the past five years at getting our organization structured right. We neither wanted to be a loosely federated set of business units with no corporate marketing support nor a highly centralized corporation that may become a hindrance to local business units getting close to the customer. We have worked together to create a hybrid model in which the corporate marketing function supports the business units where necessary.' At Parker, each year sees an improved strategic marketing department. The department was recently simplified into three basic legs: market intelligence, business intelligence and economic intelligence, each with their associated staffing. Furthermore, there is now a major transition underway to change their role from marketers with tools to a consulting team that provides valuable insights, forecasts and strategic advice to Parker business units.

■ Processes

Whatever your implementation program, it is likely to cover many different processes within the business. It might even disrupt or change those processes. So there is usually plenty of scope to improve the processes that your implemented solution depends on. At Globalserve, in their final future-proofing phase, they added in a new executive sponsorship process, integrated the various business planning processes more closely together and included the client more in the planning process. At IEB, they introduced a regular global KAM forum as part of the communication process.

7

■ Metrics

Peter Drucker (1954) said, 'what gets measured gets done.' Whatever the metrics you implement, people will find a way to play the system so that the metrics improve even if the reality is different. The last thing you want is metrics that say implementation is successful when the reality is quite different. Consequently, there is scope for refinement here. Firstly, there is the speed at which the metric is updated. Both European eCards and Lafarge are looking to establish real-time metrics so they can spot changes quickly. Secondly, there is the quality of the metric itself. Austro worked hard to ensure the individual metrics in their scorecard were aligned to overall program goals. The scorecard is not a static object though. They will keep refining it to improve its relevance, accuracy, capability and insights.

The financial resources

In Chapter 6 we explained the importance of getting the right amount of funds delivered at the right time to deliver both the solution and its supporting infrastructure. Refinements can be made in any of these areas. For example, now that the implementation is nearly complete, there should be a better understanding of the return on the investment of funds already committed. This track record can be used to justify seeking additional funds for more discretionary investments (like better IT). Clear understanding of the program costs, benefits and risks – in the past, present and future – can help the business target investments in the right areas to secure the implementation and boost its benefits.

The strategy

Refinements can be made to either the marketing strategy or its implementation strategy. There is plenty of scope to refine the strategy by adjusting its direction, focus, timing and value proposition. The tactical elements of the marketing mix (e.g., product, price, place, promotion) can be adjusted to help with this exercise. This is an exercise that will be familiar to most marketers but see Chapter 8 for more insight into how technology is making a difference here. It is worth revisiting the assumed risks at this point. Often this is something done in a few minutes at the end of a marketing plan. However, wrong assumptions have been the downfall of many a good company (Olson et al., 2008). At Lafarge, they looked at the risks and counter-measures before introducing their 'scratch card' refinement.

Adjustments can also be made to the implementation strategy. Your experience in rolling out the implementation may have given you valuable experience on how to address the final few customers in your marketplace. These could be the hardest to reach or the most difficult to convert. At Globalserve, their future-proofing work included contracting with a third party to undertake a deep client relationship survey of how well the program had been implemented. The findings from the survey were presented back to Globalserve and were used to evaluate what was going well, what could be done better and to set the vision, goals and action of the program for the next three years.

■ Confirming implementation is complete

When is implementation complete? There are two parts to this. As we saw at the start of this chapter, the program is complete when it is perceived by key stakeholders to have delivered its desired outcomes.

However, the process of embedding implementation and extracting ever higher benefits from the solution should continue long after the program itself has finished.

The boundary conditions to exit this final phase are shown at the end of this chapter.

■ Refining Winmap

From July 2010 onwards, the focus was firmly on integrating Winmap further into the DNA of the corporation.

In terms of human resources, both the quality and quantity of strategic marketing staff were improved.

The vast majority of people doing a Winmap project are smart people. But professional business development is simply very different to what they have been doing in the past. So there was a significant effort to increase the quality of the Parker staff. Initially, 11 Winmap champions had been trained across each of the eight groups to provide local support to the divisional project teams. Later, a broader and more formalized strategic marketing coaching program was established with its own certification process – 40 volunteers from around the world went through this program which produced a hard core of high standard strategic marketing professionals. This also reinforced the network of strategic marketers and further embedded the Winmap philosophy in key points within the organization.

There is also now a greater quantity of business development staff across the corporation. Winmap has underlined the importance of this skill to the corporation and has highlighted where there are gaps. These gaps are now being filled, especially at group level, and these dedicated resources will help the divisions to develop and implement local MAPs more effectively.

The central strategic marketing team, the champions and the coaches provided support to the divisions in choosing and pursuing their Winmap projects. This could vary from helping local divisions to make good business cases for additional resources to helping them develop their own sales and marketing organizations. Winmap therefore became a stronger composite brand with a powerful network of high-strength fibers.

As the team's abilities grew, they also were able to move some services in-house. One of these was the collection and analysis of economic data from around the world. The team was now better than any known external agency in sourcing and converting key indicators into specific forecasts for Parker's own markets.

Parker has also drilled down to identify the fundamental needs of mankind over the next few decades. Eight key areas have been identified and internal symposiums will be held on each of these over the next two years. All Parker groups will be invited and it is hoped this will help the whole corporation coalesce around these eight fundamental challenges in the future.

The organization has also changed. By the summer of 2010, both the EVPs who had championed Winmap had retired. However, the momentum and commitment was such that there was barely a missed heartbeat in the implementation effort. Indeed, the new leader was also the champion of the Winovation process so knew a thing or two about getting a good process installed across the corporation!

The culture of Parker has also changed. Ten years ago, it was primarily an operations-driven culture with the primary focus being on how to manufacture products more efficiently and more profitably. The Win Strategy was a major step forward in balancing lean operations with good customer service, financial performance and profitable growth (see Chapter 4 for more details). Now, Parker has a much more commercial culture with a higher appreciation for the role of marketing. This has not been achieved by simply putting operations staff through Winmap workshops. The best Winmap coaches use real success stories that they personally have witnessed personally across the Parker corporation. They use these to help staff think about solving common commercial problems in new ways. They would often kick off a workshop or training session by saying, 'Let me tell you a story' and would then tell a real story about how a division had been tasked with growing their business but could see no opportunities for growth. The coach would then ask the attendees how they would solve the problem, before explaining what actually happened as a result of using Winmap.

In some cases, the coach would invite a successful division to share its experience of implementation with other divisions, or they would organize a trip to the successful division. If appropriate, the coach would organize a trip to a Parker customer to see the successful product/service solution in action. This makes marketing a much more credible activity and the use of 'credible witnesses' has become a key feature of their change management.

As the successes of the strategic marketing program grew, so did the financial resources channeled to the Winmap projects.

All the while, there was – and still is – a compelling vision and strategy for Winmap. Without such a strategy, Winmap would not have made as much progress. Some elements of this strategy are:

- *Better branding:* Position strategic marketing as the parent brand and Winmap as the sub-brand.

- *Better segmentation:* Undertake a worldwide segmentation exercise so that the whole corporation uses standard terms and definitions of its markets, speaks one market language and is able to capture intelligence in a consistent way. For example, 'oil and gas' is the segment, not 'oil' or 'petroleum'.

- *Gain executive commitment:* Use the Winmap Dashboards to provide executive visibility of the performance of each division. These Dashboards will become part of the standard quarterly reports presented by the group presidents to the Parker Management Committee quarterly.

- *Strengthen peer support:* Develop an open source network that will create internal communities of practice (CoP) around the key areas of the marketing process, market research, economic intelligence, business intelligence, customer intelligence and competitor intelligence. Each of these CoPs will each become the global Parker brain for its chosen area.

■ *Improved Processes:* Continue to define the Parker Business Development Process by integrating marketing, sales, engineering and operations. Also, continue to define the right multi-functional teams that need to be involved in the process at each stage.

■ *Leverage IT:*

☐ Create a set of standards so that marketing data will be automatically captured with the same level of clarity as financial data. This will enable a clear global view of past, current and future market share positions in any chosen division, geography, technology or market.

☐ Use the Marketing Research Center to help disseminate information horizontally and vertically around the organization. Information entered into the MRC is tagged with key words that are then searchable by others. This will also help the strategic marketing department to find marketing talent around the corporation, regardless of their title, function and educational background.

Overall, in this phase, there has been much reflection on what has been successful and why – and a consequent refinement to the Winmap solution.

The reflection and refinement are already being used to think ahead and plan Winmap 3.0. This will follow a similar test and rollout philosophy as previous versions. The difference is that with every implementation, the steps get better defined, the timescales get shorter and the success rate gets higher.

■ Testing/evaluation

Much of the refinement work has involved developing better metrics in which to evaluate the performance of Winmap.

This can be divided into two areas:

First, work is underway to provide more visibility of the Winmap opportunity pipeline. Currently, this is focused on creating a comprehensive Winmap Dashboard with a simple graphical interface. When complete, this will show the implementation status of all Winmap projects by market, division/group, product, technology, geography and fundamental human need. Such intelligence will help:

■ People to find and see the progress of other Winmap project teams working across the organization

- People to slice and dice the value of opportunities in the pipeline in a number of different ways and answer three fundamental questions for Parker itself, for any group or any division: Are we growing? Where are we growing? How are we growing?

- Winmap teams better challenge divisions by asking: 'How are you going to grow when you have no growth opportunities in the pipeline and no projects being worked on?'

Second, work is underway to display the sales pipeline of Winmap projects which will show the commercial success of Winmap projects. The information will be tagged to the relevant Winmap project so that the team can track the growth of sales years after it has completed its first market action plan.

The Winmap Dashboard will help the whole corporation evaluate the success of Winmap and allocate its resources in a more effective manner.

■ Navigation Dashboard example

Concluding our Parker OEM system example from Chapter 6:

All the machinery had been successfully delivered and installed at the end of the rollout phase. In this phase, the focus changed to a more reflective mindset. The Parker team was interested in what went well, what could be done better, and how they could get ready for the next big order (either from this account or another).

It is interesting to note that although this project was complete in terms of getting the machinery successfully in place at the OEM's facility, there were now new challenges to overcome. This moved the project more towards being at risk from going off course (see Figure 7.3).

These new challenges involved both new commercial risks and new commitment risks. On the commercial side, Parker's focus needed to shift from short-term production help to on-going assistance/support for the OEM and end user. There was a risk that Parker's relationship with both parties would degrade after the project was completed. If there was a problem with any machine at the end user, Parker still needed to respond quickly and effectively. Otherwise it could sour Parker's relationship with the end user and the OEM. Recognizing the dangers, they made sure that strategies and tests were in place to counter them (see R7 and R8 in Figure 7.4).

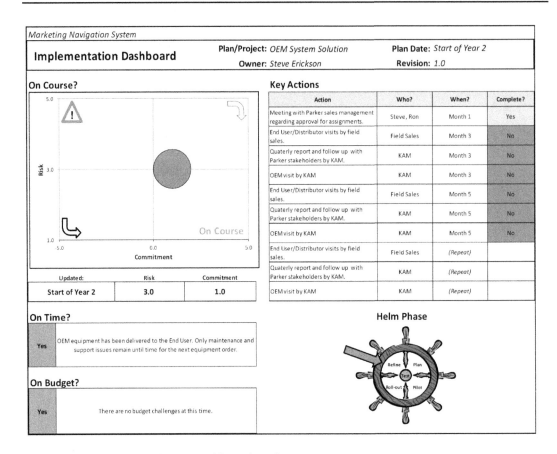

Figure 7.3: Parker OEM System Dashboard – refine

The challenge had now evolved from being a project management issue to being a relationship management issue. Consequently, a key account manager (KAM) was given the task of developing the relationship for mutual long-term gain. In fact, the KAM had worked closely on the project over the previous phases so was well experienced in the relationships between the parties. However, this did present new commitment risks. There are always risks in introducing a new point of coordination into a relationship and these are reflected in the scores (see Figure 7.4).

In fact, with good support, the KAM did take over the relationships seamlessly.

Top Risk Issues

No.	Risk	Desired State	Strategy	Test	Current Status	Rating
R7	Allowing the commercial and technical support for OEM degrade after the initial project would allow a foothold for the competition.	Ongoing superior commercial and technical support for OEM.	Continue Parker KAM assignment to coordinate and monitor Parker's commercial and technical support approach. KAM to personally visit key OEM stakeholers on a bi-monthly basis.	Agreement by Parker sales management to the KAM assignment.	Pending	3
R8	Allowing the commercial and technical support for End User to degrade after the initial project would hinder Parker's ability to win the next order.	Ongoing superior commercial and technical support for End User plant.	Work with Parker field sales to coordinate and monitor Parker's support for the End User plant (divisions, distributors). Field sales to set up regular visits to End User plant and distributors.	Agreement by Parker sales management to this field sales assignment.	Pending	3

	Score	3.0

Top Commitment Issues

No.	Desired State	Stakeholders	Strategy	Test	Current Status	Rating
C1	OEM Management committed to Parker solution	General Manager	Ongoing follow up by KAM	Continuing commitment voiced in 1:1 meetings.	Just started; no feedback yet	2
C2	OEM Purchasing committed to Parker solution	Purchasing Manager	Ongoing follow up by KAM	Continuing commitment voiced in 1:1 meetings.	Just started; no feedback yet	1
C3	OEM Engineering committed to Parker solution	Engineering Manager	Ongoing follow up by KAM	Continuing commitment voiced in 1:1 meetings.	Just started; no feedback yet	1
C4	Parker Sales Team unified and committed to the project	Field sales team (all Groups)	Ongoing follow up by KAM	Continuing commitment voiced in 1:1 meetings.	Just started; no feedback yet	1
C5	End User Plant Maintenance Manager satisfied with Parker support plan.	End User Plant Maintenance Manager	Ongoing follow up by field sales.	Continuing commitment voiced in 1:1 meetings.	Just started; no feedback yet	0

	Score	1.0

Figure 7.4: Parker OEM System Diagnostic – refine

7

Implementation outcome and result

The outcomes of this multi-million dollar project were significant:

- During the two years of its implementation, it earned Parker a total of *six times* (600%) more revenue from the OEM than the previous five years combined.

- Even after implementation was complete, the on-going support meant that Parker's annual revenues were higher. For the five years after implementation, average annual revenues were *five times* (500%) higher than they were for the five years before implementation.

- The OEM not only successfully replaced its main competitor as the End User's primary supplier of this type of machinery, it subsequently became the number one supplier of this type of equipment to the whole North America sector.

- The End User had higher quality products delivered on time (a rare occurrence in the industry and vital for its own production plans).

The result of this was that this project was seen as a tremendously successful implementation by the stakeholders of Parker, the OEM and the End User. Even to this day, the General Manager of the OEM credits Parker's approach to propelling them to the lead position in their market.

Boundary conditions

The boundary conditions to exit this final phase are:

Condition	Yes/No
99%+ of your rollout map is green (signifying implementation is complete)	
The vast majority of key stakeholders say implementation was successful	
Your relationships are green where they matter	
The solution met or exceeded expectations*	
The solution has been embedded with a good infrastructure	
The cost of implementation is within the budget set (or over-spends accepted)	
Implementation has been achieved on time (or delays accepted)	
You know how you can improve implementation in the future (including engaging stakeholders better and reducing commercial risks)	
You have completed a Marketing Navigation Dashboard for this phase	
All sensors on the Dashboard say GO	

* If stakeholders have previously accepted and supported lower expectations, higher budgets or delayed timings then you can still answer 'Yes' to these conditions.

If you can answer 'Yes' to all these, then you can now do it all again with another program. But next time (to adapt the Olympian motto) sail swifter, straighter, stronger!

Conclusions

The refinement phase is about looking for targeted improvement areas that will complete the implementation journey and lock-in the solution for the long-term. Its speed, scale and thinking are quite different from previous phases.

Good work here will make sure your change sticks. However, although this phase does not contain an ambitious plan of work, it should not be underestimated. It is like navigating your ship upriver to its final port. Now is not the time to retire to your cabin or delegate to a junior crew member. There will be difficult submergedThere will be difficult currents heading out to sea, other new ships to avoid, treacherous tides and submerged sandbanks that could easily stop you. These final few miles will require new skills and a renewed focus.

When you have navigated these final challenges, then you can relax, reflect on the journey and start planning your next great implementation voyage!

References

Bradford, E. and Viner, Paul(2010) 'Getting started with strategic account management, winning hearts and minds at Cushman and Wakefield Investors', *Velocity*, Q1, 33–38

Bradford, E., Bamford, N. and Higgins, M. (2001) 'Managing property clients properly, the journey to client excellence of Jones Lang LaSalle', *Journal of Selling and Major Account Management*, **3** (3).

Cardoso, Carlos (2012) Speech at Marketing Educators Conference, Dallas, Texas, March 2012.

Drucker, P. (1954) *The Practice of Management*, New York: Harper and Row

Jones Lang LaSalle (2012) www.joneslanglasalle.com, accessed July 2012.

Kotter, J.P. (1996) *Leading Change*, Harvard Business School

Landsberg, M. (2003) *The Tao of Coaching*, 2nd edn, Profie Books

Maister, D.H. (1997) *True Professionalism*, The Free Press

Olson, M.S., van Bever, D. and Very, S. (2008) 'When growth stalls', *Harvard Business Review*, March , 86(3) 50–61.

Peters, T., and Waterman, R.H. Jr. (1982), *In Search of Excellence*, New York: Harper & Row.

7

8 The technology of testing

This, then, is the test we must set for ourselves; not to march alone but to march in such a way that others will wish to join us.

Hubert H Humphrey

Summary

In this chapter we:

- Look more deeply at testing methods
- Show how technology is revolutionizing implementation
- Discuss how simulations are changing the implementation game.

■ Introduction

We have discussed testing throughout this book but in this chapter we will look more deeply at the impact of new technology on implementation. This offers a significant opportunity for marketers to create more robust strategies and implement them better than ever before.

Key principles

- Scientific, entrepreneurial approach
- Dynamic implementation testing
- Testing and measuring.

Case study: using a strategy simulator in a small enterprise

War games are no longer expensive exercises enjoyed by wealthy companies. Simulations have become easier to build and can now even be accessed by small companies with limited budgets.

Some of the best results come from engaging the whole leadership team in a simulation. Strategy formulation is not something that should be guarded selfishly by the CMO but something with which all senior executives should be involved. Indeed, because the entire leadership team of a small business can be involved in a simulation, they often see greater benefits than larger corporations.

A small logistics company had been writing good marketing plans every year but wanted to get better at anticipating competitors' reactions to their implementation of the plan. With a little help from a simulation developer they built their very own simulation.

A day was scheduled for the whole cross-functional leadership team to play with the simulator and test out the strategy that they had developed in their latest draft marketing plan. On the day, the team was divided up so that two executives (including the CEO) played their own business, two played one key competitor and another two played another key competitor. In the simulation, the CEO implemented the planned strategy in the simulation but was surprised at how the two competitors reacted. This resulted in revisions to the marketing plan in both the nature of the strategy and its timed implementation.

The other executives discovered much about their competitors. They not only picked up a lot of useful competitive intelligence but also gained insights into why a competitor behaved in a certain way. This helped not just to understand their past behavior better, but to predict their behavior and strategic responses in the future.

8

■ The importance of testing

Testing is not the most exciting subject. It may not get the pulse racing in the C-Suite and, let's be honest, running loads of experiments may not be why you chose the marketing profession. However, testing is a powerful device for ensuring good marketing plans are both created and implemented successfully.

Testing is a continuous exercise that needs to be done throughout the planning and implementation phases. Without testing, you will be relying on the opinions of others to tell you if your plan is on course or not. These others are probably salespeople, marketers and accountants. But for gauging accurate fixes of our position, the salespeople cannot be trusted (see Box 8.1), the marketers cannot do measurements and the accountants can only tell you where you were last month! Relying on the opinions of others is dead reckoning marketing. You will not really know your current position, your heading or the dangers that lie ahead.

Box 8.1 Don't trust the sales force!

Research by the Marketing Leadership Council in 2005 looked at how one of its members (a global communications company) had discovered it could not trust the sales force to say whether its strategy was working. The company found this out when it decided to undertake a major review of their win:loss ratio from bidding for contracts. If the bid was won, the sales force would typically say it was their hard work and relationship building that nailed the deal. If it was lost, the sales force would typically say it was lost on price. This notion that business was won on relationships but was lost on price was the accepted truth for many years.

However, this was simply the opinion of the sales force and there was no hard evidence to back it up. So to test it, the company first conducted an extensive root-cause analysis to identify all the possible causes of bid failure. Next, they turned these into testable hypotheses. They then commissioned two separate independent research companies to test the hypotheses by conducting monthly interviews with 70 customers and prospects who were going through a live bid process.

They discovered that the drivers of success were more complicated than had been thought. Some bids were lost because of systematic weaknesses in the company which a lone salesman could never have resolved. They therefore established a new senior bid review board who could address these issues and drive up their chance of success on all bids.

They also established a new scorecard that showed on a monthly basis if bids were on course or not. In three years, this new scientific sense-and-respond mechanism had resolved several major issues and contributed to additional sales of $780m.

Source: Marketing Leadership Council, 2005

■ The new technologies

Technology offers a huge opportunity for marketers to test both strategy and implementation as never before. Nor is it necessarily expensive and time-consuming. Extraordinarily powerful technology can be accessed for very little investment and is certainly affordable for even micro businesses.

Here are just some of them (in no particular order): Google Adwords, display advertising, Facebook, email marketing, online surveys, LinkedIn, video marketing, website analytics, apps, mobile marketing, high end enterprise analytics, simulations.

There are four main benefits to using these technologies:

1 **Improved quality of the marketing plan**. In particular, ensuring that the strategy and tactics within the plan have been tested and are right.

2 **Improved threat assessment**. Continuous sensing of the internal and external environment will highlight significant threats earlier and clearer.

3 **Improved opportunism**. Good sensing will quickly spot changes in customer needs, competitor actions and market forces that could allow you to be first to see an opportunity and first to exploit it.

4 **Improved responses**. You do not necessarily need to get your response right first time. Continuous testing will allow you to adjust your response and to move more quickly than your competitors.

8

■ Testing methods

Testing is not a new science and some testing methods provide a proven foundation for implementation success. Other methods leverage technology to professionalize implementation further. One method sits in the advanced level.

This is not an exhaustive list of methods and new methods are evolving continuously.

Basic testing

These provide basic governance for implementation and should be routinely adopted. We have split these into project management and change management tests. Both should be part of your everyday implementation evaluation.

Basic project (program) management tests

- **Formal implementation reviews:** Frequent (e.g., weekly) reviews with the program team leader, regular (e.g., monthly) reviews with the key program sponsor, periodic (e.g., quarterly) reviews with the full steering group.

- **Threat assessment:** Review of hazards facing the program and use of a hazard reporting mechanism to the steering group.

- **Project plan stress tests:** Input of different hazard scenarios to the project plan (or Gantt chart) to sense the impact on timescales and resources.

Basic change management tests

- *Nemawashi*: the Japanese method of many 1:1 conversations with stakeholders to sense their individual responses before planning and executing the change. By gaining their support one at a time, the plan should be rubber-stamped quickly and implementation will run more smoothly.

- **Asking 'How is it going?'** This single open question can be asked frequently to gauge progress and acceptance of implementation. This is the implementation version of the important 'How am I doing question' and should be asked 'clearly, confidently, consistently, creatively and sincerely' (Canfield, 2012).

- **Spontaneous feedback:** This is usually done during or at the end of meetings, presentations, training and workshops. It can be done verbally, via audience response tools or by simple feedback sheets handed in. The questions are variations of 'Do you agree with the vision? Do you understand how we need to change? Do you see where you fit in? Do you support the change? Is this change important to you?'

- **Market research:** The traditional methods are either deep qualitative tests (using focus groups, in-depth surveys and face-to-face interviews) or broad quantitative tests (using carefully chosen samples, short questionnaires and phone interviews). The questions could be testing everything including the customer needs, the target audience, the solution, the value proposition, the strategy, the marketing mix tactics, the timing, the likely payoff and the investment required.

Professional testing

True professional marketers will be taking testing to an even higher level. A strong advocate of testing and measuring every aspect of marketing implementation is one of Europe's most popular entrepreneurial advisors, Chris Cardell. Chris goes as far as saying that marketing is testing (see Box 8.2).

Box 8.2 Marketing means testing

'If you're familiar with marketing you'll know that testing is a vital part of all effective marketing.

But the most successful marketers understand that marketing doesn't just involve testing – marketing is testing.

If you're running a new business or you're new to the world of marketing, the concept of 'testing' might not sound particularly exciting. But for the entrepreneur who is serious about growing their business, grasping its power can be a real turning point in the life of the business.

Stop trying to choose the 'right' marketing solution

Anyone who's come from the corporate world will know the hours wasted trying to make a decision on the 'right' marketing approach.

A commitment to testing ends this problem once and for all. The smart marketer knows that the only way to be certain that a specific marketing approach will work, is to test it. As long as you test small (meaning you never spend more than you're willing to lose) you have the freedom to go out to the market and test an array of marketing initiatives: pay per click, print advertising, telephone marketing, email marketing, Facebook advertising, etc. – and we let the market (your customers) decide which is going to work.

When we've found marketing approaches that our prospective customers respond to, we then test different elements within each method (different headlines on an ad, for example) to increase our response.

At the very least, you should be testing one new marketing approach every month. If you do that, this time next year you'll have the results of twelve new marketing methods and chances are, several of those will be winners that you can roll out on a larger scale.

The small business advantage

Small business owners have several very important advantages over their big-business counterparts when it comes to marketing and testing.

First, you are closer to the action. You are in a position to see and understand the direct and immediate connection between marketing and profits: you send out a sales letter on Monday, and by Friday you're looking at your online sales figures. It's clearly a case of cause and effect, and not just some random fluctuation in your income.

But the question is, how do we know what's going to work?

And the answer is… we don't. We can't.

We do know what tends to work. For example, we know that an ad with an attention-grabbing headline and compelling body copy leading to a strong call to action is going to work better than one not having these elements (although the two bestselling sales letters in history didn't have headlines – another argument for testing).

So what we do as marketers is we begin with what we know tends to work best, and we go from there.

In other words we test.

As Claude Hopkins, the father of advertising wrote in *Scientific Advertising*:

"Now we let the thousands decide what the millions will do. We make a small venture and watch cost and result. When we learn what a thousand customers cost, we know almost exactly what a million will cost. When we learn what they buy, we know what a million will buy. We establish averages on a small scale, and those averages always hold. We know our cost, we know our sale, and we know our profit and loss."

This is the essence of marketing: testing.

Marketing is testing

We begin with something small. Maybe a small ad, a low price cost per click campaign – or a small direct mail campaign.

Then we send it out once to a small list, say 1000 names, or run it once in a publication. Because we will be measuring response by hits on our website, calls to our dedicated phone number, or even coupons through the post, we know how much profit that piece brought in.

If that revenue is more than the ad costs us to run or the letter to send, we have a winner. If we break even, it can still be a winner because our greater profits are in the long-term relationship with the customers.

If we make a loss we cannot justify even with the long-term profits, then we know we have to test again with a small sample before rolling it out to the wider audience.

This is why there is no such thing as failure in marketing – there is only a result. The only time you can fail is if you stop testing to ensure and increase profits.

Testing never stops. There are two reasons for this:

First, circumstances change. A web page or ad or sales letter that's working today is unlikely to work forever. If you're not continually testing and improving your marketing, then when the day comes that response drops off, you will be caught unprepared. So we spend much of our time testing new approaches to beat our own best results.

Secondly, great marketing systems almost never come into existence fully formed. They are always the result of much step by step refinement and testing. Even the best copywriter would struggle to get more than a 3% conversion rate from a sales letter the first time round; but if he or she can test different headlines, body copy, offers and other elements it then becomes possible to increase that 3% to 10% or even more.

In conclusion

There's a pervasive myth that effective marketing is like a military operation, where the strike is fast and furious and the withdrawal to count the profits swift and complete.

But the truth is it's more like a migration. It's slow, methodical and planned, with each step being measured tentatively by scouts before greater resources are brought to bear and risked in the search for higher profits.

As straightforward as it may sound, successful marketing is nothing more than rigorous, relentless and almost obsessive testing.'

Source: Chris Cardell, Cardell Media Ltd, http://www.cardellmedia.com/marketing-testing.html

Much of the testing methods around the marketing mix below are based on the research and experience of Chris Cardell and his team.

Price testing

Price testing is in many ways the easiest element of the marketing mix to test. The numbers are right in front of you and the impact on profitability quite measurable.

Testing price levels

This is not about lowering prices to see what happens. The sad news is that if you are redu cing your prices, your marketing is not working. An objective of good marketing is to provide so much value to customers and be so differentiated to the competition that you can safely raise your prices with little impact on volume.

Brett Matthews, the owner of Cambridge Laptop Repair, makes this clear. 'We're definitely not the cheapest and I won't be the cheapest. I came away from the Entrepreneur Summit last year and did one thing. I put my prices up. ...We didn't get any knockbacks at all. In fact I think we've had two more price increases since then. We've gone from a 10% price increase to another 7.5% to another 7.5%. In total, we've done a 25% price increase. I must point this out. The way we handled it is that on our home page it says, 'We're more than just repair. We include this with every repair. You need a 12-month warranty. A 100% money back guarantee, antibacterial clean, hardware stress test,' and all the stuff relative to what a customer would like to hear about. There's free phone support after the repair. All these things are things we do anyway. They're incidentals. If you look into any business, you're providing some unique things in your sales process that you can just wrap up and include in your price increase. It adds great value.' (Cardell, n.d.)

Testing different price points is something that marketers should do on a regular basis. In particular, you should be testing higher prices rather than lower prices, with additional value packed in.

Testing pricing options

Also, different pricing options can be tested. At Oxford Learning Labs they are refining their Freemium pricing model. Payment terms can also be varied. In many industries, they have experimented with leasing, renting, financing and outsourcing to reduce the upfront costs.

The closer you can match price and value to customer needs segment by segment, day by day, the more you will be protected from economic storms, competitor moves and sudden shifts in customer demand.

Product testing

Modern manufacturing involves regular testing all the way through the product development and manufacturing processes. However, according to National Instruments (2012), the trend is for earlier testing and seeing proper product testing as a route to competitive advantage.

The Research Triangle Institute conducted a study for the National Institute of Standards and Technology in 2002 to estimate the impact of inadequate software testing on US automotive and aerospace industries. It found that the industry-level impact for underappreciating testing was $1.47 billion. Another study conducted by researchers at NASA Johnson Space Center in 2004 stated that the cost of finding a product defect during production was 21 to 78 times more expensive than during design. The primary recommendation from both studies was to increase testing during design because of the dramatic reduction in relative cost to repair defects. By catching defects earlier in product development and collecting the data to improve a design or process, testing delivers tremendous value to the organization. The apparent conclusion is that most companies underinvest in testing and therefore suffer from slower product development, longer manufacturing cycles, and expensive repair and recall costs.

An emerging trend for electronics manufacturing companies is using product test for competitive differentiation. This has resulted in elevating the test engineering function from a cost center to a strategic asset. This shift was confirmed by a recent global National Instruments survey of test engineering leaders who said their top goal over the next one to two years is to reorganize their test organization structures for increased efficiency. This strategic realignment reduces the cost of quality and impacts a company's financials by getting better products to market faster. Research has revealed that 'optimized' is the ideal maturity level—when a test engineering organization provides a centralized test strategy that spans the product life cycle. (National Instruments, 2012)

Place testing

The Internet has made a significant difference in our ability to test different markets and routes to market. Software like Google Analytics can tell us a lot about who has visited our website, for how long, where they went, what they searched for, where they are logging in from, etc.

More recently, Facebook has become a significant additional tool here. One of the most important benefits of Facebook over Google is that it provides much more demographic information about its users. The ethics of this is for others to discuss but for marketers it is an enormous opportunity. Campaigns can be tested on highly targeted segments. You can test different age bands or test male versus female responses. You can even target users with specific interests.

At Oxford Learning Labs, they are doing their research on Facebook, then using those insights to ensure they are targeting the right segments through other channels (like YouTube, www.5min.com and www. ehowto.com).

Promotion testing

There are several different elements to the promotion mix. Here are some examples of how to test them (separated into modern online and traditional offline marketing)

Online marketing promotion testing

Social media marketing

Jon McCulloch is a marketing advisor to small businesses. In 2012 he had been experimenting with ads on Facebook. But he had a low opt-in-rate of about 4.5%. He decided to test simply changing the color of his ad. This made the opt-in-rate leap to nearly 16%. He then changed the background of the ad from white to blue. This increased the opt-in rate to nearly 29%. Why the success? His theory is that the closer the colors of the Ad match the site it is displayed within, the better the response rate. As he says, 'The general point is: don't take anything on faith. You MUST test these things for yourself.'(Cardell, n.d.)

Google Adwords

Google Adwords have been around for a while now but many marketers have not seized upon its potential to test their strategy and its implementation. Many different aspects of the strategy can be tested at any time and little risk. At the time of writing, a small UK company is developing its new three-year marketing plan. It is looking to expand beyond Europe and is using Google Adwords to test different response rates around the world to different product lines that it sells, or could sell. It is now running over 40 different ads to test various hypotheses. This will provide valuable intelligence in deciding its growth strategy.

A small UK health spa has used Google Ads to test different promotional offers. Its promotional tactics are now quite different to how they were originally framed in the marketing plan.

Small refinements can produce very different results. A slightly different word, or a new keyword linked to the ad, or even capitalization can make a difference. In one split test, the capitalized Ad brought in three times the traffic than the non-capitalized ad.

'The key to winning with Google Adwords and indeed, with any of the Pay Per Click (PPC) systems out there is testing, measurement and stepwise refinement' says Chris.(Cardell, n.d.)

Display ads

Display advertising has recently become much more powerful and is far removed from the banner advertising of the late 1990s. It has a very flexible cost model and has got a lot cheaper. Costs can be just 15 US cents per click. You can also be far more specific about where display ads are targeted, which means that if you are a small local business, you can use them just in your local area. You can also specify the type of websites they are displayed on. The really big technology shift here is that the big display ad networks (like Google) are collecting web surfing history via cookies so that they can serve up relevant ads to them. You can therefore test your marketing strategy in highly targeted ways. For example, you can run the same display ad in two different target segments or you can create two slightly different display ads to see which one generates the most traffic. The feedback data are comprehensive and fast so you can make small or large adjustments quickly to improve your success. This can be incredibly powerful. For example, Chris Cardell 'recently got 10,000 clicks in one day with just one test campaign.'(Cardell, n.d.)

Websites

8

A 'landing page' is key to website success. This is not the home page but a specific page that has been created to receive enquiries from a specific campaign. Professional marketers will have many different landing pages linked to multiple campaigns. Since most visitors only stay for a few seconds, of all the website's pages the landing pages are the most important to get right. There is always plenty of scope to experiment with them (e.g., by changing the copy, colors, offer and adding audio and video) but you can also be more scientific.

You can split test landing pages by creating two different versions and see which one works best. Google can help here with its Website Optimizer tool which presents random versions of both pages and tracks results. You can even go further with this tool and use the Taguchi Method which can test multiple variations of landing pages at the same time.

Small differences in the copy can produce dramatic differences in results. A copywriter did a split test on a web sales page where the only difference between them was that one emphasized words and phrases in bold, while the other had them underlined. The underlined page was twice as successful as the bold page.(Cardell, n.d.)

Emails

Despite the enormous amount of spam on the internet, email marketing is still one of the most popular forms of marketing and according to email specialist MailChimp (2011) is still trending upwards.

Like direct mail (see below) there are several elements that can be tested but some of the additional things to tests here are:

- *The subject header.* With so many emails in everyone's inbox, the subject header is the most important copy on the whole email. Different variations should be tested in pilots, in split tests or both.
- *Embedded* links, graphics and video.
- *The response method,* e.g., email reply vs. link to a website landing page vs. phone number.

Offline marketing promotion testing

Traditional advertising

Magazine, journal and press advertising can be tested in numerous ways and every element of the ad should be tested. You can experiment by removing unnecessary white space and graphics, changing the font size, making the offer more compelling, adding a time-limited proposition, adding response channels (e.g., phone + web + email) and changing the size and position of the ad.

This last point is particularly interesting. In one case, a regular ad for Chris Cardell in a UK national newspaper was placed on the left-hand page instead of the right-hand page. It is well-known in the advertising world that the right-hand page has a better response rate because that is where the eye is naturally drawn. In this case, the error led to a fourfold drop in enquiries! As Chris says, 'The big lesson here is the power of testing and the huge difference testing and small shifts in the way you do things can make. Imagine if I was a small business owner who has been running an ad that was doing OK. Without knowing it, just one small change could have increased my responses by [over] 400%!'(Cardell, n.d.)

In another ad that he ran in the New York Times, the simple switch to a different font doubled the response rate.

Direct mail

There are five elements to direct mail (Cardell, n.d):

1 The quality of the mail list
2 The offer

3 The timing

4 The creative content

5 The response method.

Each of these elements can be tested and improved, for example:

- The mail list can be tested by comparing their details to your current customers. If you are looking to penetrate an existing market further, see how close the mail list fits your current customer list.

- The offer can be tested by doing split tests with different variations in an initial pilot.

- The timing can be tested by dividing the list into 12-month pieces and sending one a month. One business divided their list into 52 pieces and sent the same pack out every week. They found the best week was 12 times better than the worst week!

- The creative content can be tested with different variations. The copy is extremely important and different openers, styles, length, ideas and pathways to response should be tested. The packaging is key and businesses have had much success trying different types of envelopes, handwriting styles and stamps (Kennedy, 2009).

- The response method can be tested by changing the wording of the time-limited offer, providing different response routes (phone, email, web, reply coupon, etc.) and any additional incentive (e.g., entry into a prize draw).

8

Sales

The quality of new customers can be tested. For example you can test if they are really buyers (or just browsers) with small bite-sized sales offers. (Cardell, n.d.)This can also be applied to online marketing.

Online + online marketing promotion testing

This can be the most powerful combination of all and testing an integrated online + offline campaign is smart professional marketing.

Telesales

The speed at which you respond to an online enquiry can be tested. Brett Matthews of Cambridge Laptop Repair learned that. 'I employ somebody full-time to make phone calls within two minutes of receiving an enquiry. That was something I learned quite recently. The speed with which you respond to an enquiry is very powerful. We tested it. Not only did I test it myself but I had the [telesales] people around me listen in. We tested the kind of responses we got. It was amazing. People were saying, 'Wow! I couldn't even get to my phone quick enough since I pressed Send on that email.' It blew them away. That is a major tip. Please do it.'(Cardell, n.d.)

Professionally testing the implementation/change strategy

We highlighted above some of the basic tests that can be done around your implementation plan.

There are three other testing methods worth mentioning here. The first, which we have mentioned in Chapter 5, is piloting. As discussed, this is a carefully crafted experiment to test the key elements of the solution and its implementation.

The second is surveys. Technology now makes it easier than ever to conduct online surveys of employees and/or customers. Obviously any activity here must be consistent with company policies, local laws and done responsibly. It may also need the approval of a senior executive and HR. However, assuming the above to be in place, valuable surveys can be constructed at little or no cost. SurveyMonkey is one example.

Marketers should be good at this sort of thing and able to create short, effective surveys that test specific hypotheses about implementation. One hypothesis might be: 'The leadership is committed but we have yet to gain the support of management.'

The third is polls. Short polls can be conducted very quickly (e.g., on LinkedIn) to gain a snapshot of an issue. These can be restricted to invited participants only if required. They take less than a minute to complete and can be targeted at critical groups or sent right across the company. Also, because they are not time consuming, they can be done regularly (e.g., monthly or quarterly) to see how an issue is progressing – and whether a swift change of tactics is required.

Both surveys and polls also have the benefit of allowing people to email further comments about the implementation if required.

Using an independent third party researcher will help to increase the trust in confidentiality, anonymity and willingness to share concerns.

■ Advanced testing with simulations

Here, we will reveal a relatively simple way to assess whether our strategy is robust, fit-for-purpose and future-proof. We will not go into the complexities of strategy creation as there are many other books that do a fine job of that. Instead, we will introduce a simple but powerful tool with which you can both develop and test your marketing strategy. Moreover, although a sprinkling of strategic understanding helps, the people developing and testing the strategy can be from any functional and cultural background. In other words, the whole leadership team can get involved in developing the strategy themselves. That will also pay handsome dividends when it comes to implementation.

The lesson of chess

The first question to ask here is, 'Have you ever played chess or checkers ('draughts' in Europe)?' If you have, you will know that you will NOT do very well if you make up your moves as you go along. For example, in chess, you need to have a goal (like capture the opponent's queen) and a strategy (like box her into the corner and then remove her with one of the knights). The best chess players anticipate their opponent's reactions to their decisions, many moves ahead.

Yet in the business world, where the stakes are much higher, companies are generally poor at anticipating their opponents' reactions to their marketing decisions. As Coyne and Horn (2009) note, 'In chess we are told that the best players look ahead five or more moves...When asked the number of moves and countermoves they analyzed, about 25% of our respondents said that they modeled no interactions...Fewer than 10% of the managers we surveyed looked at more than one round of response by more than one competitor.'

So, despite all the teaching on strategy and competitor analysis in business schools, there is still a lot of inertia in marketing planning and implementation. Strategies are devised with scant thought given to how competitors will react to those strategies. It is as if competitors only exist on paper, have no influence on us or the marketplace and our three-year strategy will simply become a self-fulfilling prophecy.

Marketing myopia does not work. The marketing plan needs to capture a strategy that is not only right but also robust. The strategy needs to be tested against likely reactions and scenarios that may occur over the planning period.

War games and the new strategic generation

Some of the best examples of this type of strategy formulation, of course, are done in war games. Today, many military forces around the world, including the US military and UK armed forces, conduct war games both in computerized simulations and in the field. These are used to develop and test different battle scenarios and strategies. Indeed, there have been some historic successes with war games. Leon Cooper (2006) describes how they were used to develop the US naval strategy in the Pacific in World War II:

> 'Certain islands in the Central Pacific were to be taken in the advance toward Japan. 'Island hopping,' as it became known, was deemed to be the key to ultimate victory. War games based on Island-Hopping were played out in the U.S. Naval War College.'

The interesting development over the past 15 years is that playing war games is no longer the domain of just the military. Anyone with a games console can play games like Advance Wars™ either on their own or against other players online. Anyone with a reasonable internet connection can join in 'massive multi-player online games' like World of Warcraft™ – which alone is reported to have over 11 million players worldwide (Digital Media Wire News, 2008).

Any reader with children who play war games will know that they, with little formal education and experience in marketing, are far better at strategy than we are!

In fact, this has led to some commentators talking of a new generation of strategy-savvy employees entering the workforce in the future. They will be confident strategists and much better at dealing with unexpected shocks to their strategic plans than we are today. Essentially, they have what John Brown and Douglas Thomas (2008) call a 'Gamer Disposition'. 'Each generation of [massive multiplayer on-line] games begets a new generation of participants who develop what we call the gamer disposition. It's exactly the disposition you would want in your workforce:

- 'they are bottom-line oriented
- they understand the power of diversity
- they thrive on change
- they see learning as fun
- they thrive on the edge'

These are useful attributes of leadership. In another interesting research study, 'IBM surveyed 135 of its employees who had led business teams and had also been a leader or member of a guild in a multiplayer online game...They found games to be surprisingly relevant to their day-to-day work. Of these, 75% said their [gaming experience] could be applied to enhance leadership effectiveness in a global enterprise. Nearly 50% said their game playing had already improved their leadership' (Reeves et al., 2008). This trend has caught the attention of companies like Airbus, BNP Paribas (Tieman, 2009) and BP (Little, 2009) who now use simulations as part of their undergraduate recruitment program.

The advantage of simulations as a learning tool

If we want to develop our strategic marketing skills, why not simply attend a traditional strategic marketing course run by a reputable marketing association, institute or university?

We could, but there are some useful advantages to learning with simulations. In a Thinkbalm study (2009) on the use of simulations in 66 different organizations, the following were seen to be the primary benefits:

- Increased engagement
- Increased innovation
- Valuable experience at little cost.

The increased engagement of the participants is a result of the immersive experience of simulations. In our experience of running simulations, the participants get very much into their role as chief marketing officer of the business. Moreover, there is a basic human enjoyment in playing games. This ability to learn by play works for many different cultures and backgrounds from around the world. The competitive spirit kicks in and the desire to win drives the enthusiasm to learn new ideas that might give players an edge over their competitors. This is far more engaging than sitting through dozens and dozens of slides on strategic theory.

Increased innovation develops from the cross-functional involvement in the simulation. People from many different functions can enjoy working within the same simulation. Simulations have been used by companies like Siemens to develop new products (see their Second Life site online) and Schneider Electric to drive collaborative innovation with IBM, one of their key accounts (Sullivan, 2009).

The cost advantage is big, especially where large numbers of participants are involved. Simulations allow participants to meet online rather than physically, thus saving a large portion of the travel and meeting costs. IBM reported a cost saving of 80% on their travel and meetings expenses (Linden Lab, 2009) and BP claimed to have saved around $4.5m on its global undergraduate recruitment program (Little, 2009).

From our experience, we would also add the following advantages to the above list:

- **Increased flexibility**: Simulations can be undertaken either as concentrated workshops over, say, one to two days, or as online exercises conducted over several weeks. In the latter case, this can fit around current job commitments quite easily. Participants may be given a week to make their decisions. They can share their thoughts about the market conditions and strategic options by email, chat, telephone, webinar etc. They can be free to self-organize as best suits them – both in terms of their diary and their roles in the team.

- **Greater competence:** In order to develop competent strategic leaders, we need to develop their knowledge, skills and behavior. Traditional training and development methods (like seminars and workshops) are good at developing knowledge, OK at developing skills and poor at developing behavior. This is because the participants learn the theory but do not have enough time to practice it. Like many other things in life, like learning a musical instrument, learning a new language or becoming good at a chosen sport, practice makes perfect. It is understandable why so many business leaders are poor at strategy when they have not had the opportunity to practice the art in a safe environment.

- **Increased relevance**: Because simulations can be tailored to the specific challenges of a business they are more relevant to the participants. For example, simulations can be tailored to product or service based businesses, specific industries, B2B and B2C, and to large or small companies.

- **More practical outputs:** This leads to our final point that simulations deliver more practical outputs. For example, in our simulations we offer either a universal marketing plan template (described in McDonald, 2007) or allow clients to use their own templates. With a tailored simulation, participants can write their marketing plans as they engage in the simulation. At the end of the exercise, they have a draft plan already written, with the engaged input of many of the stakeholders who will be involved in its implementation.

We may conclude by noting that the authors of the Thinkbalm survey mentioned above reported that '94% of respondents think their [simulation] project is seen as a success' and 'nearly three-quarters of respondents say they will increase their investment in [simulations].'

■ Using marketing simulations

In the marketing profession, a decade into the 21st century, we need to do something similar. Implementing a marketing strategy that has not been battle-tested is like sending soldiers into battle with no backup plan. Strategy is too important to be made up on the fly, lurching from one idea to another, panicking at competitor attacks and failing to hit marketing targets because the market did not move as we expected. Simulations help to deal with both anticipated and unanticipated risks.

Fortunately, adopting a simulator-supported approach to strategy is not difficult. You do not need to invest heavily in a vast simulator. There are many simulators that can help to develop your product marketing skills. These will provide you with a good grounding in the relevant tools and techniques of tactical product marketing. They typically cover tactical issues like the price of the product, its design features and how you promote it. Your product will compete with others in a defined market segment and you will be able to test your tactics against your competitors. You can play on these simulators, become familiar with the key concepts, and then apply the learning to one of your own key products for real. In essence, they teach you how to be a good product manager.

However, before practicing how to sell a particular product in a segment, we need to go back a step and ask whether we want to be selling that product in that segment at all. Is that product-market segment important to us? Are there other products in other segments that are more important to us? If we are a service-based company (and many product businesses have significant services connected to the product as well), we need to consider services not just the physical products. What if we have multiple products and services being sold into multiple market segments? Most global businesses have a vast array of product and service lines that they sell into multiple countries and industries. Even small businesses will generally sell multiple products or services into multiple customer segments. Often, the strategic marketing issue for a business is not one of zooming in to the tactical detail of one product and selling it better, but more about zooming out to the total marketplace and deciding where to focus the product and marketing investment for the next three years.

A good marketing simulator will help the business take a truly strategic approach to their specific challenges (see Table 8.1's Note).

We have run many simulations for businesses, universities and associations. Before proceeding further, we need to split simulations into two main types:

- *Learning simulations* where the participants are immersed in a stand-ard off-the-shelf simulation. The participants learn the key tools and concepts of strategic marketing by practicing their use in a fictional case.

- *Real simulations* where participants are immersed in the specific chal-lenges faced by their business. Here, the simulation is set up to mirror the actual market conditions they face and where real strategies are developed and tested.

From the simulations that we have run (covering the experience of hun-dreds of participants), we have seen the results shown in Table 8.1.

Table 8.1

Benefit	Learning simulations	Real simulation
Improved knowledge of key tools of strategic marketing	Yes	Yes
Improved confidence in dealing with strategic marketing issues	Yes	Yes
Improved strategic marketing skills	Yes	Yes
Improved ability to use key strategic marketing tools	Yes	Yes
Improved confidence in dealing with strategic marketing issues	Yes	Yes
Improved communication of strategy to others	Yes	Yes
A more common language and framework with which to discuss strategic marketing issues	Yes	Yes
Improved understanding of our current marketplace (including market segments, sizes and shares, customer needs, competitors and key issues)	No	Yes
Improved understanding of how our market will evolve in the future (including changing market landscape, customer needs, competitor development and key trends/shocks).	No	Yes
Improved agility in dealing with our competitors and shocks to our market	No	Yes
Development of a more robust strategy for our business that can withstand expected and unexpected shocks	No	Yes
Increased cross-functional alignment and commitment to our strategy	No	Yes
Better implementation	Yes	Yes

Note: Two of the authors of this book have developed a strategic marketing simulator for doing this. See www.market2win.com for more details.

Before we proceed, we offer a word of caution. Although we are using the term 'real' we actually mean 'realistic.' No simulation is going to model exactly the intricacies of your complex market place and your business. There are simply too many variables and too much irrational behavior! However, in the same way that pilots use simulators to learn to fly, business leaders should use them to learn to lead. Flight simulators model different hazardous scenarios and help pilots deal with different scenarios, make the right decisions swiftly and implement them effectively. The exact hazard that a pilot encounters will probably differ from the simulated hazard. But the hours spent in the simulator builds the knowledge, skills and behavior of a good pilot. Similarly, the hours spent in a marketing simulator builds good leaders, able to recognize threats quickly, respond to them correctly and implement the actions effectively and confidently.

As can be seen from Table 8.1, our experience demonstrates that even participating in a basic simulation exercise can provide significant benefits to the participants. Just one senior participant from your company attending a well-conceived learning simulation exercise will bring back a high standard of strategic thinking.

With more participants involved, the payoff is greater. Let's look at a couple of these.

Learning simulations

Case 1: Executing a new marketing campaign in a pharmaceutical company

We were invited to help a pharmaceutical company implement their new marketing campaign. The campaign relied on some segmentation work that had been done earlier. Rather than just present the new campaign to the national sales teams and tell them to follow it, the leaders of the business wanted the sales teams to understand the importance of segmentation in developing a marketing strategy and to feel more motivated to compete strategically rather than tactically. They also wanted to step outside their industry to make the exercise less sensitive and more educational.

We therefore used a standard non-pharmaceutical simulation but with a particular emphasis on segmentation. The level of engagement from the sales teams was excellent and, being sales guys, their competitive spirit kicked in. Indeed, we had to force them to take rest breaks, such was their enthusiasm to beat their fellow competitors. This immersive experience at the start of three-days of training and workshops really helped the teams to 'get' what strategy was all about, how it was incorporated into the campaign and why it was so important to act strategically in their day-to-day sales efforts.

Case 2: Studying strategic marketing at business schools

Business schools are major users of simulations. The teaching of marketing is a core discipline at these schools and the best ones are keen to use new and innovative teaching tools.

We have found that, in general, both male and female students, of all nationalities, age groups and with varied seniority and work experience engage well with simulations. In particular, they increase their appetite for learning. This is shown as increased attentiveness in class and extra hours invested outside class. We can track student log-ins to the simulation and have found many students working till midnight on developing and executing their strategies.

Although all the learning benefits in Table 8.1 apply, we have also discovered that the benefits of simulations are not just in understanding the concepts better. They have been found to be very useful in developing softer skills like team-working and leadership. We have seen how the teams that work well together do better in the simulation. We have also seen that with a good team leader there is better direction, coordination and motivation amongst the students in the team.

In most business schools where simulations are used, the students are not evaluated on how they performed in the game, but on the lessons they have learned from it. This is either assessed by a set examination question about their experience or a revised marketing plan that they submit (to take their simulated business forward from its current position). Simulations have proven to be very useful to these schools in developing the strategic leaders of tomorrow.

The greatest benefits, however, come from real simulations. Here are some specific cases where we have been involved.

Real simulations

Case 3: The marketing of independent schools

The UK independent schools market is big business. Thousands of school children from all over the world are educated privately in the UK at world famous fee-paying schools like Eton, Harrow and Rugby. Sometimes (confusingly) called either 'private' or 'public' schools, there are hundreds of independent schools across the UK that are independent enterprises outside the state education system. The bigger ones are multi-million pound enterprises and often a major employer in their area.

The market is very competitive with many independent schools reliant on overseas students. They often have their own marketing manager who must ensure that their brand is front of mind in key student recruitment markets like China, Russia and India as well as the UK. So more than ever, good segmentation, targeting and positioning have become key to their success.

We were invited to run a simulation for about 80 marketing staff from the leading UK independent schools to help them understand and practice strategic marketing. Before the session, we worked with one of the headmasters of a leading private school to pull together all the latest research on the market. We used this to segment the market, size its segments and forecast the growth of each segment year-by-year.

We also identified the key buying factors of parents. Understanding key buying factors is a critical task of strategic marketing. Buying a private education for one's child is a major decision for parents and there are many factors that may go into the decision. However, strategically, we cannot work with such a large range of factors and must consolidate them into a few key ones (see Figure 8.1).

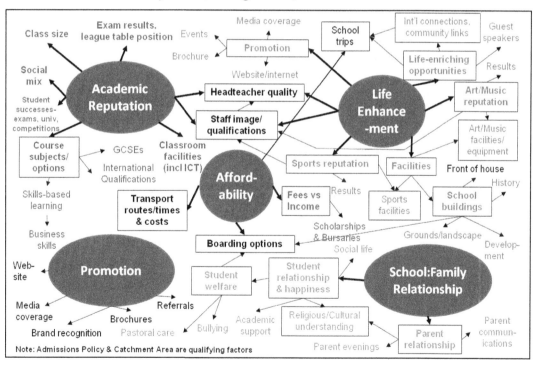

Figure 8.1: Five key buying factors for UK independent schools

We then created a customized simulation that was not only relevant to the schools but also provided key insights into how their market looks now and how it should evolve in the future.

This gave them the opportunity to develop and implement strategies that were relevant to their world of the future.

Conclusions

Each month, new technological improvements allow marketing plans to be tested in new ways. These improvements can affect every step in the planning and implementation process. To do testing properly, you should:

- Test everything and test multiple channels to market
- Recognize that smart marketing is both an art and a science
- Acquire the new skills required to use the technology and analyze the data
- Understand that the right response cannot be predicted and it will evolve from tests
- Be more entrepreneurial. Test options and implement changes swiftly
- Dynamic implementation testing is needed.

Simulations are a relatively new but important addition to the marketing process. They not only change that process but also build the right strategic skills of all stakeholders. The more stakeholders that go through a simulation exercise and the more you tailor that exercise to your own markets, the better your strategy and the more alignment you will achieve. Furthermore, because these participants are more likely to be intrinsically motivated (i.e. believe in the strategy because they helped to develop and test it) rather than just extrinsically motivated (i.e. told what the strategy is and then rewarded for executing it well), the more they will understand and be committed to the strategy. That will greatly enhance the chances of it being implemented successfully.

References

Brown, J.S. and Thomas, D. (2008) 'The gamer disposition', *Harvard Business Review Blogs*, February.

Canfield, J. (2012) 'How am I Doing', The One Question that can Change all of your Relationships, http://www.huffingtonpost.com

Cardell, C. (n.d.) Business Breakthroughs, various issues, www.cardellme-dia.com

Cooper, L. (2006) The War in the Pacific, a Retrospective, 90 Day Wonder Publishing

Coyne, K.P. and Horn, J. (2009) 'Predicting your competitor's reaction', Harvard Business Review, April.

Digital Media Wire (2008) '"World of Warcraft" players top 11 million worldwide', *Digital Media Wire News*, October 28.

Kennedy, D. (2009) *Outrageous Advertising*, Glazer Kennedy Publishing

Linden Labs (2009) 'How meeting in Second Life transformed IBM's technology elite into virtual world believers', Second Life case study on IBM, February.

Little, J. (2009) 'Enterprise virtual worlds', presentation at the Serious Virtual Worlds Conference, University of Coventry, 17 September. (Joe Little, Senior Technology Consultant, Chief Technology Office, BP)

MailChimp (2011) 'Major email trends update', blogmailchimp.com, 1 August.

Marketing Leadership Council (2005) 'Building marketing's credibility', Foundational Marketing Capsule, Marketing Leadership Council, May.

McDonald, M. (2007) *Marketing Plans: How to Prepare Them, How to Use Them*, Oxford: Butterworth-Heinemann.

National Instruments (2012) 'Optimizing test organizations', white paper, National Instruments, June 27.

Reeves, B., Malone, T.W. and O'Driscoll, A. (2008) 'Leadership's online labs', Harvard Business Review, May.

Sullivan, M. (2009) presentation at the European Conference of the Strategic Account Management Association, Berlin, March.

ThinkBalm (2009) Thinkbalm Immersive Internet Business Value Study, Q2, www.thinkbalm.com

Tieman, R. (2009) 'Recruits fired up by virtual rivalry', *Financial Times*, 4 May.

8

Part 3

Summary and Implications

9 The new marketing leader

Leadership is not a matter of ordering people around but of first taking action yourself. By initiating action yourself you will win others' trust and they in turn will take action. After fully hearing out the views of everyone, one should judge things impartially and come to a decision. And once one has done so, one should rise to implement it without vacillation.

Daisaku Ikeda

Summary

In this chapter we:

- Look at the real root cause of implementation failure
- Flip it over to view it as a key success factor
- Look at the differences between marketing management and leadership
- Define the competencies that make a good marketing leader
- Anticipate what the CMO of tomorrow will look like.

Introduction

Proper diagnosis is essential to effective treatment. Here we diagnose the root cause of marketing plan implementation failure and show how its improvement can be a key lever for implementation success. Treatment may not be easy or painless, but of all the interventions you can make, progress here should have the most dramatic impact on implementation success. Finally, if we are to become serious about implementation, there are serious implications for the marketing profession.

Key principles

- Diagnose the underlying problem not the symptom
- Use engineering's root cause analysis to do this
- Use competency profiling to define the skillset of a good CMO
- Use simulations to safely test and develop the right competencies
- Leadership is different to management.

Case study: failed implementation in a consultancy

When Georgina arrived at the consultancy she was full of high spirits. She had been recruited by the CMO to implement the client management program agreed in the marketing plan. She had run a client relationship program in a professional services company before and was looking forward to delivering a new program this time. Furthermore, this was a consultancy that advised its clients on change and so would understand the challenges of implementation. Yet, within six months she had resigned.

What went wrong? The consultancy was run by the senior partners who each had their own city office across the country. These partners were rewarded on the profits made by their office and could collect large bonuses at the end of the year. They had all agreed that coordinating their selling and delivery on common key clients would be a good idea. However, when it came to agreeing overall ownership of each client, no partner was prepared to relinquish control. They were protective of their client relationships and did not want any other office to have overall control. The CEO and CMO were not prepared to persuade them all to change. Consequently, the ambitious program was reduced to merely developing a common database for client intelligence. To this day, different offices within the same firm still compete with each other for business with the same client.

■ The real root cause of success and failure

We discussed in Chapters 1 and 4 why marketing plans fail to get implemented. We said that poor implementation was an outcome and symptom, that poor management was an underlying problem and that a poor implementation environment was a cause of failure.

However, the alert reader will note that we have not dug down to the root cause. We have not worked our way down to the bottom of the issue yet. To do this we simply need to ask the 'why' question one more time i.e. 'Why is there a poor implementation environment?' The answer is simple: poor leadership. It is the leaders of the business who set the strategy, who demand the degree of change required, who recruit and develop the employees, who decide funding issues and who mold the organization to their liking.

But we can be more specific. There are three areas of leadership at fault:

Root cause 1: poor business leadership

Although it is the responsibility of marketing to coordinate the development of the marketing strategy and to capture it effectively in a good plan, the marketing function relies on the other leaders of the business to have understanding of and commitment to the planning and implementation steps. This is not something they can opt into when they feel like it. A good business leader needs to be competent in strategy and implementation and be passionate about their importance to overall business performance.

Dave Ulrich and Norm Smallwood (2007) reviewed 150 successful leadership-driven firms and developed a code of successful leadership:

'As a prerequisite to building a leadership brand, firms must master what we call the Leadership Code. Roughly speaking, the code consists of these requirements: First, leaders must master strategy; they need to have a point of view about the future and be able to position the firm for continued success with customers. Next, they must be able to execute, which means they must be able to build organizational systems that work, to deliver results, and to make change happen. Additionally, they must manage today's talent, knowing how to motivate, engage, and communicate with employees. They must also find ways to develop tomorrow's talent and groom employees for future leadership. Finally, they must show personal proficiency – demonstrating an ability to learn, act with integrity, exercise social and emotional intelligence, make bold decisions, and engender trust.'

For Ulrich and Smallwood, these five qualities: strategy, implementation, talent management, talent development and personal proficiency are what define a good or bad business leader. Leaders must be competent in all of these. That means they must have the skills, knowledge and behavior required to discharge them effectively.

For example, if the CEO has a poor grasp of the business's relative strengths and weaknesses versus the key competitors, spends more time with shareholders than with customers, accepts sales targets without understanding how those targets will be achieved, has a poor understanding of how their market is segmented, spends too much time auditing the past financial statements and not enough time understanding the future, then they have a poor mastery of strategy. They do not have the skills required to do a basic SWOT analysis, nor the knowledge about what strategy actually is, nor do they exhibit the behavior required to demonstrate how important customers are to the business.

The more these concerns are spread throughout the board (C-Suite), the harder will be the job of marketing to both develop and execute a good strategic marketing plan.

Root cause 2: poor marketing leadership

BUT, however poor the rest of the street is, the marketing function must make sure its own house is in order. In particular, the chief marketing officer must be a good leader. Whether part of the leadership team or not, they need to demonstrate the same five factors listed above for all leaders.

In particular, they must demonstrate the factors as it concerns strategic marketing. They must be at the top of their profession and masters of strategy formulation themselves.

Sadly, as we saw in Chapter 3, research undertaken by Cranfield University and reported by McDonald (1992, 2007, p. 478) there appears to be widespread incompetence by marketing leaders. For example:

- *Confusion between marketing tactics and strategy:* A plan that only covers how the organization intends to promote specific products/services for the next 12 months is not a strategic plan but a tactical plan. The strategic questions are fewer, bigger and longer. These are: Where should we compete (which market segments should we target as an organization)? How should we compete (in those chosen segments with a superior competitive strategy)? When should we compete (what is the timing of our investment and returns)? They cover all the SBUs in the organization over three or more years. Many marketing plans pretend to be strategic while in reality they are very tactical in nature.

■ *Confusion with planning terms*: Plans often have their own specialist vocabulary. While it is always important to simplify as far as possible, the CMO needs to be clear about the differences between strategic marketing terms like: vision, mission, goals, objectives, strategies, tactics, sector, segment, product, category; strategic marketing tools like; DPM and the BCG; and financial terms like: ROI, payback and net present value.

■ *Lack of in-depth analysis*: The key tools of conducting a market audit have been around for many years yet still they are used badly. Furthermore, more sophisticated technology and research specialists have made it ever easier to analyze what has, is and will be happening in your markets and the markets of your customers. Yet still managers of failing companies hide behind excuses like 'poor trading conditions' to explain their lack of market understanding.

■ *Failure to prioritize objectives*: Marketing goals, objectives and ideas written into the marketing plan are not prioritized clearly. This means that limited resources are spread too thinly and poor resourcing decisions made before or during implementation. Also, poor prioritization dilutes executive focus, resulting in a lack of progress on the most important challenges and general inertia across a broad front.

■ *Numbers in lieu of written objectives and strategies*: Too many plans are content to show a series of sales and marketing targets heading upwards and outwards without the necessary discussion of how these will be achieved. McDonald (1992) talks about the 'emphasis which the planning system places on the physical counting of things, that encourages the questionnaire-completion, mentality and hinders the development of the creative analysis so essential to effective strategic planning.' This lack of a quality discussion is a root cause of poor marketing strategies.

■ *Isolating the marketing function from operations*: When the marketing team becomes remote from customers and competitors, it loses insight and credibility. The operations teams are dealing with these issues every day and making decisions that routinely affect the customer experience. Marketing must not be disengaged from operations. It needs to be in the trenches helping operations teams get those decisions right in addition to quickly sensing changes to the marketplace.

■ *Confusion between process and output*: Like any other function, marketing has many outputs at different levels. At a high level, the CMO who works hard to write better marketing plans every year is focusing on just one output of the marketing planning process. However, if the process does not involve enough of the stakeholders responsible for executing the plan, they would do better to improve the process rather than just the plan. Indeed, by getting the process right, they will improve their chances that the output will be right. At a lower level, the SWOT analysis is a key output of the market audit. If the market audit process is badly defined (e.g., asking only the sales force for customer and competitor intelligence) then there is little chance that the SWOT insights resulting from that will be correct.

■ *Lack of a systematic approach to marketing planning*: Many organizations have no system capable of developing and executing their marketing plans. By this we mean the system is poorly defined, not approved by the right people, invisible or misunderstood by the key stakeholders involved in its development and delivery, relies too much on hearsay rather than fact, provides too much detail, too far ahead, is not auditable, does not integrate with other key processes (like the operational planning and corporate planning processes), delivers poor non-strategic plans or is used inconsistently across the organization (sometimes fighting with alternative versions of the plan format).

■ *Lack of strategic marketing knowledge and skills*: CMOs are responsible for leading their organizations into the best marketing waters and beating their competitors to the rewards that lie there. This combines insight, leadership and implementation excellence. To do this, they need to be competent strategic managers and leaders. Sadly, many CMOs are competent only in tactical marketing management.

■ *Confusion between the marketing function and the marketing concept*: 'The marketing concept implies that all the activities of an organization are driven by a desire to satisfy customer needs (McDonald, 1992). In other words, the mission is to become a market-driven company. The marketing function is there to lead this change, to help the company migrate from being product-driven to sales-driven to market-driven. This is not just about delivering sales targets and managing the marketing mix. Marketing is a process and an attitude that involves everyone in the organization.

Led by Japanese manufacturing successes, in the 1980s, quality was changed from being something done just by the quality department's team of inspectors to becoming ingrained across the whole company. 'Quality is everyone's responsibility' was the phrase. 20 years later and marketing has yet to go through the same modernization program. Marketing plans written by the marketing function and sold to the rest of the business are doomed to failure.

■ *Organizational barriers*: These issues can arise at any stage in the marketing planning and implementation process. Here, organization refers to the organization structure and people's role within it. There are five challenges here:

1 *Organizational complexity.* This is found in large organizations where many different business units and committees need to be influenced in order for change to be implemented. It is sometimes difficult even to work out what the key decision-making units look like, what the decision-making process is and who are the key stakeholders!

2 *Organizational misalignment.* In these organizations, different departments and business units are pulling in different directions and at different speeds. There could be misaligned strategies or key performance indicators across the organization. Kaplan and Norton have written much about this issue.

3 *Organizational duplication.* In these organizations there are different people with similar jobs. The head of sales, head of marketing, head of business development, head of innovation, head of acquisitions, CEO, general manager, product manager, territory manager (and others) may all want to do their own marketing planning and implementation work. Moreover, there may be other heads in other business units that do their own work on this as well.

4 *Job/role ambiguity.* Being unclear about the role to be performed is one of the six major causes of stress in the workplace (Health and Safety Executive, 2012). When people are tasked with supporting implementation work, they may not be sure how it fits in with their job/role definition and, unless it is clarified or redefined to include it, they may resist doing the work.

5 *Marketing demotion.* Marketing often reports too low in an organization. Many companies do not have a CMO in the C-Suite and so major implementation projects have to be sold upwards before they can be implemented downwards.

The ITSalesco case (in Part 4 of this book) shows how some of these combined to frustrate attempts to implement marketing plans there.

■ *Hostile corporate cultures*: 'Culture eats strategy for breakfast' said Peter Drucker.[1] A culture that places relatively little value on marketing and implementation will be hard to navigate through. McDonald talks about the 'marketing zit' where marketing is sometimes seen as a spot on the edge of the organization. Something that is alien to the rest of the company and not necessary wanted. Symptoms of a hostile culture to

---

1   Popularized in 2006 by Mark Fields, President of the Ford Motor Company.

the implementation of marketing plans include: executives spending too much time discussing past cost performance and not enough time discussing future top line growth, insufficient coverage of marketing issues during the business planning process, no marketing officer in the C-Suite, no systematic prioritization of implementation programs, no overall change plan for the business, insufficient senior engagement in reviewing implementation programs, unwillingness of staff at all levels to make decisions, lack of ownership in following through on actions, etc.

To this list we could add poor strategic marketing talent development. By this we mean the failure of marketing to influence the process by which its own future business leaders are defined, spotted and developed. This does not just relate to the C-Suite but all senior management positions within the company.

You will notice that most of the issues above trace back to the lack of professionalism of the marketing function. Only the last two points (organization and culture) are contextual and lie outside the direct control of the CMO. The more the CMO fails on these issues, the greater the risk of implementation failure.

Root cause 3: poor change leadership

Marketing plans are not the only plans that organizations fail to implement well. We could add business plans, IT plans, HR plans, product development plans, operational improvement plans, account plans and cross-functional project plans. How many plans have you seen which fail to get executed well? There is something inherently risky about implementing plans. To quote the Scottish poet, Robert Burns (1785):

'But Mousie, thou art no thy lane,
In proving foresight may be vain:
The best laid schemes o' mice an' men
Gang aft agley,
An' lea'e us nought but grief an' pain,
For promis'd joy!'

In other words…

'But Mouse, you are not alone,
In proving foresight may be vain:
The best laid schemes of mice and men
Go often askew,
And leaves us nothing but grief and pain,
For promised joy.'

So for hundreds of years, our best laid plans have gone astray. This is often due to the leader of the project team being incompetent in their own discipline. But, there is another common issue too. There is something that causes even great functional managers, who are masters of their own subject to get shipwrecked on the rocks of implementation.

This common adversary is change. Plans are about changing things. Marketing plans are often full of proposals to change products, services, customers, prices, processes and people. The more ambitious marketing plans will seek to change the very structure, systems and culture of the organization itself – its very design. Change carries its own risks, regardless of the technical merits of the plan itself. Even the most brilliant plans can go askew if it has no allies.

Box 9.1: Great strategy De Gaulle, shame about its implementation!

In a recent biography of the French wartime leader, Charles de Gaulle, Jonathan Fenby (2010) describes how, in 1932, de Gaulle invented the idea of using tanks as a 'strategic battering ram.' His plans were ignored in France but read enthusiastically by the future Panzer general Heinz Guderian and, it appears, Adolf Hitler. At the end of the war a copy of de Gaulle's book was found in Hitler's HQ – marked with a mass of favorable comments.

Being good at leading change is an essential competence. To quote US General George S. Patton, 'A poor plan executed well is far better than a good plan executed poorly.'

But, again, there is plenty of evidence that this is not something companies are good at. Based on an analysis of dozens of change initiatives over 15 years, John P. Kotter (1995) has defined eight 'mistakes' that people make when attempting to lead change programs.

Kotter's eight mistakes:

1 Allowing too much complacency
2 Failing to create a sufficiently powerful guiding coalition
3 Underestimating the power of vision
4 Under-communicating the vision
5 Permitting obstacles to block the new vision
6 Failing to create short-term wins

7 Declaring victory too soon

8 Neglecting to anchor changes firmly in the corporate culture.

In essence, the above points to a failure of change leadership. Change leadership is very different to change management. We are drawing upon both Abraham Zaleznik's (1977) and Kotter's (2001) separate works on the difference between management and leadership in making this conclusion here and for describing the failures in business and marketing leadership above.

We would like to add one more mistake/barrier to this list: Underestimating the change required. Although this is alluded to in Kotter's first mistake we would like to make it more explicit. Many marketing plans fail because the plan owner believes the change either to be more obvious, rational, needed or simpler than it actually is. Like poor army commanders, they are unprepared for the long war ahead, have no battle plan, have poorly trained and ill-equipped troops, poor intelligence and have not predicted the likely casualties or damage to their position and plans.

Root causes conclusion

So, the root cause of implementation failure is an incompetent leadership team. Any business is essentially the product of its leaders. It can be redesigned and reshaped if the understanding, skills and motivation is there to do it.

9

■ What does good leadership look like?

Let us look at the flip side of this issue. Just as poor leadership is a root cause of failure, so is good leadership a key factor for success. Good leadership can transform the environment to give our strategy a good chance of success (see Figure 9.1). It can:

- ■ Demand an appropriate degree of change; one that balances external competitive pressures with internal change capabilities
- ■ Develop the human resources across the organization that are necessary for good implementation
- ■ Develop a good organization itself that has implementation-friendly structure, culture, metrics, processes, reward mechanisms and information management
- ■ Provide sufficient financial resources (funding) for the implementa-

tion work

- Develop a good marketing strategy to be implemented in the first place.

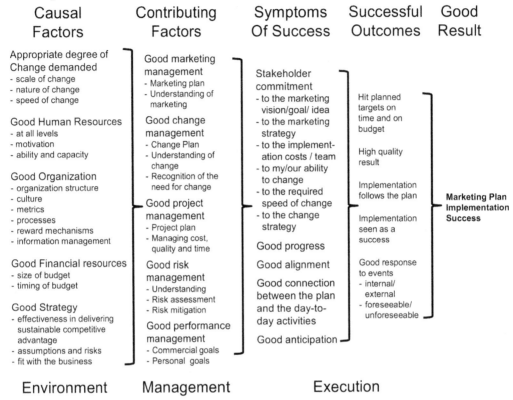

Figure 9.1: Leadership– the key lever for implementation success

Good business leadership is required to get the human resources, organization and financial resources in place. Without this, the corporation will forever be handicapped in its people, design and funding. This is the responsibility of the whole leadership team (the full C-Suite) and in particular, the CEO.

Good marketing leadership is required to get a good market strategy in place. Without this, the corporation will forever be trapped in detailed cost analysis of the current position rather than working out how to get to a desired position that will improve revenues dramatically. This is the responsibility of the chief marketing officer.

Good change leadership is required to get the degree of change right and to implement the strategy successfully. Without this, all the great strategies and plans will struggle to reach their desired goals. Whose responsibility is this? We shall pick this up later in this chapter.

The characteristics of these leadership roles are described in Table 9.1.

Table 9.1: The characteristics of good leadership

Good business leadership

Good mastery of business strategy (e.g., not too focused on short-term results, not too focused on tactics)

Good business plan

Good integration of marketing:
- ➤ Integration of operational planning, strategic planning and marketing planning with corporate planning
- ➤ Keeping the marketing function close to operations

Good accountability, measurement and alignment (between strategy and day-to-day actions, not too focused on short-term results; no silos or units with competing agendas)

Good development of tomorrow's strategic leaders

Good demonstration of the importance of strategy

Good marketing leadership

Good mastery of marketing strategy

Good marketing plan including:
- ➤ Clarity of marketing tactics and strategy; and with planning terms
- ➤ Proper in-depth analysis
- ➤ Prioritized objectives
- ➤ Written objectives and strategies, not just numbers

Good co-development of the plan
- ➤ A systematic approach to marketing planning (e.g., not too much detail, too far ahead; clarity between process and output)

Good management of current strategic marketing talent

Good demonstration of the importance of strategic marketing excellence

Good implementation leadership

Good mastery of implementation strategy

Good implementation plan

Good implementation framework including:
- ➤ Creating a sufficiently powerful guiding coalition (that overcomes the organizational barriers)
- ➤ Finding short-term wins
- ➤ Anchoring changes firmly in the corporate culture (even hostile cultures)
- ➤ Not declaring victory too soon

Good visionary leadership:
- ➤ Using the power of a clear and compelling vision
- ➤ Repeated communication of the vision and strategy

Convincing people of the urgency
- ➤ Not allowing complacency
- ➤ Not permitting obstacles to block the new change
- ➤ Not underestimating the change required

Good management of current implementation talent

Good development of tomorrow's implementation talent

Good demonstration of the importance of implementation excellence

9

▪ Leadership's overlapping roles

At this point we should make it clear that these leadership roles are not distinct from each other. For example, business leadership must combine with marketing leadership to ensure the marketing and business plans are aligned. Business leadership and change leadership must combine to ensure required changes to the corporate infrastructure are planned and implemented well. Marketing and change leadership must combine to ensure the core marketing strategy is implemented well. All three roles must combine to ensure the alignment of planning and implementation across all functions and all stakeholders. So, rather than three distinct jigsaw pieces, these are more like overlapping circles as shown in Figure 9.2.

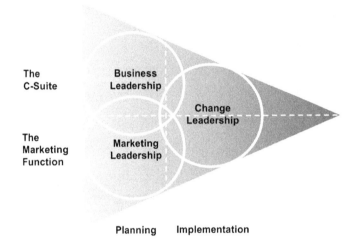

Figure 9.2: The three leadership roles

■ The implications for leadership

1 Accept the importance of marketing in planning the business strategy

In Chapter 3 we laid out the empirical and practical arguments for moving marketing out of the low-level promotional role and into the C-Suite (boardroom) as the driver of market strategy. Planning should be a market-led exercise, starting with a full understanding of the changing external conditions. It should never be last year's numbers plus the required percentage uplift. Building a leadership brand requires leaders to master strategy.

For implementation to succeed there must be a good strategic marketer in the leadership team.

2 Accept the importance of change leadership in implementation

Change leadership is not the same as change management. Some larger corporations have full-time change leaders. They need to demonstrate the characteristics shown in Table 9.1. If they do not, or you are in an organization that does not have a designated change leader, you need to ensure that these characteristics are developed within (or close to) the leadership team.

For implementation to succeed there must be a good leader of change at the top, not just a good project/change manager lower down.

3 Accept that there is joint accountability for strategic success

The more the whole leadership team understands and is personally committed to implementing the strategy the better. Good implementation of the strategy should be written into the personal development plans and the reward mechanisms of the leadership team. This is not just about setting bonuses based on profit targets and share price. Short-term profits and share prices can rise and fall with market demand unrelated to the long-term benefits of implementation success. Specific implementation SMART objectives should be included.

For implementation to succeed, its progress should form a significant contributing factor to reward and recognition of the whole leadership team.

9

4 Ensure the leadership team has competencies in all three areas

It will be a very rare individual that demonstrates strong abilities in all three areas. The requirement is to have all abilities somewhere within the leadership team. If the CEO demonstrates strong marketing leadership, then the whole business planning is likely to be done well. If the chief technology officer demonstrates a talent for change leadership then their skills will be important in getting the marketing plan implemented and their counsel sought by the CMO. Furthermore, our experience across many organizations is that good marketing leadership and change leadership can combine to overcome an unfriendly implementation environment caused by poor business leadership.

For implementation to succeed all three roles need to be developed within the leadership team.

■ Do we really care?

A senior program manager at a UK bank said it quite clearly to one of the authors of this book, 'In my experience, the problem is that marketing executives do not really care about implementation. They are creative ideas people, not detailed implementers. It is not in their psyche to do implementation and they would much rather let others deal with that issue so they can get onto the next creative campaign.'

We do not have any reliable research on this issue but it is worth considering. There is no doubt that many marketers enter the profession because they are creative, good at building relationships, good at sales, interested in strategy or interested in innovative marketing ideas. Implementing change may not have been high on their wish list!

However, as we have said before in this book, strategy is about implementation and there is no point in having a marketing plan to capture that strategy if it is not implemented. Marketers need to become as passionate about leading real and sustainable change as they are about developing the strategies in the first place.

This is best summed up by Carlos Cardoso, CEO of Kennametal. In a speech to CMOs he said,

> After process, deployment is the most important thing in a business. An organization without good deployment is called chaos. If you have a deployment issue you should take it on yourself. Define the value proposition to the business and sell it to the C-Suite. If not, then you can get in touch with a recruitment consultant to find another job. But you will find the same challenges in the next company you go to and the next. You must take ownership of deployment. Do it and test it.

> (Cardoso, 2012).

This is not to say that the CMO should do all the work of implementation. Rather, that they should be personally passionate about owning the implementation activity. They should take a close interest in setting up, reviewing and supporting the work of the implementation teams to ensure the right strategy is carried through to reality.

This may take marketers outside their comfort zone and require the development of new competencies (see below) but it is a key implementation success factor.

■ The competent CMO

A competent CMO needs to have the minimum knowledge, skills and behavior required for the job. Anything less and they are, by definition, incompetent. A great CMO will have qualities well beyond these minimum requirements.

In our work with clients we use 14 competency traits required of a good CMO (see Figure 9.3):

Figure 9.3: The competencies of a CMO

All the competencies have descriptions against them in the documentation, so that the CMO (or candidate) is clear what they mean. For example, the description for change agent is:

'He/she has a passion for improved performance, recognizes that change is necessary to deliver sustainable competitive advantage and has the courage to drive the change process. This person is capable of dealing with all aspects of change including processes, people, systems, structure and culture. He/she has a good knowledge of change leadership and change management principles, tools and ideas. He/she has a clear approach to diagnosing change barriers, creating change strategies and personally leads the change agenda.'

We have found these very useful in helping organizations set the right vision of a CMO profile and helping existing or potential CMOs identify their strengths and weaknesses.

A good exercise, for each competency, is to:

1 Score the *desired performance* level for a CMO (on a 1–5 scale)

2 Score the CMO's current performance level (on the same scale).

3 Rate the *importance* of each competency for the business as a whole (on a separate 1–5 scale).

This can be done by the existing CMO as a quick self-discovery exercise, by the CEO to establish planning versus implementation priorities, or by various stakeholders to see how much alignment there is on the implementation competencies required of a good CMO. Good practice is to have a neutral third party to also score the CMO on their current performance based on assessments (e.g., interviews, simulations, assignments etc.)

If you do this, you will find some interesting results. Do not be surprised if:

■ The current CMO does not fit the desired profile of a great CMO.

■ There is little agreement between the stakeholders of what the desired competency profile of a CMO should look like.

■ The CMO performs well on the least important competencies and badly on the most important.

These issues should trigger a healthy debate within your business about the job of a CMO and the leadership qualities required to perform it.

Testing and developing competencies

There are a number of ways that the CMO can be tested against the desired profile. These include self-assessment, interviews, assessment centers, projects, assignments, challenges, presentations, psychometric and online tests, etc. However, we would suggest you consider simulations as an extremely powerful and low-risk method. Specific challenges can be set up in simulations that will test the abilities of the CMO and develop their skills in strategy formulation, planning and implementation. Simulations can speed through simulated years in just hours and do not put any of the company's real assets at risk! Mistakes can be made, hard lessons learned and the improved knowledge, skills and behavior taken back to the business.

Simulations also provide a consistent standard for all who go through them. As we saw in Chapter 8, at one end, standard off-the-shelf simulations can be used as a training tool. These may not even be in your industry but help develop key universal strategy implementation skills. At the other end, customized simulations can be built that replicate your real market challenges closely and allow you to practice real war games using your actual marketing plans.

Moreover, where we have run them in larger corporations, simulations provide an excellent opportunity to spot new strategic talent from all functions and build a strategic implementation community.

■ **The CMO of tomorrow**

Currently CMOs are (or should be) masters of their profession. They excel at marketing strategy, marketing tactics and marketing operations. However, this is a long way from being a marketing leader (see Figure 9.4).

- Establishing direction*
- Aligning people*
- Motivating and inspiring*

- Political Entrepreneur
- Trusted Advisor
- Innovator

- Planning and budgeting*
- Organizing and staffing*
- Controlling and problem-solving*

- Risk awareness
- Risk assessment
- Risk mitigation

- Change strategy
- Change tactics
- Getting buy-in where needed

- Marketing strategy
- Marketing tactics
- Marketing operations

Marketing Leadership · Relationship Management · Project Management · Risk Management · Change Management · Marketing Management

Figure 9.4: The CMO of tomorrow

Leaders excel at implementation. This means they already possess all the management skills of marketing and implementation, i.e. marketing management, change management, project management, relationship management and risk management. But leaders go further. They translate the technical marketing strategy into a motivating and inspiring journey for all, align people around the specific direction to be travelled and take personal ownership of getting there successfully.

They have made the transition from marketing manager to Marketing Implementation Leader.

9

Conclusions

The job of a CMO is one of the most perilous roles in organizations today. A recent US study (Spencer Stuart, 2011) gives the average CMO tenure in their job as 42 months compared to 111 months for a CEO. In industries like communications, media and restaurants, the CMO tenure is 22–25 months! Clearly, there is often a low value place on either the job or the incumbent. Something needs to change drastically. The answer is better leadership.

As the authors of the study say: 'Top CMOs ... view themselves as leaders first and marketers second.' Good leadership means being good at both strategy and implementation. This will require new knowledge, skills and behaviour. However, the rewards are huge, both for your business and for you. This combination provides the ideal platform in which to take on the broad business leadership role of a great CEO.

References

Burns, R. (1785) 'To a mouse', (verse 7: 'On turning her up in her nest with the plough'), *Poems, Chiefly in the Scottish Dialect.*

Cardoso, C.M. (2012) presentation to ISBM Conference, Dallas, Texas, March (Chairman, President and CEO of Kennametal).

Fenby, J. (2010) *Charles de Gaulle and the France he Saved,* Simon & Schuster.

Health and Safety Executive (2012) 'Causes of stress', UK Government Health and Safety Executive website, July.

Kaplan, R.S. and Norton, D.P. (2006) *Alignment: Using the Balance Scorecard to Create Corporate Synergies*, Harvrad Business School Press.

Kotter, J.P. (1995) 'Leading change, why transformation efforts fail', Harvard Business Review, Spring.

Kotter, J.P. (2001) 'What leaders really do', Harvard Business Review, Dec.

McDonald, M. (1992) 'Ten barriers to marketing planning', *Journal of Business and Industrial Marketing*, Autumn, 7(1), 5–19.

McDonald, M. (2007) *Marketing Plans, How to Prepare Them, How to Use Them,* Oxford: Butterworth-Heinemann.

Spencer Stuart (2011) 'Average Chief Marketing Officer Tenure Hits New High', www.spencerstuart.com

Ulrich, D. and Smallwood, N. (2007) 'Building a leadership brand', *Harvard Business Review*, July–August.

Zaleznick, A. (1977) 'Managers and leaders: are they different?', Harvard Business Review, May-June, 67-68 .

10 Conclusions

Implementation pronunciation: /ˌɪmplɪmənˈteɪʃ(ə)n/ *the process of putting a decision or plan into effect; implementation: she was responsible for the implementation of the plan.*

Oxford English Dictionary

Summary

In this chapter we:

■ Summarize the key points in the book

■ Help you get started in applying the thinking to your own implementation challenges

■ Complete the marine chronometer story.

■ Introduction

Implementation is both an art and a science. As with any artist or scientist, there are many instruments from which to choose. However, there are only a few that you need to master. In this chapter we go through the main points of the book and the essential tools to put them into practice. Mastering these points and these instruments will take you a long way to becoming a marketing implementation leader – and beyond.

Key principles

■ Implementation matters

■ The old way of implementation does not work

■ Implementation is a process not a program

■ Planning is still vital

■ Implementation needs to respond to unexpected events

■ We must learn from other professions and use new tools

■ Sense and respond is key

■ Marketing Navigation changes the planning and implementation process

■ Strategy is implementation and implementation must include change

■ Leadership means being good at market strategy and change

■ Marketing leaders should make natural implementation leaders.

■ Implementation matters

Implementing a marketing plan may not be the most exciting subject but it is crucial. Billions of dollars are wasted in the global economy every year from poor implementation of planned strategies. Billions more are lost from failing to implement mid-term strategies that exploit new and unexpected opportunities or counter new threats.

Apart from the commercial cost, there is the frustration (ranked number one in our survey) about the wasted time and effort involved in poor implementation.

The nature of implementation is that often we do not see these problems. So long as we hit the targets in the plan, everyone is happy. Yet failing to implement well, failing to hit higher targets and not knowing we are off course until too late, can cost the business dear.

For any organization, large or small, better implementation is a sure way to improve its performance at relatively little cost.

The old way of implementation does not work

In the traditional marketing planning process (and many books on strategy), implementation is treated as a single step (see Figure 10.1).

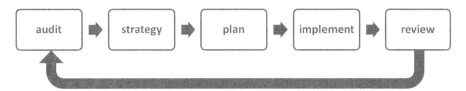

Figure 10.1: The traditional marketing planning process

The key steps are commonly:

1 Undertake a marketing audit (internal and external assessment of your situation)

2 Develop your marketing strategy

3 Capture the strategy and its rationale in a marketing plan

4 Implement the plan

5 Review its implementation (and feed results back to the marketing audit for next year's plan).

The results of implementation are reviewed and fed back into the marketing audit. The market strategy, marketing plan and its implementation can then be improved accordingly. This seems a logical process but it has severe limitations:

■ Implementation is not a single step, but a process in its own right.

■ Each of these five steps takes time and typically takes a year to complete. It is a rigid process and organizations following it cannot respond quickly to unplanned events. Events overtake the marketing plan.

■ Once agreed, marketing plans tend to be shelved and quickly become out of date.

Implementation requires a phased approach that provides guidance to the marketer but also retains flexibility in handling unplanned events.

10

■ Implementation is a process not a program

Figure 10.2 repeats Figure 3.8 in showing that implementation is a continuous, never-ending process and is actually taking place during the preparation of the next strategic marketing plan.

All organizations, of course, have a fiscal year end, but this is purely an accounting convention required by law and the day after the year ends, implementation of the next one-year plan begins and in reality this is just a continuation of the previous day's implementation, even though it is a new fiscal year – the world of business does not suddenly change because of an accounting convention!

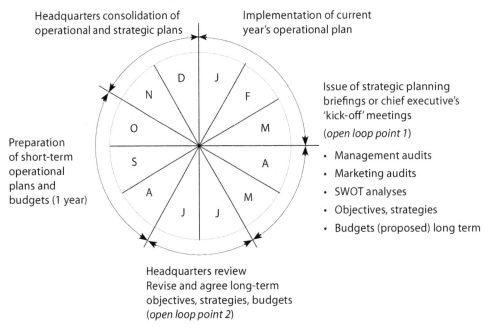

Figure 10.2: Strategic and operational planning

From reading Chapter 3 you will also observe that preparing the strategic marketing plan can take up to six months before the detailed plan for the first year of the strategic plan is prepared prior to implementation at the beginning of the next fiscal year. Meanwhile, of course, implementing the current one year plan continues apace.

A marketing plan may contain one or more growth strategies. Each of these may contain one or more growth programs requiring implementation. The implementation of each of these programs should follow the same process: plan, pilot, rollout, refine. This is a circular process as defined by our helm model and different programs can be at different phases at any point in time.

Defining implementation as a process rather than a program demonstrates that it is an on-going exercise requiring continuous improvement. This is particularly useful for large on-going programs (e.g., customer research, competitor intelligence, key account management, IT-development) which will always be continuously improving and therefore can never really be checked as complete. At the end of one major implementation cycle, another one starts.

■ Planning is still vital

The marketing plan is still as important as ever. The right strategy has to be developed carefully and implementation cannot be done without one (Booz, 2012). The marketing planning process is the vehicle for doing this and its resultant marketing plan is the document to define the strategy, tactics and actions to be implemented.

This will ensure your business is not dragged into the wrong strategy by your customers and competitors. It ensures you set the right course to blue oceans (Kim and Mauborgne, 2005) of profitability and will not get blown into the red oceans of head-to-head competition.

Risk assessment is a vital part of marketing planning. The known key risks should be anticipated in the marketing plan. Once these have been defined, the plan should also state how they are to be minimized and how the business will respond to them should they occur.

This will ensure you are ready for the problems that you know will threaten implementation. A good risk assessment ensures your ship, its procedures and crew are ready for the storms and battles that you know will lie ahead.

Appendix 10.1 provides the implementation templates to add to your marketing plan.

Implementation needs to respond to unplanned events

While a good marketing plan can anticipate known risks, the implementation of that plan has to deal with unknown and unanticipated risks.

These unplanned risks can either be:

- A relative improvement/decline in your competitive position, a new opportunity or a new threat

- A test result that indicates implementation will be easier or more difficult than expected.

In our helm model, any particular implementation program can move forwards and backwards through the process. For example, after the Lehman Brothers collapse in September 2008, many programs dealing with financial services should have moved back to the plan phase. In another example, in programs where next year's government funding has suddenly become at risk, implementation might move swiftly through the phases to ensure earlier implementation.

10

The helm can be turned to deal with unplanned events. Sometimes this involves changing course in order to reach the target destination safely. Other times, the unexpected challenges are so great that they involve re-planning a new course to a new destination.

We must learn from other professions and use new tools

To get to a new way of doing implementation, we must look to non-marketing professions that are involved in implementation on a daily basis.

In particular, we can adapt the tools of failure mode and effect analysis from engineering, relationship maps from key account management and change loop thinking from change management. We should also adapt Kotter's (1996) work on change leadership.

Central to the answer is risk management. Successful implementation is all about managing the commercial risks and the commitment risks involved in any program. These risks need to be identified and kept under constant scrutiny.

Using proven tools in new ways will help you to keep a close eye on the changing risks and stay on course throughout your implementation journey.

Sense and respond is key

Constant, regular testing is vital to implementation. It is through testing that we can regularly scrutinize the risks.

Constant testing helps you sense:

- That you have not misread your position
- New strategic opportunities and threats (e.g., a subtle shift in customer needs)
- New implementation opportunities and threats (e.g., unexpected arrival/departure of a key stakeholder)
- Changes to your competitive position that affect implementation (e.g., development by a competitor of a similar solution)
- New ways of doing things that you would never have dreamed of through conventional means (e.g., changing the capitalization of your ad messages, ensuring you call the prospect within minutes of the online enquiry being received)
- All of the above quickly.

Your response should also be tested to ensure:

- You have responded correctly (e.g., your enquiries have increased, the level of commitment has increased)
- You have responded quickly (e.g., within one week of the issue being raised).

Good implementation requires constant navigational fixes to ensure we have not drifted off course or fallen behind schedule.

Marketing Navigation changes the planning and implementation process

The Marketing Navigation approach changes the way that marketing plans are written and implemented.

We have seen how testing is central to implementation. In practice there is much parallel working between planning and implementation. We can easily expand our thinking to show testing at the heart of the full planning and implementation process (see Figure 10.3).

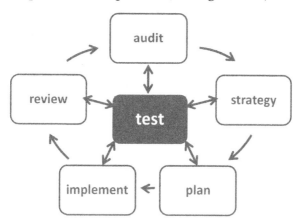

Figure 10.3: The new marketing planning process

1 The results of the marketing audit can be tested by speaking with independent industry experts.

2 This helps us develop a better strategy, which can itself be tested with a marketing simulator.

3 This helps us develop a better marketing plan, which can be tested by performing an FMEA exercise to identify the key risks.

4 This helps us implement it better, which can be tested throughout by constant checks.

5 This gives us more data, intelligence and insight to review the implementation performance and constantly refines it.

6 This helps us perform a better marketing audit...and so on.

The planning and implementation process therefore becomes circular. As with implementation, we can test any step at any time and turn it around for any program in response to unplanned events.

The more we practice Marketing Navigation, the better we become at dealing with unplanned events and implementing programs faster and more effectively.

Box 10.1: Using simulations throughout the marketing planning process

Simulations are used not only to improve strategy formulation. They are a powerful tool that can be used throughout the planning and implementation process. For example, they improve the quality of implementation by:

- Modeling the market landscape (market segments, market shares, growth rates, competitor positions, new products/technologies, key trends) that is uncovered by the marketing audit

- Developing and testing different strategies to find the one that is most effective

- Testing the marketing plan to make sure it is robust and future-proof

- Practicing and refining the implementation of the plan at any time to help ensure all stakeholders understand the strategy and their role in its implementation and are well rehearsed in how to respond to different competitor responses

- Using the review of implementation to re-calibrate the simulation (e.g., adjusting market segment sizes and growth rates) and improving the accuracy of the marketing audit.

Simulations also improve the speed of implementation by allowing participants to fast forward through the process. The participants can then see how well their intended strategies were implemented in practice and can rehearse the responses needed. Not only do participants get an insight into the implementation challenges and required responses, they also become more skillful in dealing with complexity, unexpected events, virtual resources they do not formally control and strategic analysis.

In this way, strategy does not need to be a separate step but can emerge from the process – what Cares and Miskel (2007) call 'co-evolutionary gaming.' The marketing planning process becomes less of an annual ritual and more of a live exercise where stakeholders step into and out of the simulator continuously.

It also builds understanding, alignment and commitment across the business. This reduces the gaps between the steps, speeds up the cycle and improves the quality of the thinking and decision-making.

The end result is better strategies implemented faster.

Use the Marketing Navigation System to keep your plan on course

The Marketing Navigation System can be used by all organizations large and small to help keep their implementation programs on course. A simple version should be used for small businesses and small scale programs. A full version should be used for large organizations and large-scale programs. A portfolio version should be used where multiple programs need to be managed.

The system has considerable benefits, namely, it:

- Is based on solid principles
- Is scalable
- Provides instant feedback and course correction advice
- Is easy to use
- Has proven results.

■ Strategy is implementation and implementation must include change

Although most conventional diagrams show implementation as an add-on at the end of the planning process, it should not be seen as such. The planning for implementation and the awareness of 'implementability' should happen during the marketing audit, market strategy and marketing plan steps. The marketing plan itself should have a good implementation plan section. Planning and implementation are iterative and entwined.

Implementation is not just about getting the funding for the marketing tactics and actions required. According to our survey, the organizational environment is the greatest challenge followed by the human resources.

Many of the issues here will not be marketing-specific. They will be common for all implementation programs in your and any organization. For your strategy to successfully navigate through these issues it must include a credible change plan within its implementation plan.

■ Leadership means being good at market strategy and change

A key part of leadership is formulating and implementing a strategy that will take the business to a point of greater sustainable competitive advantage.

This requires a good understanding of strategy, change, projects, relationships, risk and leadership. If you want to become or remain a successful marketing leader, you should identify your gaps and ensure you have a personal development plan to close them.

Furthermore, you should become interested in the subject of implementation. By reading this book you have clearly demonstrated some interest. Now you should seek to develop it.

Chris Cardell runs one of Europe's biggest marketing networks and has hundreds of businesses on his client list. Here is what he has to say:

> While most of our members are doing well at the moment, it's no secret that some are doing ten times better than the norm – defying the economy and raking in profits that many find hard to believe. There is normally only one thing that sets these people apart – massive implementation. They don't have a higher IQ...they're not in better businesses. They just take 10 times more action.

> (Cardell, 2012)

If you are interested in implementation, see if you can get excited about it. If you are excited, see if you can get obsessed about it. If you are obsessed, see if you can get passionate about it. The more passionate you are about it, the more enthusiastic those around you will become as well.

Marketing leaders should make natural implementation leaders

The good news is that many of the concepts of marketing can be applied easily to the issue of implementation. You should be able to:

- ■ Define the internal market and the competition for internal resources
- ■ Segment the market into meaningful stakeholders

- Understand their different needs (and look for unmet needs)
- Target the right stakeholders who will most influence the change
- Plan your internal and external marketing change strategy (e.g., how to convince your market to adopt your solution)
- Define your value proposition for each stakeholder segment
- Communicate, communicate, communicate (frequently with multiple channels and to multiple audiences)
- Use every marketing trick in the book to promote and measure the change.

These are significant inherent skills and a great foundation for a change leader. You may even find new opportunities in change leadership!

■ The four key factors for implementation success

In order of importance, the following are the key factors that will drive sustained implementation success in your organization:

1. **Improved implementation leadership** (business leadership, marketing leadership, change leadership) drives:

2. **A more implementation-friendly environment** (the degree of change demanded, the human resources available, the organization environment, the financial resources available and the quality of the strategy) which drives:

3. **Better implementation management** (marketing management, change management, project management, risk management and performance management) which drives:

4. **Better execution** (stakeholder commitment, implementation progress, alignment, plan-to-action integration).

The Marketing Navigation System drives improvement in all four areas and helps to identify any additional development required in 1 and 2.

10

■ Seven steps to successful implementation

So how can you apply the thinking in this book to improve the implementation of your own marketing programs? The recommended steps are as follows:

1   Choose a real marketing plan or marketing program(s) to work on.

2   Configure your own Marketing Navigation Dashboard template, e.g., single vs. multiple programs, portrait vs. landscape view (see Chapter 2).

3   Ensure you have a good strategy in a good marketing plan, ready for implementation (see Chapters 3 and 4).

4   Add an implementation section at the back of the plan (see Chapter 4 and Appendix 10.1 at the end of this chapter).

5   Plot your position for the implementation phase you are in e.g., plan phase (see Part 2).

6   Keep plotting your position on a regular basis to ensure you remain on course (see Part 2).

7   Find out your own competency gaps and write a personal development plan to become a good marketing implementation leader (see Chapter 9).

Remember, you do not need to be perfect at implementation. You only need to be better at it than the competition.

Further support

For further information on marketing navigation including its philosophy, tools, training, reading and case examples, visit www.marketing-navigation.com.

■ Finally...from Harrison to Hamilton and beyond

What happened to Harrison's magnificent marine chronometer? For the next 150 years 'succeeding generations of horological craftsmen refined and improved the chronometer. They contributed steadily to its value and importance to the sea-faring men of all nations, making it the most treasured and carefully guarded piece of equipment aboard ship' (Drescher, 1946).

Its production remained a craft-based industry right up to the Second World War, with Britain a key producer. The onset of war brought a huge demand for mass produced chronometers, felt most keenly by the US Navy. The US Naval Observatory issued its own challenge for a domestic producer to come up with the world's first high quality mass-produced marine chronometer. This challenge was accepted, planned and implemented by the Hamilton Watch Company which, in a short space of time, had designed and mass-produced thousands of 'Model 21' and 'Model 22' world-class chronometers.

In the 1970s more accurate satellite navigation took over and there was less need for the mechanics of the marine chronometer. However, even today some mariner qualifications such as Officer in Charge of Navigational Watch, Master and Chief Mate deck officers still require the ability to use celestial navigation and a precise chronometer (Wikepedia, 7 July 2012).

240 years after dead reckoning was abandoned by mariners, it is time for the marketing profession to do the same. Good navigational skills using solid techniques may even one day be a certified requirement of a Chief Marketing Officer.

References

Booz & Co (2012) 'Strategy or Implementation: Which is More Important?', www.booz.com

Cardell, C. (2012) 'Winner takes all', Business Breakthroughs, available via www.cardellmedia.com.

Cares, J. and Miskell, J. (2007) 'Take your third move first', *Harvard Business Review*, March.

Drescher, E.W. (1946) 'The hairspring and balance wheel assembly of the Hamilton marine chronometer', reprinted from the H.A.A. Journal, available from http://www.militarywatchmuseum.com/HMCH&BW.htm

Kim, W. Chan and Mauborgne, R. (2005) *Blue Ocean Strategy, How to Create Uncontested Market Space and Make the Competition Irrelevant*, Harvard Business School Press.

Kotter, J.P. (1996) *Leading Change*, Harvard Business School Press.

10

■ Appendix 10.1: An Implementation Plan Template

Program:

Marketing Plan: Date:

Owner: Version:

1.0 Program Specification

1.1 Program Background

1.2 Program Summary

1.3 Program Deliverables

1.4 Program Scope

1.5 Program Steps and Plan

1.6 Key Resources and Investment

1.7 Program Management and Reviews

2.0 Program Roadmap for Change

3.0 Key Activity Planner

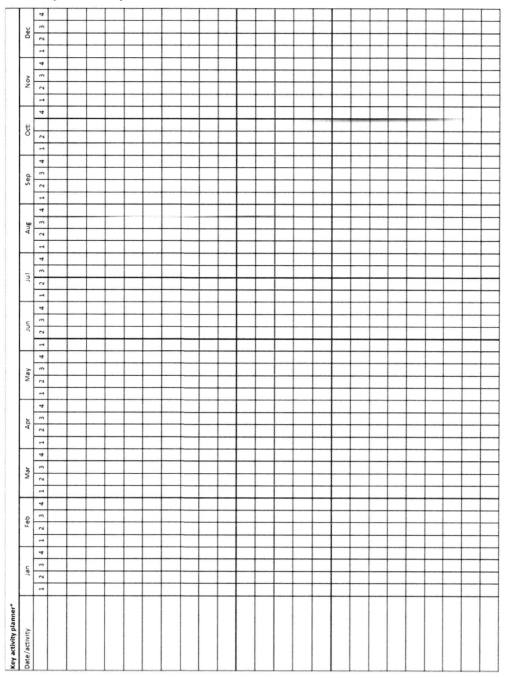

10

* Source: *Marketing Plans, How to Prepare Them, How to Use Them*, Form 7, p549, Malcolm McDonald, Seventh Edition, Wiley

4.0 Monitoring Tool: The Marketing Navigation Dashboard

Marketing Navigation System

Navigation Dashboard

Plan/Project:

Owner:

Date:

Revision:

On Course?   Yes/No

The Risk-Commitment Matrix: Current Position

High

!

Risk

✕

Low

Low   Commitment   High

Key Actions

Action	Who	By When	Done?

On Time?   Yes/No

Comments here

On Budget?   Yes/No

Comments here

The Helm

Implementation Phase: Pilot

Refine   Plan

Test

Roll-out   Pilot

Risk - Commitment Diagnostic

Top Risk Issues   Conclusion | GO/ NO GO

Ref	Desired State	Risk Area	Failure Threat	Test	Current Status	GO, NO GO

Top Commitment Issues   Conclusion | GO/ NO GO

Ref	Desired State	Stakeholder	Failure Threat	Test	Current Status	GO, NO GO

11 The seven steps to implementation success (fast track)

Billions of dollars are lost every year from marketing plans that fail to get implemented properly. The risks around implementation are high and the challenges are many. To help overcome them, good marketing leaders need new knowledge, skills and tools. This book draws upon fresh research, new technology and decades of experience to help marketers improve their chances of success. We propose a simple marketing navigation system to help all businesses ensure their plan identifies the implementation risks and remains on course to deliver its targets. This releases significant profits for the business and helps ensure it continues its journey to sustainable competitive success.

Implementing a marketing plan is one of the most perilous journeys that anyone can undertake. Our research suggests that over 60% of marketing plans fail to achieve their targets. Overall, there is more chance a marketing plan will fail than succeed.

This is a multi-billion dollar problem. Across the top 50 corporations of America, we estimate the total lost profits from poor implementation to be well over $50billion, four times the annual profits of Apple! Add to that the lost profits from the thousands of companies further down the ranking and repeat it for the other global regions and you can see this is a considerable global goldmine.

However, this is no easy task. If you are not armed with the right knowledge, skills and tools, then there is a good chance that your marketing plan will simply be dashed on the rocks of fate, like so many others before it. Your plan will be like a ship, sailing swiftly and blindly towards submerged rocks, uncharted icebergs and unforeseen storms, without any navigation aids to help you.

Here is how you can successfully navigate the implementation journey.

1   Learn to use the Marketing Navigation System (Chapter 2)

To help you maintain control of implementation, we recommend you use the Marketing Navigation System. This is a suite of tools to help you implement your marketing plan more successfully. It has four core tools:

- The Marketing Helm
- The Marketing Navigation Dashboard
- The Risk–Commitment Diagnostic
- The Risk–Commitment Matrix.

The core tools are based on good demonstrated practice in a range of professions. We have identified the best tools, imported their essential ingredients into our system and adapted them for our use. The end result is a powerful system with solid foundations.

The Dashboard pulls together the key elements of the tools onto one page (see Figure 11.1).

2   Plan your implementation carefully (Chapters 3 and 4)

This is the first phase of the implementation journey. In this phase you will need to understand what your marketing strategy (and plan) is seeking to achieve and then plan a route to get you there. This is done by being crystal clear about your marketing orders, diagnosing your current implementation issues, anticipating implementation problems ahead and planning your best route to success. This implementation plan is a vital additional element of an excellent marketing plan. Good work today will save many a weary night later.

Key principles

- The marketing plan must be ready for implementation
- Do the implementation diagnostics
- Write a change plan
- Test this in a variety of ways
- Move firmly to the next phase only when ready.

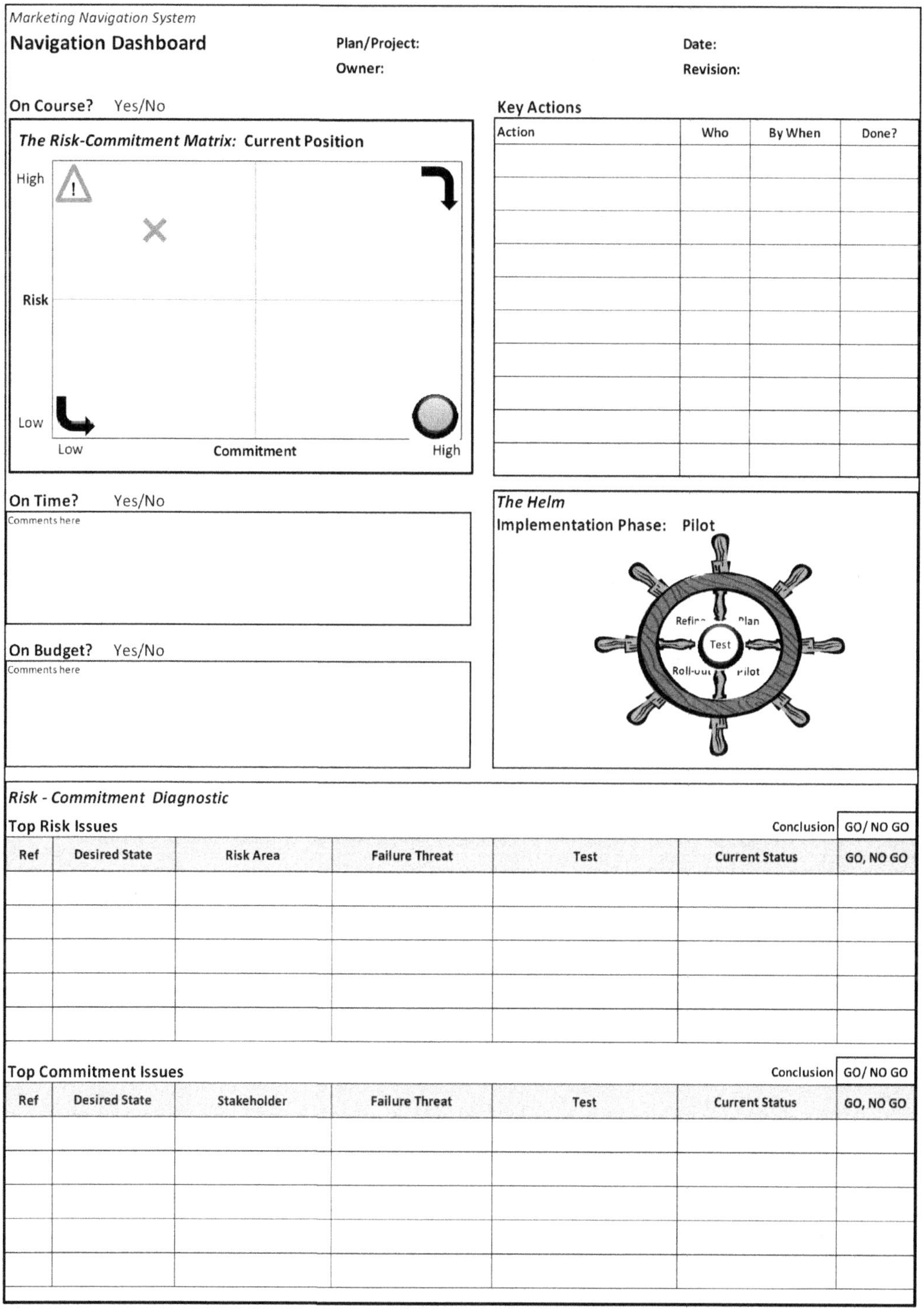

Figure 11.1: The Marketing Navigation Dashboard

Within the figure:

Marketing Navigation System

Navigation Dashboard

Plan/Project:

Owner:

Date:

Revision:

On Course?   Yes/No

The Risk-Commitment Matrix: Current Position

High

Risk

Low

Low

Commitment

High

Key Actions

Action	Who	By When	Done?

On Time?   Yes/No

Comments here

On Budget?   Yes/No

Comments here

The Helm

Implementation Phase: Pilot

Refine   Plan

Test

Roll-out   Pilot

Risk - Commitment Diagnostic

Top Risk Issues   Conclusion GO/ NO GO

Ref	Desired State	Risk Area	Failure Threat	Test	Current Status	GO, NO GO

Top Commitment Issues   Conclusion GO/ NO GO

Ref	Desired State	Stakeholder	Failure Threat	Test	Current Status	GO, NO GO

11

How to plan your implementation course

Much time and money can be wasted on implementing strategies that have not been properly thought through. Many programs fail even before they get started because they have not been planned properly.

So, to begin with, you must plan your journey ahead. As the old saying goes, 'failing to plan means planning to fail.'   Here are the key steps to do it:

2.1   Determine if your marketing plan is ready for implementation

2.2   Do the implementation diagnostics

2.3   Develop a change plan

2.4   Use the plans to improve your position immediately

2.5   Confirm your readiness for the next phase

Boundary conditions

The conditions to exit the plan phase are.

Condition	Yes/No
You have a clear vision of your goal and a good market strategy to get there	
These are captured in a good marketing plan	
You understand the impact of the strategy on the organization	
You understand the implementation environment	
You have identified the key supporters and opponents of implementation	
You have a good change plan that shows how the strategy will be implemented in your organization	
You have completed a Marketing Navigation Dashboard for this phase	
All sensors on the Dashboard say GO	

3   Test your implementation plan with a pilot exercise (Chapter 5)

You should now have a good marketing plan brimming with growth programs ready for implementation. However complex your plan and its programs, before you commit all the resources required you should conduct a simple pilot test first to ensure that the proposed solution will work with your intended audience. This will give you valuable feedback and confidence before you proceed to full rollout.

Key principles

- Walk before you can run
- Use *lab testing* and *prototype* thinking
- Build the solution dynamically
- Improve your navigation instruments
- Recalibrate as you progress.

How to pilot your plan

Getting the pilot right is important and is a mini-implementation exercise in its own right. Here are the key steps to do it:

3.1 Develop the solution to a testable state

3.2 Choose your pilots wisely

3.3 Decide how to run the pilot

3.4 Look for early wins

3.5 Improve the pilot as you go along

3.6 Test and re-test.

Boundary conditions

If the following boundary conditions have been met, then you are ready to proceed to the next phase of the journey:

The conditions to exit the pilot phase are:

Condition	Yes/No
You carefully chose a sample of users for your pilot	
You have tested your solution on them	
You have reviewed the results and made the necessary improvements to the solution, its supporting infrastructure and to the implementation plan itself	
Commitment is sufficiently strong across the stakeholders to proceed	
You have completed a Marketing Navigation Dashboard for this phase	
All sensors on the Dashboard say GO	

11

4   Rollout implementation (Chapter 6)

In this phase, we use the results from the pilot to accelerate implementation. This is the major action phase and covers most of the implementation journey. We will make the transition from a few users of our solution(s) to a full market rollout. By the end of this phase, implementation should be around 95% complete.

Key principles

- Use rolling wave planning
- Use strategic marketing thinking to get your rollout strategy right
- Use market maps to plan your rollout
- Use SAM principles to build buy-in
- Adopt continuous improvement
- Use sports thinking to consolidate and progress.

How to roll out your plan

We are now leaving the safety of the harbor and heading out towards the vastness of the ocean. All the planning and prototyping of the previous two phases (plan and pilot) can now be used to help us proceed safely. Our final destination, on the other side of that ocean, is known and we have performed all the necessary safety checks. Our instruments have helped us become aware of many threats, from many quarters, but we are monitoring them and are confident that we can overcome them.

This is a major part of the implementation journey which we have divided into six steps:

4.1 Finalize the rollout plan

4.2 Ensure the resources are ready to deliver it

4.3 Implement with certainty and flexibility

4.4 Improve the rollout as you go along

4.5 Test and re-test

4.6 Confirm your readiness for the next phase.

Boundary conditions

The conditions to exit the rollout phase are:

Condition	Yes/No
Over 90% of your rollout map is green (signifying implementation is virtually complete)	
The vast majority of key stakeholders say implementation will be a success	
Your relationships are green where it matters	
Powerful opponents of implementation have been won over or their influence is under control	
The solution currently meets or exceeds expectations	
The solution is supported with a good infrastructure	
You have completed a Marketing Navigation Dashboard for this phase	
All sensors on the Dashboard say GO	

5   Refine the implementation (see Chapter 7)

During this stage of the journey we will reach our destination. We have covered 95% of our route and simply need to bring our plan safely home. However, we should not be over-confident. A common failure of implementation is declaring victory too soon. That is, too many change leaders think they have implemented their solution when, unseen to them, little has really changed. New CRM tools may lie unused, new behavior reverts back to the old bad ways, new approaches lie abandoned because new behaviors are not rewarded. Indeed, we should think of this part of the journey as being the most challenging. There are so many things to do in order to get our implementation firmly anchored into the business but often with so little time. There will be new risks as we enter the harbor waters. We must reach port safely and ensure no navigational errors, submerged objects, adverse currents nor wayward ships will sink us as we steer our plan into port.

Key principles

- Embed the change
- Final 5% but it could be the small hole that sinks your ship.
- Recognize what drives embedded, successful implementation
- Use root cause analysis
- Consider the drivers of success
- Adopt a continuous improvement philosophy
- Process, not a program.

How to refine implementation

In order to refine our implementation, we need to understand a little better the levers for improvement. In particular, it is useful to separate out those levers that produce superficial improvements from those that provide deep-rooted change.

To get to these, we need to ask the question, 'Why are the all the stakeholders not committed?' In doing so, we may find a variety of contributing factors: a poorly written marketing plan, a poor understanding of marketing itself, little recognition of why we need to change, disapproval of the speed of change or the investment required, etc. Once we know these, we can seek to improve them. We can clarify the plan, adjust the marketing strategy within it, explain how good marketing is vital for the future of the business, change the speed and cost of implementation, etc.

11

However, we can go even deeper than this to identify the causal factors. We need to ensure the change being demanded is appropriate for the business, that the human resources required to implement the change are motivated and able to do it, that the organizational environment is fertile for implementation, that the financial resources are sufficient and that the strategy is good in the first place.

The more we can refine the causal factors, the more we can lay the foundations for repeated good implementation results.

5.1 Refine the contributing factors

The contributing factors are:

- Good marketing management
  - ☐ Good marketing plan
  - ☐ Good understanding of marketing
- Good change management
  - ☐ Good change plan
  - ☐ Good understanding of change
  - ☐ Good recognition of the need for change
- Good project management
  - ☐ Good project plan
  - ☐ Good management of project cost, quality and time
- Good risk management
  - ☐ Good understanding of risk
  - ☐ Good at risk assessment
  - ☐ Good at risk mitigation
- Good performance management
  - ☐ Good fit with commercial goals including their key performance indicators
  - ☐ Good fit with personal goals of stakeholders.

Together, these contributing factors define the management of marketing implementation.

5.2 Refine the causal factors

The causal factors are:

- The degree of change demanded
- The human resources
- The organization

- The financial resources and
- The strategy in the marketing plan.

Together, these causal factors these define the implementation environment. If they are all good then there are healthy conditions for the implementation of the plan.

Boundary conditions

The boundary conditions to exit this phase are therefore:

Condition	Yes/No
99%+ of your rollout map is green (signifying implementation is complete)	
The vast majority of key stakeholders say implementation was successful	
Your relationships are green where it matters	
The solution met or exceeded expectations*	
The solution has been embedded with a good infrastructure	
The cost of implementation is within the budget set (or over-spends accepted)	
Implementation has been achieved on time (or delays accepted)	
You know how you can improve implementation in the future (including engaging stakeholders better and reducing commercial risks)	
You have completed a Marketing Navigation Dashboard for this phase	
All sensors on the Dashboard say GO	

* If stakeholders have previously accepted and supported lower expectations, higher budgets, or delayed timings then you can still answer 'Yes' to these conditions.

Congratulations! Your implementation should now have been successfully completed. We now need to work on improving how you do implementation itself...

6   Use technology to improve your implementation testing (Chapter 8)

Technology offers a significant opportunity for marketers to create more robust strategies and implement them better than ever before.

Key principles

- Scientific, entrepreneurial approach
- Dynamic implementation testing
- Testing and measuring.

The new technologies

Extraordinarily powerful technology can be accessed for very little investment and is certainly affordable for even micro businesses.

Here are just some of them (in no particular order): Google Adwords, Display Advertising, Facebook, Email marketing, Online surveys, LinkedIn, Video marketing, Website analytics, Apps, Mobile marketing, High end enterprise analytics, Simulations.

There are four main benefits to using these technologies:

1 **Improved quality of the marketing plan**. In particular, ensuring that the strategy and tactics within the plan have been tested and are right.

2 **Improved threat assessment**. Continuous sensing of the internal and external environment will highlight significant threats earlier and clearer.

3 **Improved opportunism**. Good sensing will quickly spot changes in customer needs, competitor actions and market forces that could allow you to be first to see an opportunity and first to exploit it.

4 **Improved responses**. You do not necessarily need to get your response right first time. Continuous testing will allow you to adjust your response and to move more quickly than your competitors.

Use technology to test all aspects of the marketing mix and make changes to the mix, the plan and the strategy based on the results.

Do advanced testing with simulations

Implementing a marketing strategy that has not been battle-tested is like sending soldiers into battle with no backup plan. Strategy is too important to be made up on the fly, lurching from one idea to another, panicking at competitor attacks and failing to hit marketing targets because the market moved more slowly or differently than anticipated.

Fortunately, adopting a simulator-supported approach to strategy is not difficult. You do not need to invest heavily in a vast simulator.

A good marketing simulator will help the business take a truly strategic approach to their specific challenges. They offer the following benefits:

- Improved knowledge of key tools of strategic marketing
- Improved confidence in dealing with strategic marketing issues
- Improved strategic marketing skills
- Improved ability to use key strategic marketing tools
- Improved confidence in dealing with strategic marketing issues

- Improved communication of strategy to others
- A more common language and framework with which to discuss strategic marketing issues
- Improved understanding of our current marketplace (including market segments, sizes and shares, customer needs, competitors and key issues)
- Improved understanding of how our market will evolve in the future (including changing market landscape, customer needs, competitor development and key trends/shocks)
- Improved agility in dealing with our competitors and shocks to our market
- Development of a more robust strategy for our business that can withstand expected and unexpected shocks
- Increased cross-functional alignment and commitment to our strategy
- Better implementation.

Simulations are a relatively new but important addition to the marketing planning and implementation process. They not only change that process but also build the right strategic skills of all stakeholders. The more stakeholders that go through a simulation exercise and the more you tailor that exercise to your own markets, the better your strategy and the more alignment you will achieve. Furthermore, because these participants are more likely to be intrinsically motivated (i.e. believe in the strategy because they helped to develop and test it) rather than just extrinsically motivated (i.e. told what the strategy is and then rewarded for executing it well), the more they understand and are committed to the strategy. That will greatly enhance the chances of it being implemented successfully.

7 Improve implementation leadership (Chapter 9)

Like any issue, proper diagnosis leads to effective treatment. Here we diagnose the real root cause of marketing plan implementation failure and show how its improvement can be a key lever for implementation success. Treatment may not be easy or painless, but of all the interventions you can make, progress here should have the most dramatic impact on implementation success.

Key principles

- Diagnose the underlying problem not the symptom
- Use engineering's root cause analysis to do this
- Use competency profiling to define the skillset of a good CMO
- Use simulations to safely test and develop the right competencies
- Leadership is different to management.

The root causes of implementation success and failure

- Business leadership
- Marketing leadership
- Change leadership.

The characteristics of good marketing leadership are shown in the table below:

Good business leadership

Good mastery of business strategy (e.g., not too focused on short-term results, not too focused on tactics)

Good business plan

Good integration of marketing:

- ➢ Integration of operational planning, strategic planning and marketing planning with corporate planning
- ➢ Keeping the marketing function close to operations

Good accountability, measurement and alignment (between strategy and day-to-day actions, not too focused on short-term results; no silos or units with competing agendas)

Good development of tomorrow's strategic leaders

Good demonstration of the importance of strategy

Good marketing leadership

Good mastery of marketing strategy

Good marketing plan including:

- ➢ Clarity of marketing tactics and strategy; and with planning terms
- ➢ Proper in-depth analysis
- ➢ Prioritized objectives
- ➢ Written objectives and strategies, not just numbers

Good co-development of the plan

- ➢ A systematic approach to marketing planning (e.g., not too much detail, too far ahead; clarity between process and output)

Good management of current strategic marketing talent

Good demonstration of the importance of strategic marketing excellence

---

Good implementation leadership

Good mastery of implementation strategy

Good implementation plan

Good implementation framework including:

- ➢ Creating a sufficiently powerful guiding coalition (that overcomes the organizational barriers)
- ➢ Finding short-term wins
- ➢ Anchoring changes firmly in the corporate culture (even hostile cultures)
- ➢ Not declaring victory too soon

Good visionary leadership:

- ➢ Using the power of a clear and compelling vision
- ➢ Repeated communication of the vision and strategy

Convincing people of the urgency

- ➢ Not allowing complacency
- ➢ Not permitting obstacles to block the new change
- ➢ Not underestimating the change required

Good management of current implementation talent

Good development of tomorrow's implementation talent

Good demonstration of the importance of implementation excellence

The implications for leadership

1 Accept the importance of marketing in planning the business strategy

2 Accept the importance of change leadership in implementation

3 Accept that there is joint accountability for strategic success

4 Ensure the leadership team has competencies in all three areas.

Great leaders are ultimately the key success factor for great implementation.

11

Marketing Navigation: Quick Reference Guide

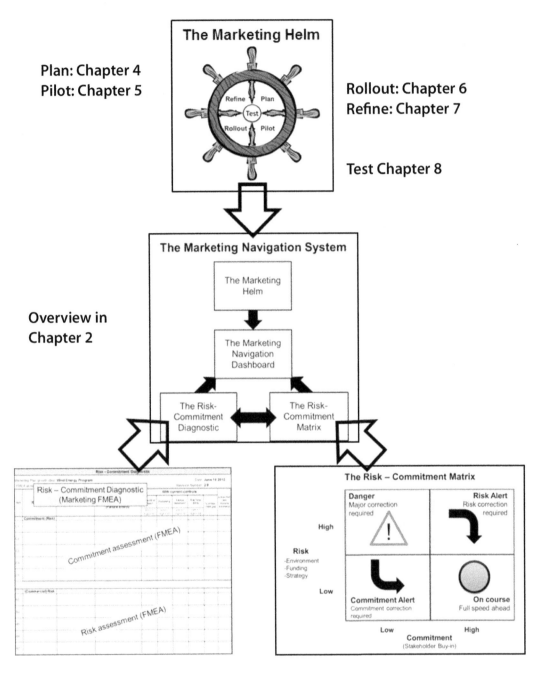

Plan: Chapter 4
Pilot: Chapter 5

Rollout: Chapter 6
Refine: Chapter 7

Test Chapter 8

Overview in
Chapter 2

Chapter 4   Chapter 2

Part 4

Marketing Implementation Case Examples

Contents

Austro: Accelerated implementation   270

English Energy*: Implementing a new market entry strategy   275

European eCards*: Successful implementation of smart marketing   280

Global Language Partner Consulting: Charting an implementation course in China   284

Globalserve*: Combining account management with change management   288

IEB*: Implementing a new mindset   297

ITSalesco*: The challenge of a complex sales-driven company   302

Kennametal: Keeping marketing plans on track   304

Lafarge Jordan: Re-cementing a leadership position   307

Medic*: Implementation enlightenment in India   324

Oxford Learning Lab: Online implementation   328

Tuntex*: A cautionary tale from the textiles industry   332

* Names have been disguised to maintain anonymity. There is no connection between these organizations and any other using a similar name.

All interviews conducted by the authors between September 2011 and March 2012.

Austro: Accelerated implementation

Charles Jacobs, CEO and Peter Ivanoff, National Marketing Manager, Austro Group Limited

■ Background

Austro entered the South African woodworking market as an agent/ distributor of European sourced equipment in 1980. Some ten years later it commenced with the distribution of tooling and invested in equipment to sharpen such tooling on behalf of its customers.

During the first two decades of trading the company grew in line with the general expansion of the South African economy at that time. However, with the economic boom of the early 2000s the company flourished.

The company developed into the largest distributor in South Africa which was attributable to:

- The drive and energy of its founder.
- The company's range of products included most of the leading brands at that time.
- The value proposition of the business which was to provide superior after-sales service. Amazingly it was the only distributor to offer such after-sales care.

The company listed in 2007 on the Johannesburg Stock Exchange (JSE), at which time the founder retired from the business. He was succeeded by a sales orientated CEO with limited management experience. Not surprisingly, during the highly optimistic period which prevailed at the time, overheads became bloated with crony appointments earning extravagant salaries and asset management was totally neglected. As the business previously focused primarily on equipment sales, it considered its service department to be a cost center and as a consequence of not having profit responsibility, the service department was staffed with overpaid technicians.

Subsequently to the economic crash in 2008, management was unable to cope with the changed environment and the Board was compelled to intervene with the appointment of a temporary CEO tasked with bringing overheads in line with the new levels of economic activity.

The management baton was subsequently passed to the manager of a small subsidiary who continued to focus on cost cutting and accounting controls. The company's technical service was consequently drastically pruned during this period. Unfortunately, as the after-sales service was a key element in the value proposition, the baby was proverbially thrown out with the bath water.

With the focus on cost cutting, sales continued its downward trend.

■ Environmental scan and development of a revised business model

On New Year's Day 2011 a new CEO, Charles Jacobs, was appointed to turn around the company's fortunes. A task force was assembled to undertake a strategic marketing review for the first time in the company's history. The review included an external audit of the company's customers utilizing the Malcolm MacDonald template.

Some of the more important issues revealed by the audit were:

The business had not segmented its market and had a 'one-size fits all' value proposition. Because the business considered its service department to be a cost center, which incurred significant losses, the value offered was not recovered in the selling price of the products.

The business had previously targeted only one segment of the market and had no defined value proposition to enter other segments of the market. The business was growing well at the time. It was able to report significant sales growth during the boom period in the early 2000s but this disguised the fact that sales were simply rising with demand and that sales personnel were not equipped to pro-actively pursue sales. Moreover, sales were conducted on a transactional basis with no attempt made to negotiate sustainable long-term customer value through integrated solution offerings.

In summary:

- In line with many companies at the time, the company's sales force had become order takers whose skills were primarily product orientated.
- Sales were transactional in nature which consequently resulted in the company's customers buying their products from competitors of the company as well.
- The company had lost its most profitable product agency and there were signs that some of its other key agencies were in jeopardy.

Cases

- The company's business model was heavily focused on capital equipment sales, which is intrinsically linked to gross domestic fixed investment, and by nature, is highly cyclical.

With the low business confidence prevailing after the 2008 economic crash, and likely to continue for the foreseeable future, the diminishing sales trend was likely to remain. The sale of consumable products, such as tooling and service, was the responsibility of the equipment sales personnel who in the main, considered these products as mere tools to support the sale of equipment.

Further cost cutting in such an environment of dwindling sales was not an option as the business had relatively high and entrenched fixed overheads (such as property rental commitments, etc.).

In light of these circumstances, the management's only viable option was to re-focus the business by restructuring the business model with the objective to increase the sale of consumables and service-based products. These sales are driven by the less volatile GDP business cycle which could sustain the business in the long term.

■ Implementation

As the management of the day-to-day sales of consumable products differed from the sale of service-based products and the long selling cycles of capital goods sales, it was necessary to restructure the business into the following three distinctive profit centers, each with its own focused management:

- Equipment sales
- Supplies – incorporating the sharpening service
- Technical services – incorporating spare part sales.

These divisions needed to be staffed with sales orientated management capable of growing revenue both independently and in collaboration with each other where required. Whilst it was possible to fill one management position with an internal appointment, it was necessary to 'head hunt' externally to fill the other positions.

The initial focus of each of these divisions was to grow their revenue independently. However, with the objective of introducing sustainable sales, the products of the divisions needed to be sold in an integrated manner.

To achieve this it was necessary to:

- Develop appropriate value propositions for each of the market segments, and to support the sales thereof with extensive training and subsequent coaching and counseling.

- Develop programs to ensure that the divisions incorporate the concept of 'hunting in packs' in their day-to-day selling activities.

- Implement commission and incentive programs to reinforce the objective of selling all inclusive solutions designed to make Austro the preferred supplier on a sustainable basis.

After a comprehensive process review, it became necessary to implement a new ERP system to effectively support and manage the various programs described above.

■ Conclusion

According to Austro, the key reasons for the successful implementation of its restructure were:

- Change was initially instituted from the top down, but a broad spectrum of management developed into a collaborative leadership with buy-in from an early stage.

- A good template for change was developed by using the methodologies of global experts like Kotter, McDonald, Ansoff, Porter, Slywotzky, and Morrison, etc. While this aspect caused some delay initially, it significantly speeded up final implementation.

- The vision and mission statements that clearly reflected the company's new strategy was only formulated after establishing the needs of the market.

- A marketing strategy was developed with a three-year implementation period which incorporated a short-term tactical plan to gain quick wins before phasing in the medium and longer-term strategic programs.

- The program itself proved to be useful in moving the business culture from that of a telling style of management to a much more collaborative one. The importance of buy-in from key implementation stakeholders and the jettisoning of individuals who resisted change cannot be over-estimated.

- The sales-driven strategies were at all times aligned with asset management to achieve optimum shareholder returns.

Cases

- Austro mapped and translated the broad strategy into easily manageable key performance areas and process workflows (using Scientrix software – see *Scientrix Implementation Methodology* below). The diagram below is just one top level view of a multidimensional balanced scorecard. The sub-matrices of each top level view are intertwined and linked to each other to provide a comprehensive and holistic tool for the implementation of Austro's complex new business model.

Considering that the re-engineering process encompassed all aspects of the business (ranging from strategy to selling to supply management to supporting systems and human resources) it was a real achievement that the program was implemented swiftly and in a fully integrated manner.

Scientrix Implementation Methodology

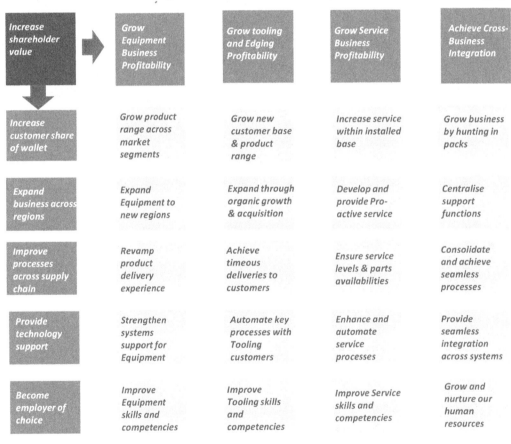

English Energy: Implementing a new market entry strategy

Ian Helps, formerly their Business Development Manager

Most marketers will be familiar with the challenge of finding new sources of growth. In many cases the marketing eye looks beyond the current market to new segments which are often seen as more attractive. Analysis will often show that the rewards here are higher if the company can only develop new products and services to access these new customers. However, as Igor Ansoff will tell you, the most dangerous of marketing strategies is the 'diversification' strategy which calls for a new service to be sold to a new market. These strategies often fail because they involve understanding new customers (better than their existing suppliers) and developing new products (with all the risk that this entails).

However, with great care, this dangerous journey can be navigated successfully and the huge rewards reaped. In this case, we will look at the story of how a major UK utilities company (which we will call English Energy) implemented such a plan to invade a new market segment.

In the early 2000s, English Energy was well established as one of the key suppliers of gas and electricity to homes and businesses across the UK. However, growth options were seen to be limited in its traditional market especially with a powerful government regulator watching every move.

After careful analysis of their options, it was decided that telecoms presented an attractive opportunity. It was felt that if the business could introduce a new credible telecoms service, it could sell that to both existing and new customers. A detailed business and marketing plan was written that demonstrated a strong business case for going ahead. Of course, the company had little experience of the telecoms industry so there was considerable unease amongst the executive about this venture.

Nevertheless, a multi-skilled taskforce was formed to put the plan into practice. Ian Helps was their Business Development Manager at the time and was recruited to be the taskforce leader. 'I think I was just making a lot of the right noises at the time about exploiting new opportunities outside our traditional business and was given this project to manage,' he explains.

Cases

The objectives of the venture were quite simple:

- Develop and launch a new telecoms offer
- Sign up the targeted number of customers to this offer
- Protect the brand (i.e. do not screw up!).

One of the first things that the team did was to find and setup a joint venture with a small telecoms Internet business. They found one which was very experienced with multi-product billing and knew the telecoms industry. The business also brought a lot of clarity to the offer (e.g., fixed versus mobile telecoms) and the systems required to support it.

'There was a large amount of detailed thinking in the early days' says Ian. 'We not only had to design the offer but also think through all the likely customer scenarios and define the processes and infrastructure required to support each scenario.'

These detailed processes then had to be mapped and programmed into the IT infrastructure. This was a huge task which required some very complex and detailed work. In fact, according to Ian, 'The single biggest challenge that the team had to overcome was IT.'

However, within a few months, the infrastructure had been set up, the internal tests had been completed and the team was ready for its first customer test. A carefully selected tranche of existing customers was chosen for a pilot. These were selected on their usage history and were seen as good prospects for the new telecoms offer. A small call handling team was also set up that could be dedicated to the new telecoms business.

Ian continues the story, 'The pilot was much more successful than we expected. We already had a good reputation with these customers and people saw telecoms as a logical extension to our services. Consequently, we over-achieved our initial sign-up target many times over.'

After just one month of pilot testing, the service was rolled out across the whole UK. A nationwide promotional campaign was undertaken to raise awareness of the telecoms service. In addition, all the necessary training was undertaken right across the customer service teams to ensure the company could handle a potential avalanche of telecoms enquiries.

The results were impressive. 'Tens of thousands of new customers quickly signed up to the deal' says Ian. 'The results dramatically beat our expectations and enhanced our brand value.'

This success did not come by accident. According to Ian, there are some specific reasons why this implementation program was successful.

1 **Clarity of the value proposition**. The value proposition was systematically simplified to make it as clear and compelling as possible. In the end, it was all about 'the same level of service as your existing supplier but at a cheaper price'. Ian underlines the importance of this point, 'In my experience, many product launches fail because of a vague value proposition. Being clear up front about the value being promised is absolutely essential'.

2 **Good plans**. A comprehensive business plan was written that contained the marketing plan and a clear business case for change. Once approved, this was then turned into a detailed project and change plan. One of the first things the team did was to define the implementation steps that would hit the time/cost/quality targets of the project and minimize the risks of implementation failure along the way.

3 **Unbending determination**. The project team also had to convince the executive that this really was going ahead. 'There is always a natural inertia in doing new things' says Ian. 'Often, it is easier *not* to do something than to do it. To overcome this issue, we were very clear about when the launch date would be and we stuck to it. Even at the eleventh hour there was a big news story in the UK involving a breach of data security in an unrelated industry and we had to investigate our own security systems. However, we just put in the extra hours and confirmed to the executive that all was secure and that the launch date was still good.'

4 **Delivering the value promised**. The service delivery must match the offer being promised. Most of the work done by the project team was to ensure that the customer experience was as good for the new service as it was for other services that the company provided.

5 **Taskforce approach**. Key to success was the quality of project team. 'We were fortunate enough to have been loaned some very talented people' says Ian. 'This included IT specialists that understood billing, the customer services director of one of our business units who understood service delivery and the managing director of our retail business who had worked in British Telecom previously.' Such people do not come easily. Although they were officially full-time on the project, the reality was that they were still being pulled back to deal with operational issues in their own areas. This would have sunk many other projects but these people really were the best of the best from each department and they wore both hats well. At the end of the project the team was disbanded and went back to their regular positions.

Cases

6 **Supportive leadership**. 'This top talent was loaned to us because the executive understood the need to grow and the strategic imperative of getting this right' says Ian.

7 **Good governance**. A carefully crafted governance mechanism was also in place to review progress. There were formal updates given regularly to the executive. This was an important opportunity to update the top team, to answer their questions directly and to overcome any significant organizational hurdles. However, in addition to the formal reviews, informal feedback was provided by the members of the team to their own line managers. Ian also had frequent 1:1 meetings with the CEO to ensure he was happy with progress. This combination of formal and informal engagement was key to building confidence in the team, their plan and the solution.

8 **Risk assessment**. A risk log was continuously updated. This included a list of what risks had been identified, which of these were considered the most important, what the response is to each of these risks and any risks that had not been properly assessed. One of the major risks that came out of this exercise was the possibility that the company could not invoice the telecoms service effectively. This was given a high priority action for the team and additional resources convened to ensure the systems were set up properly.

9 **Openness**. There was a good degree of openness between the team and the executive. If there were concerns, these were raised on both sides and there was a good deal of trust in evidence. For example, there were significant disagreements about the offer initially but these were resolved quickly and professionally.

10 **Speed**. Exploiting the limited window of opportunity was key. The telecoms industry moves fast and the business plan called for rapid implementation. There was always the danger that one of their competitors would act first or that the incumbent suppliers would change their pricing policy and blur the value proposition. Here, from 'business case approval' to 'launch' took just nine months.

It is also interesting to reflect on the role of marketing for such challenging implementations. If Ian had to find someone to lead such a project in the future, he is very clear about the qualities of that person. 'I would never put someone from marketing into that role. The marketing skills are only a small part of the overall skill-set required to implement such a program. These qualities include project and program management, change management, attention to detail and multi-disciplinary team-working. It is better suited to someone with a 'special projects' role within the business than to a marketer. In this case, the CMO was part of the executive. He was visible and supportive but he did not lead the implementation program.'

Ian believes there are useful lessons here. 'Although we did not have experience in telecoms, we knew how to handle millions of customers effectively. By careful planning and implementation we were able to use that competence to deliver a brand new service to both existing and new customers. This is a good template for any large scale strategic implementation program,' he concludes.

Cases

European eCards: Successful implementation of smart marketing

■ Background

European eCards (not its real name) is a B2C company that specializes in customizable e-cards. Customers log onto their website, then choose and customize cards that are then printed and posted to their desired address.

The CMO there knew the company was not capturing enough information about its customers and not making use of the customer data it already stored. He had the foresight to understand that with deeper customer insights the company could segment their customers better, improve the customer experience and better tailor the marketing messages to the customer needs.

He therefore hired Jacques Devalier (not his real name) to develop and implement a customer personalization strategy.

Jacques quickly analyzed the order history data and could see some basic problems. There were some very loyal customers but the company was also losing customers who would order just once and not return. The company needed to improve its retention rates of these customers.

■ The plan

Within a short time Jacques had a basic idea of what needed to be done and wrote it down in a marketing plan. He then took the CMO through the plan and secured his agreement to its main points. On his advice, it was then presented by Jacques to the Board.

The plan provided:

- A summary of what other leading web-based companies had done in this area and the results they had achieved

- An analysis of what its competitors were doing in this area

- A vision of how email marketing will transform its relationship with customers. This included how the website will look in the future, how customers will get a personalized experience on the website when they login and how offers can be adjusted for each customer segment.

- The commercial objectives including increased frequency of purchase, up-selling to higher value products, cross-selling between products and improved customer lock-in and loyalty
- The tactics of how email marketing will work in practice
- The measurements of success including:
  - ☐ Short-term measures like revenue per 1000 emails sent, activation of new customers, click-through-rates, conversion rates
  - ☐ Long-term measures like customer lifetime value, customer activity, cards per order, order frequency, data richness and share of wallet.

■ The implementation

The plan also had a phased implementation approach, i.e.

- Phase 1: Campaign automation
- Phase 2: Data enrichment
- Phase 3: Web personalization.

As the IT infrastructure developed, Jacques continuously ran small tests on chosen segments. This was very powerful in demonstrating both what the IT could do and also in making immediate improvements in performance in these segments. The positive feedback from these tests was critical to the board in approving the investment for each subsequent phase.

■ The results

Before the strategy was implemented, people worked hard but did not work smart. For example, a lot of time and stress went into writing regular newsletters. These had to be completed regularly on time and required a lot of effort to complete and send out. Now they have been dropped in favor of more personalized emails. Doing less bad marketing has been one major benefit of the new system. Dropping that one stressful exercise alone won a lot of converts to the strategy and freed up the time needed to implement it.

Another benefit of the new system is that the team can quickly test something and they get quick and powerful feedback on whether it works or not based on actual customer behavior. They can test significant things like a new pricing offer all the way down to little things like changing the color of a webpage button from red to blue.

Cases

'My team absolutely loves the new smarter marketing world' says Jacques. 'They are far more innovative now and want to keep testing and trying new ideas to see what will happen. They also get immediate feedback on how they are doing. This is not based annually on subjective assessments by managers, but by real and up-to-date customer data. It is also very low risk. We can test it in one isolated segment and if it does not work, simply stop it quickly. We can also run split campaigns and see which version of an offer works better.'

This continuous effort to keep testing and improving is now a key part of the company's smart marketing culture.

They can conduct almost real-time segmentation and offerings. Every day, segments are automatically analyzed and new segmentation options suggested. Once approved, these segments then trigger automated, customized offers via email and customized experiences on the website.

They can also keep a much closer eye on revenues. There is more granularity to historical and current revenues from specific customer segments and there is also improved forecasting accuracy from the more detailed pipeline metrics.

The commercial results from this have been impressive with a 250% increase in revenue!

■ Conclusions

Jacques considers himself fortunate in that the company did several things well to improve the chances of successful implementation: 'First, the board was very market-driven and fully understood that customer loyalty is one of the main drivers of revenue. Secondly, we had a good prioritization process to pick the best projects in the company. Hard commercial business cases were used to choose the best project and there was considerable cross-board support for the projects chosen. This clear selection process also meant that the chosen projects were not starved of the required investment. Anyone can write a plan but it means nothing without the right support. Finally, we had a good culture of accepting mistakes. We like to see our company as one that can change quickly to changing consumer needs and competitor actions. Getting the systems right is one part of this but it is also important to have a culture that appreciates new ideas and supports constant experimentation.'

Jacques is also clear about the type of marketer that can run this type of smart marketing department. 'Marketing results must be tangible and unfortunately a lot of marketing people do not like numbers. Marketers tend to like playing around with things like the color of the leaflet. Now, with so much data around, marketers must be as comfortable with the hard facts as they are with the soft creative ideas.'

Global Language Partner Consulting: Charting an implementation course in China

Zhanhong (Larissa) Liang, Founder, Global Language Partner Consulting

'In 2007 I was working as a freelance interpreter in Beijing, China. It was good work and I was benefitting from the influx of foreign businesses entering the country. However, I wanted to develop a business that was bigger than just myself. So in July 2007 I setup Global Language Partner Consulting (GLP).

One of the first things I did was to profile my existing freelance clients to learn more about the type of clients I should be targeting. I started doing this by simply asking questions about their key language challenges when I submitted my regular invoices to them. That way, I also was able to get my intelligence from the key decision-makers who signed off the invoice.

One thing I discovered was that many clients were frustrated by the variable quality they were experiencing from their language service suppliers. So I thought of a solution and proposed it to one of my clients. I simply went to the right decision-maker and asked him to divert some of his spend my way so he could try out my solution.

The trial was a success and soon another company heard about it and contacted us. This in fact was a client of my client's who had heard some good things about me. Then another one heard and contacted us, then another one. From small beginnings, my business developed like a snowball.

Within my first year of business, my clients could see that my work was of a high standard and I built up a level of trust with them. I then started to cross-sell translation and interpretation services more intensively within each client. Furthermore, this translation–interpretation combination had two additional advantages:

1 It set me apart from other competitors that tended to be better in just one of the two areas.

2 It allowed me to see how their staff performed along this spectrum and I could identify the specific language challenges (e.g., listening, speaking, reading and writing abilities in English) of specific staff (e.g.,

the C-Suite, the sales and marketing team, etc.). This then allowed me to add a major third string to my bow, customized language training courses.

So you can see that our strategy, right from the start, was not to sell one narrow service across but to develop multiple service streams and sell these deeply into each client relationship, pro-actively providing the right solution for each of them.

Our strategy also suited our very limited resources. At the start, I was the sole employee. Not only was there just one of me but also I had low skill and low will in some vital implementation areas. For example, in terms of skill, when I setup GLP I did not know what marketing was! I thought it was advertising and Google. I wanted to try Google Adwords but I came to realize that this was expensive and ineffective in helping me acquire the high quality clients that I needed. I also printed some brochures and fliers but that did not work. No one around me could tell me what the right marketing approach was.

In terms of will, at the start, I was so reluctant to sell. Even though I was a freelancer I did not need to sell. I would usually get pulled in to a client by another agency or by someone in my network of business contacts. But later on, one of my friends told me that I was not selling if I was helping other people. He told me I needed to change my mindset. Overcoming this psychological barrier was key to implementation.

We now have a full-time team of employees plus third-party translators. Our strategy now is to target specific government-sponsored bodies like the British Council who provide support and advice for their members doing business with China. We are helping them with their language services but also accessing their huge pool of overseas corporate members.

In implementing my strategy, I thought the biggest issue would be finance. Finance and budgeting are important but not top. Money is just a resource to grow. It is not a determining point for success.

Put simply, people have been my greatest implementation issue. I have had enormous challenges in recruiting and developing the right people for my business. If my team does not share my values, then the business has a problem. I need people with both the right professional (e.g., bilingual) skills and the right personal (e.g., client handling) skills. They need to be good at their core job but also demonstrate their fit to our business principles.

Cases

For example, I hired a lady who was good at project management but she turned out not to be very good with the client. After a lot of personal investment from me to help her develop these missing skills, I came to realize that she was not going to make it and had to change her for somebody who was good at both aspects. Getting the right shaped person to fill the gap has been one part of the issue.

Another part of the issue is motivating someone to change in line with our evolving strategy. For example, I had one great employee who was good at both translation and interpretation. But we wanted to develop our new training capability and she simply did not see any future for herself working within a training environment, so she said she wanted to leave.

In large corporations there are people dedicated to developing the right talent. But for small companies, the resources are not there and major strategic change happens more frequently. This is compounded by the fact that owners are so passionate about their own ideas they often don't realize that their staff are not bought in! Looking back, I should have developed my coaching skills to help my staff make the transition. Too many people have left my business because they did not understand our strategy, did not support it or did not share my business values.

Many are not interested in existing outside their comfort zone and like to work within their area of experience. To some extent, this is a function of the recent development of China where people are simply not experienced at being flexible in the work place nor appreciative of the importance of good customer service, nor have been empowered and encouraged to take risks.

People management is the top issue especially for SMEs and family businesses where competencies may not be right. The business owners need to think through the people-side of the plan and make sure they pay adequate attention to training the teams that are key to implementation.

For me, dividing my time effectively between business development tasks (like recruiting and training employees) and operational tasks has been a real personal challenge. In 2010 I decided that the best way for me to learn all the skills I needed was to do a respected MBA in a decent university. So in 2010–11 I took a year out from my business while I studied full-time for an MBA at Durham University in the UK.

After I came back to Beijing in late 2011, I saw things a lot more clearly. I now have a bigger picture of all the key management issues and am much better able to respond to them and grow the business.

Meeting other entrepreneurs from around the world during the MBA has been one of the biggest benefits for me. Realizing they had the same challenges as me and learning about how they overcame them has been a great experience. Moreover, this network is still on-going even after our course has finished. I now have a good international network of highly talented and motivated entrepreneurs with whom I can share problems and ideas.

I have also become clearer about how the business environment in China differs to the business environment in the West. This is a key factor and implementation must have local characteristics. For example, in the West everyone respects intellectual property. In China, there is simply not such a high value attached to it. We do not have a history of IP protection and for many Chinese it seems almost anti-competitive. If you are a Western company whose business model is based on licensing, you will definitely need to adjust your strategy in China. For example, you would do better to work hard on developing long-term trusted relationships than waving trade-marks around. We are a country governed by relationships not by laws. The strategy may be the same but the implementation tactics will be different.

Also, personally, I realized I needed to have more of a gambling spirit. I was very risk averse. For example, I would carefully keep to my budget every quarter. If I went over budget in one area, I would cut back in another area. However, if I had front-loaded my implementation spend, I would have speeded up implementation, increased revenues faster and probably cut out a long tail of incremental implementation (like additional training) later. This may be a bigger problem for female entrepreneurs who are used to managing household budgets. We like everything to be well-planned and steady. But we need to be more male and aggressive. Men start with the end goal and work out what investment is needed rather than seeing how much money there is in the pot and then working out what we can be achieved with it.

You definitely do not need an MBA to be a successful entrepreneur but it does help. I meet many Chinese entrepreneurs who have not studied and really have not thought enough about their market strategy and how to implement it.'

Cases

Globalserve: Combining account management with change management

■ Introduction

In 1997 a large electronics company issued their first global RFP (request for a proposal) to all their relevant service suppliers. One of these suppliers we shall call 'Globalserve'.

It was the first time a global RFP had been issued in the industry and it sent a few shock waves around the suppliers. Globalserve won that bid but the whole industry knew things would never be the same again. There would be more RFPs like this to come and everyone knew they had to figure out a way that such global service contracts could be supported in the future.

Today, Globalserve has implemented one of the best global account management (GAM) programs in their industry. This is the story of how that program was implemented and how it has helped Globalserve to become one of the industry's top performing suppliers.

■ GAM Version 1.0

The RFP triggered the appointment of a new global account director (GAD) at Globalserve who set about developing a plan to build a GAM capability. The plan was duly approved and a small team was assembled to get it into place. They quickly set about evaluating the contract and figuring out how the company could be pulled closer together to service it on a global scale. This would be no easy task. At the time, Globalserve was a very fragmented company split into multiple divisions, each with its own support functions like HR, sales, marketing and IT.

The team then spent a lot of time travelling around the divisions convincing them of the importance of serving the electronics account well. They tried to make sure that every division knew what was expected of them in delivering a consistent service to the electronics client.

This led to some good progress with the account's business. The team set up monthly and quarterly reports that looked at things like the level of client interaction and executive sponsorship. They also improved their IT capability to monitor the service levels being delivered by the divisions.

But it was still not developing a universal capability. As soon as the management of other clients was raised, the internal arguments started about where the account team should be located and which divisions should have control of the relationship. The company did not have a clear enough vision for GAM nor a good enough plan to move it forward.

One key problem was the then CEO was very supportive of GAM but was not prepared to address the divisional turf battles. Consequently, there was very slow progress in getting genuine GAM established across the business.

■ GAM Version 2.0 (International Client Management)

It was only with the appointment of a new CEO that the GAM idea received a new burst of energy. One of his first major actions was to abandon the regional division structure and strengthen the group's corporate function to implement common standards. Through this reorganization, a lot of fresh blood was infused into the leadership team. The team now had more experience in handling large international deals and a much greater interest in being the best global supplier in the industry. Even so, they did not rush to enforce a new solution.

They toured the company and spoke to all the business leaders in the major countries to learn more about the business. From this, they gained some clear insights into the status of GAM in the company:

- International client management still seemed to offer good potential.

- There was an opportunity to more effectively align the account teams and countries to deliver greater value both to clients and Globalserve. More consistency in the processes and tools used would drive this.

- The responsibilities of the key account managers needed to extend from a focus on relationship management to looking at the accounts as businesses.

- The reward process had to reflect the changing account management responsibilities.

- A more proactive approach toward business development was needed to unlock the true relationship potential.

- Globalserve's product and service development would greatly benefit from stronger client input.

Cases

Clearly the foundations needed renewed attention to develop the capability to serve and leverage Globalserve's multinational client relationships in the future. A proactive approach was required that would maximize the opportunities and also provide strong input to future service development.

One major foundation was the development of a company-wide performance framework. It identified several key drivers of success for the whole company but client sales and marketing was right at the top. It sent the message right across the company that winning and growing key account business was a major priority.

The internal environment was now much more conducive to GAM and in 2007 the company developed a 5-Step Plan to re-launch and implement it successfully (see Figure 1).

Five steps to implementation

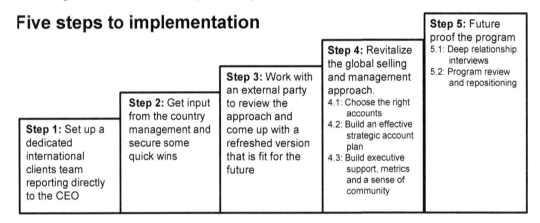

Step 1: Set up a dedicated international clients team reporting directly to the CEO

Step 2: Get input from the country management and secure some quick wins

Step 3: Work with an external party to review the approach and come up with a refreshed version that is fit for the future

Step 4: Revitalize the global selling and management approach.
4.1: Choose the right accounts
4.2: Build an effective strategic account plan
4.3: Build executive support, metrics and a sense of community

Step 5: Future proof the program
5.1: Deep relationship interviews
5.2: Program review and repositioning

Figure 1: Five steps to implementation

Step 1: Set up a dedicated international clients team reporting directly to the CEO

In 2007, Globalserve established a dedicated International Clients (IC) team with a senior director reporting directly to the CEO. The switch of name from GAM to IC was deliberate to show that this was a new initiative with the personal commitment of the CEO. The team was multifunctional and included people with experience in business development, account management, finance and IT. The IC team's mission was 'improving the top and bottom line of international clients, developing an industry-leading client management process to be implemented in a consistent way and installing a clearer, proactive business development strategy.' Quite simply, it had a brief to establish Globalserve's ability to manage international clients as a unique selling point.

Initially, twelve major international clients were selected for coordination by this team.

Step 2: Get input from the country management and score some quick wins

After installing the IC team, a more detailed review was organized with each of the main countries to gain a deeper understanding of the key concerns of the senior management team, understand its needs and promote good internal relationships. As a result of this work two key actions were implemented. First a communications plan was put in place aimed at building executive and country-level management buy-in. This plan had two aspects: resolving immediate internal issues related to how multinational contracts were handled and underlining the importance of executive management support for international client management. Secondly, meetings were set up with best-in-class Globalserve suppliers to learn how they managed their client base. Both of these actions gave the IC function some rapid internal credibility.

Step 3: Work with an external party to review the approach and come up with a refreshed version that is fit for the future

Moreover, there was a desire to consider not only the lessons learned and best practices of the program's early life but also other companies' experiences. From connecting with SAMA, including attending its conferences, Globalserve studied a case study about Jones Lang LaSalle's client management program. This led them to identify an external partner to sharpen Globalserve's own program. The company wanted an external specialist to challenge its current program in order to see how far it was from best in class. The partner provided the framework and experience for this and ran an exercise with the IC team to score Globalserve across numerous areas in a KAM Healthcheck. This was very useful in establishing a new IC program plan.

The IC program plan defined 10 key objectives for the program that kept everyone focused on the major deliverables. For example, the first two objectives were to:

'Create a vision of what world-class IC Management (ICM) looks like at Globalserve. Use this to gain agreement on the vision to achieve buy-in for necessary changes.'

Cases

'Take a program approach: Create reference terms and plan the journey to achieve the vision. Ensure that smaller countries are included in the plan. Treat the program as a challenge to embed change.'

The program was then split into the key areas as defined by the Healthcheck. Under each of these, there are specific action plans and clear definitions of success. This was Globalserve's day-to-day guide for developing its IC capability and delivering quick wins.

Step 4: Revitalize the global selling and management approach

4.1: Choosing the right accounts

The Healthcheck also highlighted the importance of good key account selection. Globalserve needed to focus more proactively on developing relationships with the right clients rather than reacting equally to problems or requests for proposals across all clients.

Even today, key account selection is not just about generating a list of top clients but also about managing a strategic sales pipeline. Globalserve required a tool to help the company populate its pipeline with the right names. Its key account selection model is actually a process that helps filter hundreds of international accounts into a short list of potential clients and then finally into its strategic account portfolio.

Important to the process is first to have a clear definition of the minimum requirements to be considered a key account. At Globalserve these are:

- The current plus potential volume of food and support/facilities services.
- A multi-country/multi-site presence.
- A willingness to sign a global agreement on a preferred/exclusive basis.
- A significant part of revenue generated outside the client's home country.

Secondly, those accounts that clear the minimum hurdle need to be prioritized. The account's importance is driven by potential (not current) business levels and the potential relationship, which are evaluated by scoring such factors as:

- Risk evaluation
- Partnering potential
- Cross-selling opportunity
- Ease of implementation.

In today's environment of fewer resources and more demanding customers it is even more important to adopt a process that distinguishes between investing in the clients of the future and the clients of the past.

4.2: Building an effective strategic account plan

Building an effective account plan is critical to ensuring relationship lock-in, uncovering new business development opportunities and driving rapid implementation. Globalserve's account plan is a true strategic, relationship-focused, comprehensive process to drive long-term account planning. It is the primary vehicle to push executive support internally and to drive better client support and alignment. The account plan is also a good tool for developing the strategic and business skills of the key account directors (KADs – i.e. Globalserve's account managers). For example, if the plan asks the right questions of the KAD, then it helps them ask the right questions to the client and question the relationship in the right way.

4.3: Building executive support, metrics and a sense of community

The Healthcheck also helped Globalserve focus on further development of the KAM infrastructure, including:

■ *Senior executive support.* One simple task was to ask the CEO to provide a statement about the importance of ICM to the company and to the achievement of the business unit objectives. In parallel, the visibility of ICM performance was raised by adding the sales and profits line of ICM to the company's strategic management and performance process. ICM is now a regular item on the board agenda and integrated into the country reports.

■ *Good internal reporting.* Standard internal management reports are now produced with the KADs that show quarterly sales, profitability, satisfaction and account penetration figures for each IC. These are used to review performance with the key account teams and are available online to the country business units.

■ *Good external reporting.* In addition to the existing financial performance reporting of its clients, Globalserve has also launched an online client loyalty/satisfaction measurement tool. This gives Globalserve a robust assessment of a client's satisfaction with the delivery of its services and how likely it is to renew a contract. The latter measure is a key indicator of loyalty and provides Globalserve with useful statistics on the progress being made across the IC portfolio.

Cases

- *Measuring client penetration.* A customer relationship management tool is used to track client penetration. A database is used to identify current market share with the ICs and the areas of largest potential growth.

- *Establishing an ICM community with the clients.* Globalserve is establishing an online ICM community that includes contacts, relevant articles and e-news for KADs. In addition the company is installing client web portals (extranets). These include contract performance reporting, contact information, a contract archive, a best-practice archive and key dates for the diary.

Together these building blocks ensure that good science is balanced with good execution and that the IC program maintains momentum.

Step 5: Refine the solution and future-proof the program

Globalserve has put many of the key components of its program in place over the past few years. However, it recognizes that this is a continuous journey requiring periodic major reviews and repositioning.

Work will always be needed to inoculate ICM from future challenges and some of the activities now being worked on are to:

1 Implement a stronger *executive sponsorship* program (modeled on Siemens AG's approach). Each executive committee member is assigned a current or prospective IC account. The sponsor then plays a significant part helping to develop business with the account. Examples of this include a sponsor becoming quickly involved with any health and safety incidents and assisting with overcoming internal or external cross-functional hurdles. The account plan plays a substantial role in keeping the sponsors updated on the client relationship.

2 Expand the key account *community* beyond just the KADs to all the stakeholders at Globalserve. This will include integrating the account plans more closely with the country business plans and seeking increased involvement of the countries in ICM.

3 Develop a universal gold standard of performance across the KADs by developing a KAD *competency model.* This will be used to assess training needs and close skill, knowledge and behavior gaps.

4 Develop *joint account plans* with selected clients to cement the relationship and further drive strategic alignment.

In 2010/11, Globalserve wanted to integrate ICM much more closely with client needs, the overall business strategy and the personal goals of the

KADs. It therefore decided to ask some of its clients for an assessment of how well the ICM approach was working for them.

Rather than undertake a shallow survey across all its clients, it decided it would be more insightful to get a deep assessment across a representative sample of clients. In order to get an honest assessment of their opinions it commissioned an outside agent to undertake a deep relationship insight survey across the decision-makers in each chosen client. Typically, this meant interviewing senior client executives from global procurement, operations and the global regions.

The findings from the survey were presented back to Globalserve and were used to evaluate what was going well, what could be done better and to set the vision, goals and action of the program for the next three years.

The major elements of this strategy have been approved by the CEO during the regular reviews that he holds with the IC team.

■ Conclusions

Not only is Globalserve growing its existing client revenues but it is also winning new prestigious clients every month. The IC program has been a key factor of this success providing:

- ■ Improved performance and service delivery with international clients
- ■ Supporting the bid process for new clients
- ■ Achieving greater consistency of service across the business
- ■ More effective, efficient and aligned global activities
- ■ A deeper, broader knowledge of clients with much greater insight about their key issues
- ■ Better appreciation of account attractiveness, a more objective account qualification process and reduced internal discussion about priorities. This has resulted in much greater focus and energy applied to the most attractive clients.
- ■ Improved communication and information flow internally with greater teamwork across the business.

The IC program is a very significant vehicle for helping the company's global business strategy get implemented locally. It has been a fundamental mechanism for delivering Globalserve's multiservice offerings into its key markets in a turbulent economic climate.

Cases

However, for any other company embarking on such a program, it should be stressed that it is no good going about it in an amateur way. The key to success is taking a pragmatic but professional change management approach and balancing sensible science with focused execution. This includes:

- Secure and maintain real senior commitment to the program
- Plan some quick victories to demonstrate early success
- Use outsiders such as consultants to provide an external best-practice solution and challenge the internal mind-set
- Make sure there is a balance between science and execution. The exercise must be quickly converted into action, otherwise momentum will be lost.
- Keep the tools and processes simple. Don't try to model everything.
- Take the program seriously by utilizing a professional change management approach. This means having a carefully constructed program plan and team and ensuring that the key players have real business experience and authority.

Throughout this journey, Globalserve has been excellent at two things:

1 Combining both the technical needs and the change needs into a single market-driven change plan required to get the solution in place successfully and globally.

2 Converting that high level plan into detailed actions and linking those actions to personal performance objectives for all the key stakeholders. For example, there is a specific process integration tracker that looks at the progress of implementing 10 elements of the ICM client by client. These elements include whether they have the following in place: an executive sponsor, an up-to-date crisis/risk mitigation plan, an up-to-date client plan, a recently completed client survey, regular client reviews, etc.

During economic downturns, not only are the good implementers better prepared for tougher client demands, but they can also take advantage of the cutbacks in their competitors' budgets to strengthen client relationships further, exploit new opportunities quicker and reap the rewards faster this year – as well as into the future.

IEB: Implementing a new mindset

Alistair Taylor, Director, TaylorHoughton

'I worked in a large international engineering business (which we will abbreviate to 'IEB') for much of the last decade. Reporting directly to the CEO, my role focused on driving 'best in class' key account management practices across several different business divisions each of which dealt with a range of blue-chip customers. The global businesses focused on premium solutions for markets including automotive, medical, drinks dispensers and oil and gas.

Throughout the 1990s the company performed reasonably well but at the start of that decade (the early 2000s) a new and highly ambitious CEO was brought in.

He quickly discovered that each division had its own key account planning process and that the majority of the resulting key account plans were inadequate. There was little real sparkle with little to get really excited about.

To open the eyes of the global sales team to the philosophies, processes and practices required for 'new growth' the CEO arranged for 110 people in sales and leadership positions to attend courses on key account management (KAM) at Cranfield School of Management in the UK.

Following this, over 60 key roles were redefined as key account managers (KAMs). Each KAM was then required to quickly develop new and more expansive key account plans.

Far from being an academic exercise and perhaps to the amazement of many in the business, each and every one of these plans was personally read from cover to cover by the CEO himself.

His conclusion? There was some improvement, but even after the training many failed to identify good customer insights, new opportunities and clearly define the actions required. The plans were too descriptive, with standard 2–3% per annum growth rates built in, rather than more expansive options. He felt that many of the KAMs were not getting to grips with leveraging the firm's full capabilities to develop deep customer relationships and bold new sources of revenue.

Cases

Recognizing that addressing such a shortfall required more than relatively straightforward adjustments to a planning process the CEO devoted more resources to KAM.

I was therefore appointed as the new KAM Director to develop the right people and processes to deliver success across all the key business divisions.

With a small centrally based team we set up assessment and development centers for the existing KAMs and sales leaders. The assessment was tough and many of the original KAMs fell short of the demanding targets we set. Several were redeployed and it became clear that some new recruitment to key roles was required.

Training and coaching programs were also put in place and an internal 'KAM Academy' was set up. This not only initiated and arranged training but provided KAMs from across the world with shared market and customer insight, internal consultancy to develop appropriate account management processes and better access to senior management.

The central team also had a key role in managing the change in philosophy across the company. Some senior managers in the various divisions were great supporters of the changes, others less so.

To increase the focus on excellent account planning, and execution of such plans, we set a target of developing 10 excellent account plans with each of the five key business divisions. Whilst this was only a small percentage of the total number of customers the company dealt with, once we had 50 good account plans in place most of our key growth and strategic opportunities would be covered to a high standard.

To foster ownership the CEO requested that each business nominate their own top 10 accounts and develop their own account plans for them. We kept track of progress by asking the presidents of each division how the account plans were coming along, how they were being used and occasionally reviewing one or two.

So long as the division's overall results were in line with the targets set, the CEO let them get on with things and deliberately kept at a distance on this area. He insisted that we needed to work with the divisions carefully and not push them too hard.

It was during one of my many discussions with him that I recommended a renewed focus be put on our key account plans. I felt things were moving along but the plans were not getting enough senior executive support. I wanted to get the CEO and executive actively and visibly engaged in reviewing the plans. It was my belief that if a handful were being formally reviewed, with detailed feedback, a powerful message would quickly be spread across the group.

I quickly received support and we managed to set up twice-yearly face-to-face account plan review sessions involving our board (our C-Suite of top executives) and a selected number of KAMs. Each account manager would present a plan for two hours, allowing wide ranging interrogation, debate and constructive sharing of ideas.

Before each of these sessions the board chose what type of account plan they wished to focus on. If they were interested in a particular industry (e.g., nuclear power), a specific area of innovation or a particular geography, then this guidance would be given to the businesses. The division (or divisions) would then choose the appropriate account plan for review.

This was the most important presentations that a KAM could make internally and so, once the account had been chosen, I would work with the KAM and help him or her develop the plan. In some cases, this involved polishing the plan and helping to summarize it effectively. In other cases, there was a serious amount of further work to be done including gathering market information and identifying key strategies, options and priority actions.

During the two hours spent going through each plan, the board would be generally positive towards the KAM but did not flinch from asking some very pointed questions such as, 'What would be required to double our market share with this customer?' or 'Are we investing too heavily in the wrong programs?'

Also, the business leaders present did not escape scrutiny. The CEO would question the relevant business leaders to make sure they also had a good handle on the activities of their account managers and key customers.

On a few occasions where the CEO thought the presentation or answers were not up to standard, he would certainly let the relevant president know in private afterwards.

There was good follow-up after these reviews. Progress with the implementation of the plan would be reported back to the board by the relevant president and, if necessary, the KAM could be recalled to give a direct update. This gave a strong message to the business units that good implementation was just as important as a good plan.

Of course, there was push back from some of the businesses who did not see why one of their top salespeople should be sidelined into spending considerable time writing a good internal presentation, rather than getting on with the immediate business of selling. Furthermore, some project-based businesses did not see the full value in KAM given that their relationships tended to be project-by-project. So some strong 'internal selling' was undertaken and a more flexible approach was put in place. Not every plan was required to follow the same templates, but adherence to core principles, practices and stretch-targets, were expected.

Other businesses, however, were much more positive about it and keen on getting a good process in place. Either way, the net effect of this was that the KAMs, their line manager and the division president became much more engaged in the whole process.

The CEO saw KAM as not just as a framework for coordinating our efforts but as an opportunity to get his whole top team aligned to develop a more strategic and global organization. Reviewing key plans was a highly relevant activity for all members of the board. I remember that during one particularly insightful presentation, the finance director (CFO) said, 'That is really helpful and I will recount some of this insight when I'm talking to analysts at next week's results presentations.'

The account planning reviews became just one of several ways that the CEO and board personally demonstrated their support for KAM.

A further approach undertaken was a twice-yearly global KAM forum. This would be a phone-in with the CEO and would typically be done 2–3 times in one day to suit different time zones. Over 100 KAMs and business leaders would call in. The CEO would provide an overview of the progress and challenges in the KAM program and I would present on best practice approaches from within and outside the business. The results of the account reviews were often discussed during these calls. The global KAMs could then ask questions directly. As well as demonstrating the CEO's support, the forums also created a sense of community amongst the scattered KAMs.

Five years later, the results have been tremendous:

- Target levels of profitability are being achieved.
- The board is much more involved in the whole process.
- There has been a dramatic improvement in the quality of plans.
- The key accounts are now much more aligned in delivering the overall business strategy.
- Significant learning took place across the company about what KAM is all about and what a good key account plan looks like.

- There is a much higher return on the investment in the key account relationships.

In particular, the cultural mindset across the business has changed from being safe and incremental to being much more ambitious and entrepreneurial.

Finally, the business has developed a new breed of KAM leader who is more like a general manager of a customer focused business rather than a salesperson. The KAMs are now great connectors who put the right people together and who are not frightened to ask for help if needed. They understand that they cannot implement plans on their own and should act as a single point of coordination for the account, leading multifunctional teams to get the right solutions in place at each key account. Indeed, we found that some of the best KAMs did not come from a sales background at all. At this level, selling is less important than leading and managing. This comes down more to their personal attributes than their functional background.

Ultimately, there are three things that made a real difference to the implementation of this program:

1 Sponsorship from the top. It was active not just words.

2 A recognition that a different type of KAM blueprint was required across the business divisions.

3 An appreciation that strategic change has a political dimension which must be managed carefully and which affects how quickly you can undertake change.

This was a significant change exercise and I was privileged to have been at the heart of making it happen.'

Cases

ITSalesco: The challenge of a complex sales-driven company

This case involves a global IT company (which we will call ITSalesco). 'Joanna' worked for it until recently and explained the problems she experienced with implementing marketing plans there.

'We had a regional organization structure and I worked in the European marketing team. The regions were pretty autonomous and we did things quite differently to how things were done elsewhere like the US. For example, we had our own matrix organization of EMEA country-level business units and EMEA-specific industry sectors. We also had our own marketing planning process where the appropriate marketing manager would present their plan and ROI forecasts to the relevant leadership team who would then allocate the marketing budget accordingly.

One problem was that despite being a global IT company, our systems could not track the performance of these marketing investments. We would know of course if sales were up or down in a particular country or industry. We could also track sales by individual accounts and by individual products and services. However, we could not make any connection between the investment in a particular marketing campaign and the sales results. If the campaign had not run at all, it was impossible to understand what the sales would have been anyway. Similarly, we might invest in a 100 promotional events across Europe but had no idea if a few other events that we had not invested in, would have given us a higher ROI. We were unable to verify what parts of the plan worked and what parts did not.

Another problem was that, at our core, we were a very sales focused company. The leadership team did not understand what marketing is all about and valued selling much more than marketing. There was always a strong focus on getting the sale and if there was a sales problem, it was often marketing that got the blame. The common view was that marketing supports sales.

This culture was apparent in the bi-annual campaign review meeting. Every six months, all the European marketing campaigns would be rolled together and reviewed. This was no simple task with anywhere between

180–260 separate campaigns to review! Unfortunately, the whole review process was unscientific and driven by gut feeling. The sales managers would run the show and axe those campaigns that they simply felt were not working in delivering immediate sales.

To make matters worse, nobody seemed to be bothered that there were hundreds of leads in the CRM system that were not being followed up properly. For example, if someone called us as a result of a campaign we had run and said they would be happy for a call-back, this was either not done at all by the relevant sales manager, or done in an ill-informed way by a junior person in our inside sales team.

Implementing strategic marketing plans in this context was always going to be an uphill struggle. We had multiple and overlapping layers of marketing across Europe and no one was sure who was in charge of what. We had a carrot and stick approach to our sales and marketing efforts: when things went well, the sales managers got rewarded and when things went wrong, marketing's budget got cut!'

Kennametal:
Keeping marketing plans on track

Francois Gau, Director of Strategic Marketing, Kennametal

When assessing the performance of a firm in keeping its marketing plans on track, I would like to frame my response based upon the type of 'plan' in question. There are two types of plans in my opinion:

The first one is around introducing to market a product or service that is basically 'more of the same', i.e. a routine modification, extension or upgrade to an existing product or service. In this case we know the customer needs fairly well and the technology/processes required to match those needs. At Kennametal we have a stage gate process that will support this well. It progresses ideas to commercialization through five key gates. The first two stages are really about business planning. Stage 3 is product development proper. Stage 4 is beta testing and Stage 5 is preparation for commercialization. We have worked hard on this award winning process and our new product development process has been cut from two years to less than six months. Indeed, this is a major objective for Kennametal and we are achieving our target of having 40% of our sales from new products which are less than five years old. Multi-functional teams look at every aspect of the issue and the team gets rewarded if they achieve their performance targets.

The second area is new-new or adjacent projects. These are new markets and/or new technologies to Kennametal. Here, the process of implementation is by design more flexible in order to address uncertainty. We basically have two tracks to follow: One led by our technology group to look at new technology introductions to market and one led by marketing to look at how to enter new markets with existing technologies. Both might converge for new/new. Our track record in both processes is pretty good. Looking backward, however, there are two important success factors:

1 Success is dependent on good executive sponsorship.
2 There must be a dedicated leader to run the project. By dedicated, I mean full-time, not part-time.

Moreover, that leader must have passion about the product or service, must be evangelical and have some authority over the required resources. He/she must be charismatic and the right person at the helm. Unfortunately, the risk is to pick the wrong person because they are available rather than because they have the right stuff. This must be watched for and acted upon swiftly through project review processes.

Regardless of the type of project there are a few generic key success factors:

- Projects need to aim at displacing old stuff with new stuff. If we don't 'kill or prune' the old, we will never get enough room or resources to grow and will be grounded in the past.

- We also need to make the distinction between approval and commitment. By commitment, we mean that not only has the plan been signed-off but all the resources are committed and will be in the right place at the right time. When a business plan is approved, it should get the total resources it needs but this might not happen for several reasons. We need to be watchful for these pitfalls. For example:

   ☐ The approval is granted off budget cycle and cannot be funded without major re-shuffling of all the other projects. Resources may be needed mid-year and may have to wait until the start of the next financial year.

   ☐ In a highly matrixed structure, decision by consensus might take a long time to get all stakeholders to commit the resources required. Executive sponsorship might be crucial there.

This all works fine for 95% of the time, and our regular review process take care of the issues. However, 5% of the time the project requires a serious commitment across the business to get it implemented. This tends to happen on new–new projects that do not necessarily follow a standard process and needs 'corporate' support. Great organizations are good at getting new and disruptive ideas embraced and applied. You can see how effective Apple is in doing that.

We have also worked hard over the past five years at getting our organization structured right. We neither wanted to be a loosely federated set of business units with no corporate marketing support nor a highly centralized corporation that may become a hindrance to local business units getting close to the customer. We have worked together to create a hybrid model in which the corporate marketing function supports the business units where necessary. We make the distinction between upstream (e.g., forecasting, strategic planning) and downstream marketing activities (e.g., customer service, application expertise, local branch management). We might get involved in any part of that value stream but only where it supports the local business units.

Key to implementation is the translation between the central marketing organization and local execution. Planning may be led by the marketing function but the best implementation successes are where these plans have been diligently converted into regional plans where the product is launched when, for example, the sales teams have been trained and the customer service teams are ready.

Another key to success is the structure of the review committees: They must be composed of senior credible executives (e.g., VPs or Directors, etc.) they have a say on resource allocation and acceptance of plans. This again, comes ultimately down to good leadership: leadership by the project leader and leadership by the company.

Lafarge Jordan: Re-cementing a leadership position

Hussam Asmar, Marketing Manager, Lafarge Jordan

■ Summary

Developing and implementing a marketing plan is not easy. The go-to-market strategy has to be right, the change strategy has to be right and then the implementation work has to be done right on both. If you get any of these steps wrong, your chances of success are much diminished.

These are also fundamental steps that apply around the world. As an example, in this article we look at the case of Lafarge Cement, Jordan (LCJ). Here, a marketing plan was successfully developed and implemented that made a significant difference to the business.

This was no accident. Good principles were put into practice that reduced the risks of failure in each step of the journey. The good news is that these principles can be copied by most organizations to improve the success rate of their own marketing plans.

■ Introduction

Lafarge is a world leader in building materials and has group sales of €16 billion. This includes cement, aggregates, concrete and gypsum. It has 76,000 employees and operates in 78 countries.

Lafarge Cement is a global division within the group and has sales of around €2 billion worldwide. Lafarge Cement, Jordan (LCJ) is one of many national business units within this division and operates with its own management team (reporting to the division and group).

■ The old simple world

Things were very different in 2005. The cement market in Jordan was then still controlled by LCJ as it was the only manufacturer. LCJ enjoyed a near monopoly of the market with minor imports occurring in the peak season. Cement buyers from all sectors had little bargaining power and

Cases

generally had to accept whatever products were made for them. At that time, LCJ's capacity matched the market demand nicely.

However, following deregulation of the market by the Jordanian Government, four new competitors then announced that they were going to build cement plants in Jordan. It was clear to Lafarge that the landscape was about to change fast. In three years' time, the new manufacturers would enter the market in force and the total market supply would exceed demand (see Figure 1). If nothing was done, LCJ's market share would shrink as customers were given much greater choice.

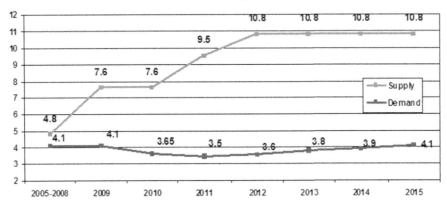

Figure 1: Forecasted supply and demand of cement in Jordan. Source: Lafarge analysis

So, in 2006 the LCJ Marketing Department was founded with the brief to develop and implement a new marketing strategy to decisively deal with this major challenge.

■ The implementation journey

Although this was a new department (and, in many ways, a new concept for the LCJ business) a very deliberate path was followed to ensure that a good marketing plan was written and implemented successfully. These are the key steps along that path:

Step 1: Develop the new marketing plan

Conduct a thorough marketing audit

First, they had to come up with the right strategy and capture it in a new marketing plan.

The first task was to complete a detailed marketing audit across the whole downward supply chain. The audit included extensive internal and external research across all channels and end-users covering customer satisfaction surveys, brand image, customer usage and customer attitudes.

The audit revealed many gaps that needed to be addressed. These were summarized into three main areas of product, image and service (see Figure 2) and formed the three pillars of the marketing strategy.

In this case, we will concentrate on the work done in the product area which includes implementation of a new product mix, a new pricing policy and new branding for the products. Nevertheless, we should emphasize that these would not have been successful without completing the full plan.

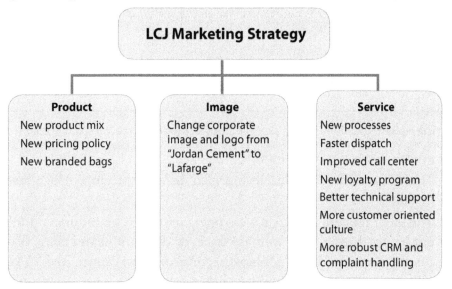

Figure 2: The three dimensions of the LCJ marketing strategy

A more detailed product-specific audit was conducted from 2006 to 2007. This used various research techniques including both qualitative and quantitative methods. The aim of the audit was to:

- Understand the usage and attitude of the end-users in various applications including the volumes consumed and preferred product characteristics for each application.

- Understand the buyer's behavior and define the role of everyone involved in the various purchasing processes (see Figure 3).

- Understand the brand image of the current product line and define what the elements of a successful cement brand would look like.

Summary: Decision making process

Engineer ➡ Contractor ➡ Home builder

- The ultimate user, the home builder, will most often ask for advice on cement brand from the contractor and sometimes from the engineer
- For masonry work (but not concrete) they will sometimes ask for advice from the mason/worker
- Contractors sometimes decide on the brand but more often are guided by the engineers and sometimes by the homeowner
- If contractors are not sure or require advice they will predominantly rely on the advice of engineers
- Engineers will often test the product in the lab with testing cubes
- Engineers therefore emerge as very important specifiers
    - Engineers are an important communications target
    - More direct marketing should be done with engineers
- Contractors also have an important role to play in the decision making process

Figure 3: The cement decision-making process (Source: Leading Edge Research, Jordan)

From this it was discovered that:

- There was only one clearly branded Lafarge product ('Tashtibat') available

- The other Lafarge products were being marketed under many different names. In fact there were up to seven different names being used for the same product! Moreover, some of these names like 'PPC',' OPC' and 'SRC' were actually technical terms, which had no meaning to consumers.

- Many building masons were confused by the terms and could not identify which bag was which. For example, OPC was often confused with PPC. Some masons simply went by the color of the bag and associated a completely different product name with it (e.g., 'Rashadieh' – which is actually the location of the manufacturing plant in Southern Jordan).

- The cement bags had detailed technical specifications written on them which meant nothing to the majority of users.

Clearly, there was a problem with the brand and the branding concept. Figure 4 shows the four old names for the product (on the left) and some of the names under which they were marketed (on the right).

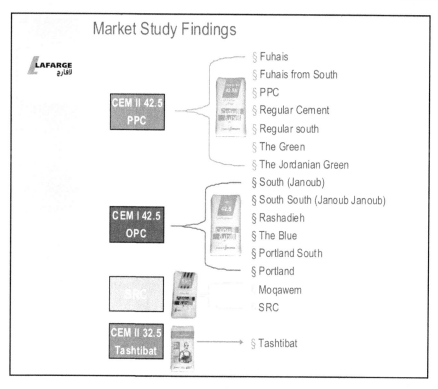

Figure 4: Lafarge product brands and names in 2006

However, the product audit also revealed some interesting opportunities:

- New domestically produced cement products made by Jordanian manufacturers would be seen as inferior to the Lafarge products.

- General building cement with a low price can have a good market share if correctly priced and positioned.

- There was an unmet need for a specialized high-strength product for concrete.

- Cement was sold as a pure commodity. Price was the only variable and there was no real value in branding.

The earlier marketing audit also uncovered some other useful insights:

- The reason there were no customer complaints logged was not because customers were happy. The problem was that there was no CRM system in place and the front-line employees were not customer oriented.

- There were no 'pull' marketing activities on the end consumer. In other words, all marketing activities were aimed at pushing products through retailers to consumers. There were no activities to stimulate demand by consumers and stimulate them to ask for Lafarge products.

Cases

The audit showed that Lafarge needed to gain a deeper understanding of its customers. Consequently, a lot of work was then done (using internal resources) to understand the needs of cement buyers and cluster those buyers into appropriate needs-based segments.

Develop a good strategy

Using the above analysis, LCJ set about developing their new marketing strategy for Jordan. A key part of this strategy was the establishment of a new brand proposition. This would involve an overhaul of the product mix with different cement products designed and targeted at specific customer segments. The strategy meant having a simplified range of three products labeled *Basic, Classic* and *Premium*. The Premium product would be a newly positioned high-end product that would work well with concrete and would be difficult for competitors to copy. Each of the new products would have faster hardening time, a new color tint (outside the traditional color specification) and be high strength.

The strategy also included creating a new brand identity across the range. This included the following changes:

- Link the product strategy to the application of the product, i.e. the product line should be designed to better reflect the real application of the product by the end-user.

- Ensure good use of the Lafarge umbrella brand to endorse products with the quality, trust and expertise of an internationally recognized company.

- Gain a deep understanding of end-user applications and use this as a basis for segmentation and product mapping.

- Labeling would be in Arabic as the majority of buyers could not understand English.

- To help customers differentiate between the products, any new brand names would be closely associated with the product usage and/or its features.

- To further distinguish the new range, colors would be unique for each product and, if necessary, different to the previous colors used (see Figure 5).

- The new brand names would be registered both locally and in key export markets.

- There would be a clear positioning and brand choice from standard application/low price up to specialized application/high price (see Figure 6).

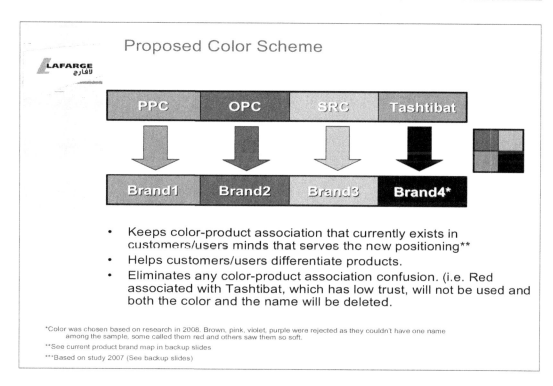

Figure 5: Old and new brand color scheme

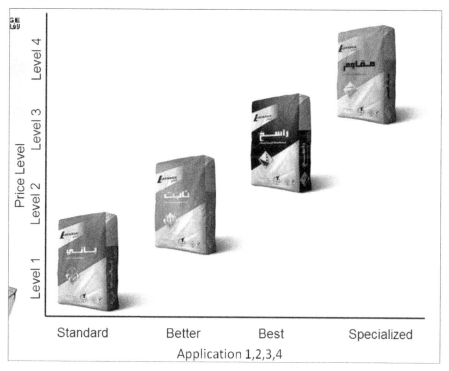

Figure 6: New product positioning

It was clear to the LCJ management team that they needed a good local media partner to help promote its new strategy. To do this, the findings from the segmentation work were also used to develop a specification for selected local media agencies to pitch against. From this exercise, a good local media partner was chosen.

With their support and further research a new promotional campaign was developed. It utilized a mix of media based on the following findings:

■ The message should be simple. Visuals on the bag and in the ads should reflect the usage.

■ The most effective way of communicating with targeted users (masons, contractors and engineers) was through point-of-sale brochures and technical sheets. It was also discovered that there would be a strong interest in awareness seminars conducted by LCJ representatives at the users' construction sites.

■ Outdoor advertising was also seen to have high levels of reach especially billboards and posters in bus stations (where masons are picked up for daily work).

■ Radio was found to be the best broadcast media. It was listened to by the target users during their daily commute to and from work and was true if travelling by public transport or by car. Some users also listened while working on site. In particular, two radio stations (*Fann FM* and *Amen FM*) were the most popular. However, it was also noted that preferences change during the month of Ramadan when radio *Hayat* briefly becomes the most popular.

■ Newspapers (such as *Al-Rai, Al Ghad* and *Addustour*) are read by site supervisors on-site but not on a daily basis.

■ TV has a very low reach amongst targeted users.

LCJ found that with this new promotional campaign, they could reach their target market at a much lower spend than their competitors. They even bought the copyright of a song from a former well-known state TV show which had run for decades but was now off-air. The words worked well and were changed from '*arms of labor* are needed to build the country' to '*cement* is needed to build the country.' The images in Figure 7 show examples of how the campaign was implemented.

Figure 7: Sample images from the promotional campaign

One of the final pieces to the strategy was pricing. It was agreed that LCJ would operate clear price gaps between the three products to underline their differentiation (see Figure 8). It would also deliberately set out to charge a premium price for each product, underlining its brand strength. This would also leave the new competitors to compete on price. When they do enter the marketplace, it was anticipated that a price war would break out and they would be left fighting for the bottom price, leaving LCJ safe in the high quality corner.

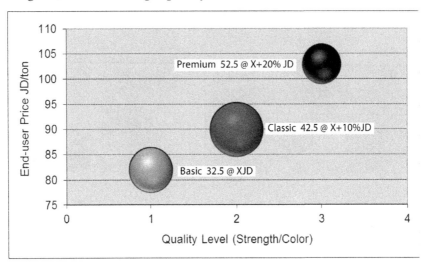

Figure 8: New pricing policy

Careful consideration was also given to retailers. To get these on board, a two-day program was set up to train their sales teams (see Figure 10). This covered all aspects of the LCJ re-branding exercise and focused on giving them some key selling skills that they could use to help improve their whole business, not just the throughput of the LCJ products.

Further consideration was given to the *internal* stakeholders within LCJ. A deliberate policy was established to treat the company as an internal market. Relationship mapping was undertaken to identify the key Lafarge staff who would significantly influence the success of the plan. Discussions were then undertaken with these influencers to understand their specific roles around the strategy. Eventually, a specific plan of action was drawn up that combined presentations, seminars, meetings and informal discussions to ensure that the key internal stakeholders understood the rationale behind the strategy, the strategy itself and how it benefitted themselves and their department (see Figure 10). These influencers played a key part in both shaping the strategy and supporting its implementation.

Figure 9: A training session for the sales team

Figure 10: An internal Lafarge briefing session

Test the plan

Throughout this step of developing the strategy, many aspects were tested both internally and externally.

Externally, working with the media partner, end consumers were recruited into focus groups which were then used to test different brand propositions. Also, the new promotional campaign was tested in two ways: first, by discussing its key points with other local agencies and second, by seeking the feedback of a global research agency (IPSOS).

The pricing tactics were tested by building a new bespoke pricing simulation model based on conjoint analysis and using all the market intelligence that had been gathered. This would establish the price elasticity of demand (price and usage) over different price points for each product and each target segment.

Internally, in addition to various technical product development tests, at each key stage of strategy development, the key stakeholders were updated and their input sought. Where necessary, support was sought from higher up the company in order to deal with any roadblocks that could not be resolved locally.

Write the plan

The 2006 the LCJ marketing plan was duly written up which defined the strategy in broad terms, e.g., 'introduce a simplified 3-product choice and establish a wider pricing pattern.' The plan also included the promotional tactics required to change the behaviors of both buyers and consumers.

Step 2: Initiate implementation with a pilot

At the end of 2008, the first batch of new cement bags had been manufactured. This batch was tested first by standard technical tests within LCJ and then by giving them away free to selected pilot retailers. The feedback from these retailers was excellent and in the second quarter of 2009 the new promotional campaign was launched.

Internally, to strengthen commitment by LCJ, the following 10 key actions were taken:

1 Re-calibrate who the key internal stakeholders are (based on experience in developing the strategy).

2 Celebrate the successes with the key *proponents* of the strategy and use hard facts and figures to argue the case with the key *opponents* of the strategy.

3 Develop FAQs and talk sheets to be used by everyone to ensure a standard and consistent message.

4 Communicate successes using real-time newsflashes about the products on the company communications network.

5 Develop a special issue of the internal *Cement Leaders* magazine with coverage on the new products, usages and their positioning.

6 Develop *product champions*. This idea was blessed by HR. Senior respected operations staff or managers were invited to become a product champion. Once recruited, they were trained in the new strategy and how to implement it. In a cascade approach, these product champions then trained more than 600 employees across the company, especially those in contact with customers either directly or indirectly. The product champions were key ambassadors for change and significantly influenced the success of the implementation by:

  ■ Communicating the company's message to all their team members through formal and informal meetings, presentations, discussions, etc.

  ■ Providing a thorough explanation to their team members and sharing positive and consistent word-of-mouth messages to the market.

7 Setup a LCJ certified salesperson training program. Through this program, the top 15 retail sales teams were trained in how to sell the new product range.

8 Bring the top 100 customers to the LCJ plant to attend free one-day seminars on the new product range.

9 Create incentives for everyone in the supply chain.

10 Measure and interpret brand performance (from the pilot).

On the last point, each month, the success of the pilot was carefully evaluated by looking at various KPIs. These findings were presented monthly to an executive committee composed of the Jordan general manager and his senior management team (typically the VP of each function). Included in this committee was:

The technical VP who played a key part in ensuring that the speed of implementation was right. If the products were introduced too quickly, then there was a danger they would not have the right quality.

The procurement VP who was kept up-to-date so he could order the right amount of raw materials, minimize overall stock levels of old bags and secure new bags on time.

Cases

Of course, not everything went to plan. Despite all the preparation and planning, some technical staff in Lafarge did not understand or like the new brand concept. After all, LCJ had enjoyed a long leadership position with the existing products so why change? Here, the hard evidence from the research and the pilots was used to convince them to give the new products a chance.

Step 3: Accelerate implementation with a rollout

After the success of the pilot implementation, the 'LCJ Certified Salesperson' training program was rolled out to the full base of retailers (including small shop owners) right across the Jordan marketplace. In addition, the one-day customer awareness seminars were rolled out to a further 500 customers who were brought in to the plant to get the briefing.

Each month, the brand performance from the full campaign was measured, interpreted and reviewed. Where necessary, adjustments were made (e.g., to the mix of media, the frequency of advertising, the training materials). This was done both to test new ideas and to reduce underperforming activities.

Indeed, the results were so impressive that the campaign was then rolled out to other countries in the Middle East.

Step 4: Refine implementation and improve everything

One of these new ideas was a bonus mechanism that would incentivize every link in the supply chain towards LCJ products. This would fill the missing 'pull' element to the marketing strategy.

The concept was quite simple. Lafarge would develop scratch cards that traders could then give to their customers for each ton of cement bought. The campaign would run during the peak May–July building period in Jordan. There were three top prizes of a brand new car, plus other prizes of air conditioning units, vouchers and home appliances. In addition, traders and Lafarge salespeople would also get gifts and holidays based on the volume of cement sold over the period.

The campaign was supported by full training and promotion including flyers, posters, SMS and radio advertising (see Figure 11). Materials would feature prominently at point-of-sale and even enclosed with Lafarge invoices to customers. Furthermore, scratch card winners would also be featured in newspapers, posters, flyers and further radio ads.

Key to the success of the campaign was a clear understanding of the risks and counter-measures required to countenance them. The key risks and actions are shown in Figure 12.

Figure 11: 'Scratch and Win' poster

Risk	Counter-measure
Competitors quickly copying the idea	Confidentiality. The planning team was kept to a small and trusted number of people. Fast execution. Make full use of the element of surprise with a bold, fast and decisive launch.
Scratch cards handed out not linked to volume	Good integrity. Strict controls and monitoring were established for handing out the cards.
Promotion bags being sold after the end of the campaign and product shortages during the campaign	Tight stock management. More frequent stock checks were undertaken during and after the campaign to ensure stock levels were right.

Figure 12: Risks and counter-measures in implementing the 'Scratch and Win' campaign

In 2010 the campaign was implemented. The results were tremendous. Not only did the campaign run without any significant competitor response but LCJ saw a significant market share gain during the campaign period, which continued after the campaign ended. Lafarge was the first cement producer to implement such a pull campaign in Jordan.

Cases

On a broader note, there is still room for improvement in every step of the process. Surveys can be more insightful, the simulation model can be more accurate, the measurement systems can be more real-time, the planning template can be more effective, and the internal change plan can be more specific. But these are all improvements that are being worked on.

■ Conclusions

This exercise shows that even for a relatively small business unit within a large global organization, using some key principles can really make a difference to implementation success. For LCJ, these are:

1 Start by getting to **really understand the market**. Market research reveals many surprising facts and new ideas

2 Use **testing** extensively to develop, refine and implement the strategy

3 **Use pilots and rollouts** to manage the change

4 **Anticipate** actions and reactions both internally and externally to the strategy – and prepare counter moves

5 Have **a clear market strategy and change strategy**. They are like two sides of the same coin.

6 Make sure your strategies are converted to **practical, detailed communication and action plans**

7 **Secure buy-in from all your key people** (not just sales and marketing). There are many functions involved in implementation. Work hard to coordinate and align with all these departments and plants.

8 **Use hard facts** to fight your corner and make the best use of whatever resources are available

9 Develop simple **Talk Sheets and FAQs** that can be used to ensure a consistent message across the company

10 **Good branding is insufficient** for strategy success. There is far more to implementation than a good idea.

■ The results

Although we cannot reveal market share data here, according to ACNielsen, LCJ has the highest brand equity score in the Jordan market.

They also say that imitation is the best form of flattery. Lafarge was flattered that a key competitor was so impressed with the LCJ strategy that they redesigned their own brands with close imitations of the LCJ products, adopting similar names and bag colors. This, of course, was anticipated and LCJ implemented another campaign highlighting the differences between the real bags and their inferior copies (see Figure 13).

Figure 13: Later campaign to protect the Lafarge 'Thabet' brand

Finally, the lessons from developing and implementing this strategy can be applied to improving the success of future marketing plans not only within LCJ but right across the company. LCJ is now seen as one of the best market-driven businesses within the Lafarge company and their skills in developing and implementing strategic marketing plans is widely sought.

Cases

Medic: Implementation enlightenment in India

Arif Fahim

At the time of writing, India has one of the fastest growing economies in the world and, if some forecasters are to be believed will overtake China by 2020 as the world's fastest growing economy. Like any large country, it is also a very diverse and complex place to do business. Global companies have for many years wanted to ride the Indian tiger, but have found it a frustrating place to implement their growth strategy.

However, as this case shows, implementing a successful strategy here does not need to be complicated. A few simple steps, properly followed, can lead to implementation enlightenment!

■ Background

In 2008, a global medical instruments company (which we will call 'MEDIC') was looking to expand its operations in India. It produced a wide range of products, many of which were integrated unto complete solutions for research (both government and privately funded), education (medical colleges) and the pharmaceutical sectors.

India is a fast growing economy with new medical colleges and companies springing up every year. MEDIC had been involved with India for many years and their global leadership team was very keen to see high sales growth there. Indeed, MEDIC India was growing faster than most MEDIC business units in other countries.

But they were not growing quickly in all these sectors. In particular, they were struggling in the education sector. This included medical schools, dental schools and pharmacy colleges.

The key problem here for MEDIC was that the colleges typically used older equipment and had no real appetite to upgrade to new equipment. Many staff at the colleges were used to teaching with the older equipment and had no real desire re-learn how to operate a machine or use the new PC-based software. They were not exposed to new research, technology and techniques and often repeated the same lessons to students year after year. Their view was, if the course was not broke, why go through the hassle and expense of fixing it? Old technology like blackboards and chalk worked fine, thank you.

Furthermore, if there was any new equipment, repairs or upgrades to be done, local companies would step in and do the work at a very low price, fitting inexpensive parts at a low labor rate. Sometimes these were local independent businesses and sometimes local agents of larger Indian businesses. If any customization work was needed for a medical college, the local supplier would do that as well. Indeed, many of these local relationships between the local agent/supplier and the college had existed successfully for decades.

This was a pretty difficult environment in which to sell state-of-the-art training laboratories! MEDIC was seen as a high end, high priced supplier, who was not suited to the Indian education market. Worse, colleges would speak to each other via informal personal networks and formal conferences so this opinion of MEDIC pervaded the whole country.

■ The plan

Persuading the key decision-makers in medical colleges across India to change their mind about MEDIC was not going to be easy.

MEDIC thought about undertaking a blanket marketing campaign across the whole country. However, this would be relatively costly and India is too large a target to attack effectively. It would be much more effective to target a specific opportunity where MEDIC could prove its value. This could have been one of the large contracts offered by the national government, but these can take two years to process from start to finish. Instead, it was decided to look for a large provincial contract. This would have sufficient volume to allow MEDIC to reduce its prices and would cover a number of colleges in one single order.

■ The pilot

Soon enough, the Southern state of Andhra Pradesh issued an invitation to tender for 25 medical systems covering five of its medical colleges. This was the opportunity that MEDIC was waiting for. Working with their local agent in the state capital of Hyderabad, they carefully completed the tender.

Cases

At the same time, they also made a special effort to showcase their products in Hyderabad. MEDIC was already well known to scientists in both the research and pharmaceutical sectors. They already had a good opinion of the value of buying MEDIC equipment. By setting up local networking opportunities, they mixed local educators together with the scientists. The scientists were very supportive of the idea that there could be state-wide use of MEDIC equipment across all the medical colleges. This began to unfreeze educators' attitudes towards MEDIC and help them become interested in what MEDIC could provide for them.

Meanwhile, MEDIC's competitors polarized into two camps. The first camp consisted of the local suppliers whose bid prices were so low that they could not afford essential aftermarket services like technical support. The second camp was made up of larger competitors who were so confident they would win the order again that they pushed up their bid prices and margins.

At the end of the tender process, the decision was announced and MEDIC had won the order!

This was a significant event for the company as it proved that they could compete and win in the education sector.

■ The rollout

The company then had to think how it could replicate this success in other Indian states. Although the Andhra Pradesh bid was a great success it also showed areas where MEDIC could improve its value proposition.

One key lesson was that the MEDIC brand names needed improving. The products were typically named using technical jargon that most educators did not understand. For example, most teachers have no idea what a 'Medical data acquisition system' actually is! This led to a rebranding of the product range using simpler, more common terms.

Secondly, pricing was reviewed across all its product range and a new limited-time promotional offer was introduced on two of the more basic MEDIC product lines to encourage rapid adoption of those technologies. This added to the existing tactic of deep discounting for high volume orders.

MEDIC also rolled out the value awareness campaign to distributors and initiated some serious research to identify which other states used a state-wide procurement process.

These changes were very successful and soon MEDIC won a similar contract in the northern state of Uttar Pradesh.

■ The refinement

The basic strategy was now working well. After they had won their second major contract, they were able to pinpoint gaps in their previous strategy and make further refinements to it.

For example, their success gave them more authority to adapt global company policies to local market conditions. One such global policy was to provide the equipment only after it has been paid for in full up front. After much discussion between head office and the local team, it was agreed they could loan the equipment (up to a certain value) to agreed prospective customers on a trial basis so that these prospects could experience its benefits before they purchase. This 'try before you buy' policy is proving very useful in winning over new converts. It also forced head office to re-examine some of its global policies and how they could be more flexibly implemented locally.

■ The results and lessons

MEDIC is now a key player in the Indian education sector and enjoys a much more balanced market portfolio in the country. Although with such rapid economic growth, it is difficult to estimate market potential – and therefore market share – MEDIC are confident they are successfully diverting spend from their competitors to themselves.

They also put their success down to following some simple principles:

- Test your strategy by focusing your energies and value proposition on a properly targeted sales opportunity
- Learn from this before you roll out to other sales opportunities. This is a form of *bid testing* which both applies the marketing strategy and feeds back to it.
- Continuously refine the strategy and value proposition as you bid on additional opportunities
- Capture your marketing and implementation strategy in a good marketing plan that can be shared across the business
- Use a small multifunctional team to coordinate the development and implementation of the plan

Cases

- Ensure the local leadership is on board and entrepreneurial. The general manager of MEDIC India was instrumental to the success of the plan. He was closely involved in all the key decisions and provided immediate support where needed. He fully backed the team and gave them a free hand to experiment and be innovative.

Even a small team can impact a huge country if there is that magical combination of a great plan coupled with great implementation.

Oxford Learning Lab: Online implementation

Giorgio Burlini, Founder and Head of Operations, Oxford Learning Lab

Oxford Learning Lab (www.oxlearn.com) specializes in producing marketing video courses that can be streamed online. It works with some of Europe's best marketing experts to produce high quality educational videos available to the general public. The company is based primarily in the UK and Italy.

They are a young company and an excellent example of how modern strategy implementation is being shaped by new online marketing tools.

Giorgio explains their journey:

'Selling online is a challenge. It requires a good 18-month period of building traffic to the website. When I setup my business I thought we could have some decent traffic coming from Google search. So at the end of 2010 and into early 2011 I tried multiple Google Pay-Per-Click (PPC) Adword campaigns to drive more traffic to my website. I also sourced external search engine specialists to help me find the most cost-effective keywords to use in the campaigns.

But after all this effort, the result was zero sales. People were clicking on the Google advert but, when they arrived, were not buying anything from my website. My products were selling anyway so I felt it was not a problem with the site.

I realized then that the Google strategy was not working.

I could have stopped the Adwords campaign there and focused on natural search engine optimization (SEO) instead. However, I knew enough of SEO to know that I had a mountain to climb to beat other bigger websites to the top of the Google search results. There is no way in the world that you can outbid them because Google's algorithm will rank those websites as more relevant. Many startup businesses do not grasp this issue at the beginning and waste a lot of money on SEO.

PPC was not working and SEO was not viable. It is fair to say that overall Google was a big disappointment for me! I needed to develop a different online marketing strategy.

Cases

So in early 2011 I put much more focus into social channels. I started experimenting by putting links and video samples on YouTube. The most important thing I discovered from these tests was that if people found free samples, they would then buy my products.

I developed a strategy to disseminate free video clips on multiple user-generated websites. I created my own channels on YouTube and other relevant websites like www.5min.com and www.ehowto.com (both of which concentrate on instructional 'How To' videos). Also, I uploaded clips to 'supersites' like www.oneload.com which distributes the video to all channels that you pre-select. They are great because they also provide viewing and download statistics.

I did not realize then that they would become predominant. In fact, this strategy was so successful that after six months, I switched most of my focus to it.

I have not stopped spending money with Google completely though. Google has proven to be a very useful market research tool. This is where PPC has been very good. I was using Google Adsense as well and I realized from the data that some channels were more effective than others.

In particular, I discovered that my single biggest route to market was not YouTube but a specialist website called www.marketingteacher.com. They offer free marketing resources and the site is very popular with students, achieving half a million hits per month!

So I used LinkedIn to find and contact their CEO. After some preliminary discussions, we met and formed a good commercial partnership. We have changed the relationship from an arm's-length affiliate model to a more relationship-based advertising model. I am now one of their key advertisers and we are collaborating on developing more videos for their site. I see partnering with chosen channels like this on marketing strategy and implementation as key to our business in the future.

Another one of my strategic partners is the Oxford College of Marketing. They are one of the UK's foremost trainers for qualifications awarded by the Chartered Institute of Marketing. My videos are a great source of value-added for their programs. They provide me with advice in a number of areas including the best subject areas to film and in doing the filming itself.

I am now also using Facebook for research. It provides additional demographic data on my customers including their country, age, gender and interests. If you are a small company, this is a very powerful tool.

It costs you just a few hundred euros to access the research. It is also cheaper than Google's PPC. For example, I understood very quickly that the market could be divided into digital marketing (DM) and marketing strategy (MS) segments. MS was converting at a far higher number.

Pricing has also evolved as we have moved further into implementation. At first, we went for a 'Freemium' subscription model. This was the model developed by Chris Anderson (who wrote *The Long Tail*). Basically, part of my website offers free clips while other parts offer a premium version with subscription. In the beginning, the model was simple and you could buy either a monthly or annual subscription. I then moved to a better model that asked for an email address in exchange for free videos. I noticed that quite a high number of visitors (about 25%) are prepared to exchange their email to get a free clip. I now proactively market to these email addresses with time-limited discount coupons and monthly updates.

In my business, I do not have a lot of people that I need to influence in order to implement my strategy. Most of my people issues are involved on the supply side. For example, a key process for my business is the sourcing and selection of subject matter experts who also perform well in front of a camera. I used to identify these people based on recommendations but now I actively find experts who have a good track-record in running training courses over a long period of time. Not only does this help identify enduring speakers but also they tend to have built up a good bank of trained delegates who may be interested in a refresher video course.

Similarly, on the IT side, there is no in-house IT team so we have to hire external resources (web agency). The downside of this arrangement is that they are not dedicated (solely) to my business and every time I need to implement something, I need to work with them to do it. I have to explain to them what needs to be done, why it is necessary and then book their time ahead to work on the change. This is an issue of time-to-market, not just money. Speed is of the essence here and what could be implemented in two weeks internally could take two months externally.

I realized pretty quickly that the same kind of problem applies in mastering all the marketing channels including Facebook and Twitter. It looks easy from the outside but in reality, the time and skills required to do it correctly are enormous. Just putting up a Facebook page is not going to achieve anything. There are also other technical issues that you only understand in time.

Cases

I am continuing to experiment with social media. We are now creating a social part of the website, focusing on the 'gamification' element. People will be presented with the opportunity to link their Oxlearn profile with their Facebook, LinkedIn or Twitter profiles. They will achieve points and badges upon completion of our video courses. They can then display their badges alongside their public social network profiles to show what they achieved. There will also be a reward system linked to referrals of their friends.

In essence, I am using my experiments and experiences here of combining online research with strategy and implementation to educate myself on how best to use social media.

Here then is the interesting thing: if your implementation relies on one vehicle, like paid advertising or free social media, you will find that success is limited and the time required is enormous. However, if you combine them both in a rich and varied way you will find that they reinforce each other and produce a powerful implementation model.

Implementing this strategy has meant traffic to my website has already risen 600% in the last 12 months. Our YouTube channel has been watched over 200,000 times and over the past 12 months alone we have had around 500,000 videos streamed across all channels. We also now sign up about 2,000 new subscribers every month and serve over 50 countries around the world.

When I started my business, I thought we could have good business generated through Google. Then I analyzed it and decided that it was not the case. I then changed my strategy to go around Google and saw it as a barrier to me. Now I see Google as a key part of the implementation program with its place firmly beside the other parts that make my program work.'

Tuntex: A cautionary tale from the textiles industry

Kaouther Kooli, Lecturer in Marketing, University of Bournemouth, UK

■ Background

'Tuntex' makes denim clothes for the retail trade. It was founded by two brothers-in-law, Karim and Zakaria, in Tunisia in 1983. They specialize in the final assembly of the garments and typically receive pre-cut parts of denim clothes (like trousers and skirts) which they sew together. They often work as an outsourced operation for international clothing manufacturers from whom they receive the parts and to whom they will ship the final assembled garment.

The company employs around 2500 people.

In 2003 I got to know the leadership team as part of a PhD I was doing at the time.

On 1 January 2005 their world changed forever when the global Multi Fibre Agreement (MFA) ended. The MFA was originally setup in 1974 to protect developed economies' textile industries from cheap imports. It operated on a quota system and permitted only limited imports from countries like China and India.

The European Union allowed nearby countries like Tunisia, Morocco and Turkey to operate inside the boundary and to trade without quotas in place. For Tuntex, almost 85% of their sales went to European customers, so the ending of the protection was a major threat.

■ The strategy

Tuntex were very dependent on one account in particular, 'Eurogarments.' Tuntex were an outsourced supplier to them and quite vulnerable to being replaced by a similar cheaper supplier elsewhere. Tuntex's relationship with Eurogarments was therefore critical to their business success.

I used the product-life-cycle (PLC) concept to explain how their relationship had evolved over the years and where it was heading now. One important thing about the PLC concept is that you can attempt to break out of the cycle and start a new cycle. So we used this simple idea to map

Cases

out what things we needed to do to kick-off a new relationship growth phase with Eurogarments.

There were several strands to this strategy:

1 Be less 'inside-out' driven and more 'outside-in' driven

2 Modernize the company and provide a higher quality of service

3 Integrate the different production departments so that the company is more efficient and responsive

4 Become more proactive and smarter with customers and suppliers

5 Become a broader one-stop shop

6 Prospect new markets and develop a more diversified portfolio of clients

7 Invest in cross company training programs to improve skills and know-how

8 Sell direct to the end consumer by developing their own branded collection of ready-to-wear clothes.

■ The implementation successes

By 2010, the company had changed dramatically:

- There was much better integration between the different production departments like pattern making, sewing lines, washing, finishing services and shipping.

- They have invested heavily in new equipment and a new wash facility was built to ensure even greater quality of the final shipped product.

- Furthermore, because they know the product better and the right inputs to make the garments, they are now at a point where they can inspect Eurogarments' own specifications and improve those to lower overall production costs and improve quality.

- Their staff developed much higher skills in quality and production excellence.

- Tuntex has become much more aware of the importance of all its supply chain relationships and they have developed close partnerships with mills and other suppliers.

- These partnerships have helped Tuntex design and manufacture its own clothing collection. It also bought a modest retail store in Paris to market these goods directly.

■ The implementation barriers

Although this strategy has been successful in saving the company from new competition, there were four major barriers that had to be overcome:

First there was a problem with the strategy. Eurogarments were uneasy about Tuntex effectively setting up as a small competitor to them with their own range of denim clothes. It took a lot of senior engagement between the two companies for Eurogarments to be satisfied that this would help them more than it hindered them. It was argued that this would happen because Tuntex would:

a) Be closer to the end consumer and able to offer Eurogarments fresh insights on their needs outside Eurogarments' normal research partners.

b) Have to produce even higher quality items to satisfy the Parisian consumer.

Secondly, there was a problem with insufficient market knowledge. Until 2005, Tuntex had been a traditional backwater textile assembly plant with little knowledge of their customers, the end consumer market and how the supply chain worked across Europe. To find out about this, Karim had to spend a significant amount of time travelling across Europe, the Middle East and Africa to meet with industry experts and develop his understanding from scratch. He also had to understand much more about Eurogarments and their competitors. This was very challenging because most organizations had been evolving ever more complex business models and demand was becoming ever more fragmented into smaller niche consumer segments.

This led to the third problem, money. In particular, the change to the ready-to-wear business needed a lot of investment both in terms of premises and advanced inventory. Also, this was not just about the size of the investment but also the cash flow issue. From the initial investment in fabric and trims through to export and payment there is typically a six-month time lag. This is a very long period for a medium-sized company like Tuntex. Moreover, there was not much of an appetite in Tunisian banks to lend in such circumstances and they had to self-finance the implementation.

Finally, and most significant of all, there was divided leadership. Although Karim and Zakaria agreed on the broad aspects of the strategy, they had major differences on how it should be implemented. For example, on selling direct, Karim wanted to move swiftly to design a new

Cases

brand, buy one or two retail locations and start design and marketing. Whereas Zakaria wanted to first restructure and consolidate the existing business before engaging in 'foreign adventures.' Whereas Karim was highly optimistic about the possibilities, Zakaria was highly cautionary, believing that the market was saturated already with many existing struggling brands.

Indeed, there were big differences between Karim and Zakaria in their outlook, approach and management style. Karim was the optimistic sales and marketing guy who moved fast and could sell sand to the Saudis. Zakaria was a much more reasoned ops guy that preferred everything to be planned in advance and implemented carefully. These differences often confused employees, clients and suppliers, especially when trying to understand the future plans for the business.

■ The end

Unfortunately, as time progressed, these differences became more pronounced. Problems increased, decision-making got slower and it led to a deteriorating relationship between Karim and Zakaria. This had a negative influence on the motivation of the employees and the overall performance of the company began to suffer.

After lengthy negotiations, the two bothers-in-law agreed to end their collaboration. Zakaria has remained at the helm of Tuntex, whereas Karim is at the helm of a new business he has started. Their customers were divided up as well with Eurogarments being transferred to Karim's new business.

Now Karim and Zakaria are competitors with Karim focusing more on standard brands and Zakaria focusing more on medium to high end brands.

Index

Ansoff Matrix 84–88, 104–105
audits, hierarchy of 68
Austro 133
  case study 270–274

budget and marketing plan 64
budget tracking tool, need for 27
business leadership, for success 222–223
business processes and implementation
      success 181
business strategy vs. market strategy 20

Cardell, Chris 199, 248
Cardoso, Carlos 234
Caulkin, Simon 83
change
  assessing risks 103
  cube 103
  leadership 227–228
  management, testing 196
  plan developing 109–114
  programs, Kotter's eight mistakes 228
chief marketing officer 223–227
  See also CMO
chronometers 4
Cloudesley Shovell, Admiral 2
CMO
  developing competencies 236
  required competencies 235–236
  See also chief marketing officer
commercial risks, FMEA 108
commitment 98–102
  continuum 98
  FMEA exercise 102
  improving 115–116
  of key stakeholders 99
  significance of for success 5
competitive advantage 71
competitors, in marketing audit 73

continuous improvement concept 176
corporate objectives 57
cost, quality, time triangle for assessing
      projects 28
CRISP-metrics 179–182
critical success factors (CSFs) 84
culture and implementation success 179
customer orientation 77

Dashboard. See Navigation Dashboard
dead reckoning 2
  in marketing, end of 9–21
degree of change and implementation
      success 177
desired state 31
Diagnostic. See Risk–Commitment
      Diagnostic
Diagnostic principles 30
differentiation 72
direct mail, testing 204
display advertising on websites 203
diversification strategy
  case example 275
downside risks 107
Drucker, Peter 182

early wins, value of 135
email marketing, testing 204
English Energy
  implementation success factors 157
  case study 275–279
environment of business operations 73
European e-Cards 133
  and testing 36
  case study 280–283

Facebook 201
failure mode and effects analysis 32
  See also FEMA

financial crisis, threat and opportunity 18
FMEA
  assessing commitment 102
  on commercial risks 108
  See also failure mode and effects analysis
forward testing 35
four Ps and marketing strategies 64

global account management programs
        288–296
Global Language Partner Consulting case
        study 284–287
Globalserve case study 288–296
GO/NO GO tests 29, 40
Google 201
Google Adwords 202, 329

Harrison, John 4
Helm. *See* Marketing Helm
Hopkins, Claude 198
human resources and implementation
        success 178

implementation
  funding 155–156
  levers for success 174
  online 329–332
  reasons for delay 27
  refining 169–191
  root cause of success or failure 221–230
  seven steps to success 250
  seven steps to success (fast track) 255–268
  skills resources 156
  when complete? 183
implementation diagnostics 95
implementation failure
  causes 5, 95–96
  costs of 10–13
  example, fire control centres 8–21
  greatest impacts 12
  hard and soft costs 10–13
implementation phases 33
implementation plan
  key principles 256
  refinement 172
  rolling out 149–160
Implementation Plan Template 252–254
implementation plan testing
  key principles 258

implementation refining
  key principles 261
implementation relationship map 100
implementation roadmap 111–114
implementation success
  four key factors 249
  importance of good leadership 230–231
  levers 174
  refining the factors 176
information management and
        implementation success 180
international engineering business (IEB) case
        study 297–301
Internet, impact on marketing 52–53
ITSalesco case study 302–303

Jobs, Steve 27–42, 94

Kelly, Sean 81–88
Kennametal case study 304–306
key account management 159
  in practice 297–301
key account management (KAM 99–100
Key Activity Planner 253
key stakeholders, identifying 99–101
killer threats, identifying 31
Kotter, John P. 228

Lafarge Jordan case study 307–323
leadership 220–238
  and change 227–228
  characteristics of good 229
  chief marketing officer 223–227
  improving, key principles 265
  of the business 222–223
  overlapping roles 232
learning simulations 213–214
Longitude Prize 3

market definitions 60
market evolution 75
marketing
  and testing 197
  measuring effectiveness 80–88
  simulations 211–215
  testing promotion 204–207
marketing audit 57
  conducting 59
marketing books market in the UK 61

marketing department, role 51
Marketing Helm 16, 33
marketing leadership
  typical problems 223–227
marketing metrics 79–86
  levels 81–88
Marketing Navigation, the approach 13
Marketing Navigation Dashboard 16
Marketing Navigation: Quick Reference
    Guide 268
Marketing Navigation System 22–42
  as a portfolio tool 38
  imported best practices 24–30
  outlined 16
  using at lower levels 38
marketing plan
  assumptions in preparation 63
  budget 64
  need for 93
  objectives and strategies 63
  stress testing 117–118
  tactical plan 66
marketing planning
  barriers to implementing 67
  for current and new products 304–306
  guidelines 70
  implications of formalized approach 66
  position within marketing 50
  process 53
  strategic planning process 69
marketing planning process
  in action 68
  new 245
  traditional v. continuous 240–241
marketing plans, implementation survey 4
marketing process, map of 51
market overview 59
market segmentation 75
Market Strategy Test 127
Maxwell, Craig 116–117
Medic case study 324–328
metrics and implementation success 182
mission statement 55–57
mplementation plan 90–128

NASA, failure mode and effects analysis 32
Navigation Dashboard 24
  example 122–126, 138–144, 165–167,
    187–190

objectives and strategies
  in marketing plan 63
on budget? 27
on course? 26
online implementation 329–332
online marketing, testing 202–204
on time? 26
organizational design and implementation
    success 179
over-performance 40–41
Oxford Learning Labs
  case study 329–332
  identifying threats to success 33
  implementation strategy 158

Parker 133, 183–187
  case study 17–18
  OEM System Dashboard
    pilot 139–145
    refine 188
    rollout 166–168
  OEM System Diagnostic
    pilot 139–145
    refine 189
    rollout 167–168
  response to credit crunch 158
  Winmap Program 111–113
  Winmap rollout 160–165
Parker Hannifin Corporation
  See Parker
pilot 129–145
  concept 132
  continuous development 136
  developing product for 133
  implementation phase 34
  running 135
  selecting customers 134
  testing implementation 138
PIMS (Profit Impact of Market Strategy)
    project 44–59
place, testing 201
plan, implementation phase 34
polls 206
press advertising, testing 204
price, testing levels 200
Principles of Play 147–149
product
  importance of assessing market 211
  testing 200

product-life-cycle (PLC) 333
professionalism, need for 78
program specification
  example 109–110
  writing 109–114
project management 26
  tests 196
promotion, testing 202
prototyping 132

refine implementation phase 35
relationship strategy 153–155
retro-testing 35
Return On Marketing Investment 81
reward mechanisms and implementation
    success 180
risk assessment in marketing planning 243
Risk–Commitment Diagnostic 16, 30
Risk–Commitment Matrix 16, 28
risks to marketing plans 7–8
risk vs. reward ratio 39
rolling wave planning 150–152
rollout 146–168
  implementation phase 34
  key principles 260
rollout plan
  example 152
  finalizing 149–151
rollout strategy 151
root cause analysis 96–97
routes to get back on course 37

Scientrix Implementation Methodology 274
search engine optimization (SEO) 329
Segment SWOT Analysis 42
simulations
  benefits of 209
  for testing 206, 264
  for learning 213
  marketing 211–215
  use in business schools 214
small business advantage 198
Smith, B D 50–53
social media marketing 202
stakeholder involvement 94
strategic marketing plan
  assessing quality 47
  component critique 48

contents of 45
  example of lack of 91
Strategic Planning Institute 44–59
strategic planning process 69
strategy
  assessing risk 104–105
  business vs. market 20
  risk profiles 106–107
strategy simulator 193
stress testing 117–118
structure of organization and
      implementation success   181
Sun Tzu 159
surveys 206
SWOT analyses 62

tactical plan in marketing plan 66
technologies for testing 195
telesales, testing 205
testing
  importance of 35, 193–194
  long-term cost of inadequate 201
  marketing promotion 204–206
  methods 195–197
  online marketing 202–204
  price levels 200
  products 200
  rollout phase 159
  technology of 192–217
  traditional advertising 204
testing technology
  key principles 263
tests, project management 196
threat testing 32
Tuntex case study 333–336

vision, need for 93

Wade, Allen 147–149
war games 207
websites, key to success of 203
Winmap 113
  pilot 140–144
  refining 183–187
  rollout 160–165

X-Factor, implementation success 170–172